**H**ow

**ag**ainst Competition

John Fenton has been called the Billy Graham of selling.

John Fenton is the author of *Within the Year* and *The A–Z of Sales Management*, also published by Pan.

Also by John Fenton in Pan Books

*How to Double Your Profits Within the Year*
*The A–Z of Sales Management*

# How to SELL against Competition

## John Fenton
of Structured Training Limited

Illustrations by Kenneth Aitken

Pan Books
in association with Heinemann

First published 1984 by William Heinemann Ltd.
This edition published 1986 by Pan Books Ltd,
Cavaye Place, London SW10 9PG
9 8 7 6 5 4 3 2 1
© John Fenton 1984
ISBN 0 330 290967
Photoset by Parker Typesetting Service, Leicester
Printed and bound in Great Britain by
Hazell Watson & Viney Limited,
Member of the BPCC Group,
Aylesbury, Bucks

# Contents

# The Importance of Selling

It is a glaring glimpse of the obvious to say that no amount of production is the slightest value unless the products are sold for cash.

Selling is the very crux of any commercial or industrial enterprise.

It therefore stands to reason that as a nation which depends so heavily on selling our products abroad, it is very much in the national interest that the highest standards and the most advanced techniques in salemanship should be encouraged.

*HRH The Prince Philip*
*Duke of Edinburgh, KG, KT*

# The Importance of Competitive Selling

Much attention has been focused – rightly – on the scope which exists for more British goods to be bought at home. But 'Buy British' is not in itself the answer. Indeed, the British products in question have to be fully competitive in price and quality for it to be even part of the answer.

It is of vital importance that we 'Sell British'.

We must leave no one in any doubt of the many areas where British goods *can* compete with all comers.

*The Rt. Hon. Mrs Margaret Thatcher, PC, MP*
*Prime Minister*

# Selling Is the Most Important Job in the World

Positive, dynamic, professional, enthusiastic Selling can do more to boost the economy, increase employment and curb competition from abroad than ten thousand sanctions and subsidies. In all walks of life Selling is as essential as food and drink. Customers don't beat a path to many doors any more!

In industry, if the Sellers at the 'sharp end' didn't sell, just about everyone employed in manufacturing and distributing would be out of a job. In retail stores and at trade exhibitions, if casual callers were just allowed to browse and the Sellers didn't try positively to generate interest and help people decide, very little would happen except for the bare essentials and the 'impulse buys'.

Sellers can be advisers, problem solvers, merchandisers, innovators, efficiency experts, cures for a buyer's headache or simply nice, helpful people – but their paramount function is to secure profitable orders for their goods or services, often against stiff competition. How they do this is the subject and purpose of this book.

Every managing director, chief executive, proprietor, of every business needs to know – in intimate detail – what his people at the sharp end, his Sellers, are up against. But all too often the occupants of the executive suites never even think about the problems of Selling the goods or services for which they are responsible overall, let alone get down there and see and live it for themselves. If they did, Wow! Wouldn't things be different – and better!

Selling is a highly developed series of skills. There is absolutely no truth in the rumour that 'salesmen are born and not made'.

Sellers are most definitely 'made'! Really good Sellers are very thoroughly **trained**.

Selling, when it is planned and carried out properly, is a most exciting profession. A career in Selling is not only highly satisfying, it is also financially very rewarding. There are vast opportunities in Selling. There is a chronic shortage of really good Sellers; real professionals; people blessed with the competitive spirit; people who know where they are going and why; people who have found the self-fulfillment that comes from making other people happy at a profit; people who are themselves looking for more out of life; people who are consistently trying to do better; people for whom, the stronger the odds against, the more they enjoy their work.

People who are the very life blood of any nation.

This book is for them – and for people who want to be like them.

# A Word about Sex Discrimination

I've spent twenty years of my life trying to make Salesmen proud to call themselves Salesmen and Saleswomen proud to call themselves Saleswomen.

Now the Sex Discrimination Act has brought another title to the forefront – the Salesperson.

In this book, Salespersons are Sellers, Salesmen and Saleswomen, depending upon which suits the case best. Customers are mostly 'He' rather than 'She' and for this, I apologize.

Because Saleswomen everywhere, in Selling – as in Government – your time has come. The fellers have had it all their own way for far too long, and a lot of them have messed it up.

From my experience, good Saleswomen beat good Salesmen almost every time – and not by using their sex. They've been beating the fellers hands down in Tele-Sales for years; and in most of Retailing. In Industrial Selling, the few Saleswomen try harder because they have to, to make the grade in the eyes of very sceptical and chauvanistic sales managers and sales directors. They are a very small minority, fighting for recognition – but they mean to win.

Winning is what this book is all about. The challenge from the ladies might even make a few more 'born' Salesmen more professional, because the key lies in the will to do something about it, and the ladies have always been best at motivating the fellers to do something about it!

*How to Sell Against Competition* is the right title, whichever way you look at it.

*John Fenton*

**If you believe in yourself
you can achieve anything
you want to achieve.**

# 1
# How to Stand Out from the Crowd and Become a 'Positive'

I want to sell you something.

It's something that will earn you more money.

It's something that will get you promotion.

It's something that will bring you more job satisfaction and more happiness out of life.

It's something that will get your boss off your back.

It might even stop your wife nagging you.

ARE YOU INTERESTED?

Can you imagine anyone saying 'no' to that?

In fact, probably 90% of the population of the world would hesitate and say 'Yes, but!' or 'Not really'.

'Negatives' I call them. The world is full of them. Selling is full of them. People who work very hard at finding reasons why something wouldn't work for them in a million years. People who are so resistant to any form of change that they are in ruts much too deep to climb out of. People who have lost faith in their own ability to do better. Abominable no men!

Read these seven lines beginning 'I want to sell you something' again. Think about how they could be made to fit your products or services. Then ask yourself – is Selling really that difficult? No, it isn't. In fact Selling is simply applied common sense. But, of course, that's the least practised thing in the world.

Well, there's a smack in the teeth at the very beginning of this book. If you bought or borrowed it thinking you were going to find some sophisticated high-faluting sales techniques to help you marmalise your competitors in three weeks flat, you're living in a dream world. Everything in this book is simply applied common sense: proven ideas which have worked for those 10% POSI-

TIVES who seem to be doing so well.

Now I want you to be completely honest with yourself. When you read the opening words of this first chapter, down to the first question – ARE YOU INTERESTED? – what *was* your initial reaction?

Was it – 'Holy Moses! Just what I've been looking for for ten years'?

Or was it – 'Oh oh! Another one of *those* books. Another smart-ass who reckons he can change my world'?

Or did you just read it with little or no personal response at all, kind of feeling that the words didn't apply to *YOU*? Which of these three reactions is *nearest* to yours?

If you got near 'Holy Moses' – great! If you moved the other way, let me let you into a secret.


## You're Much Better than You Think You Are!

Or, to be more accurate, you're much better than your mind lets you believe you are.

All through your life, your mind has been building up what we'll call your **attitude screen** – that mess of experiences you've gone through, through which your mind lets you look at life.

You're already conditioned to expect 'NO', rather than 'YES'.

Want me to prove it to you?

Who make the best closers? Children aged four to seven. They NEVER accept No. They're old enough to use our language, but not old enough to have become conditioned. From seven onwards, conditioning begins to limit their potential.

Remember that day in the park with your five year old? 'Dad, I wanna ice-cream!' 'No, it's too near your lunch time.' 'But Dad, I wanna ice-cream!' 'I said No.' 'Dad, **please** I wanna ice-cream!' 'No!'

**'I wanna ice-creammm!'**

'Oh, f'Christ's sake. All right. But don't tell your mother!'

How come we can't be that persistent and positive when we become adults? Because by then we've accepted that '**no**' rules, okay! By the time we're big enough to hit back, it's too late.

Throughout your business career, people have been telling you 'That'll never work in this business' or 'The boss'll never buy that idea', or 'We tried that five years ago and it was a disaster'. Another kind of conditioning that keeps most people in line and prevents them from putting forward new ideas or from changing the *status quo*. Another part of your attitude screen.

Then there are the nasties. The embarrassments you've suffered. Indelibly engraved on your attitude screen. No way are you going to risk going through *those* again.

But all these things on your attitude screen are holding you back. You're much better than your mind lets you believe you are. Here's the proof. Read this sentence JUST ONCE, and count how many Fs there are in it.

FINISHED FILES ARE THE RESULT OF YEARS OF SCIENTIFIC STUDY COMBINED WITH THE EXPERIENCE OF MANY YEARS.

First time I was given this test, I got three. And I cheated. I read it through three times, not just once. When I was told I was wrong, I read it through again and I **still** got three.

There are in fact six Fs in that sentence.

The three you keep missing (unless you're a speed reader, in which case you may have got it right first time, because you scanned it, you didn't actually read it from start to finish) are the three in OF, because when your mind reads OF, it doesn't read F, it reads V.

*That's* how much your mind is holding you back. 50% accuracy! Maybe, therefore, when you start thinking of all the other ways your mind could be playing tricks on you; maybe you could be TWICE as good at doing what you do now.

Maybe for the first time ever, someone is starting to break down your attitude screen instead of building it up.

You've actually gone to the trouble of reading this far. Maybe you've even bought this book with your own money, rather than been given it by your company. If it's all making sense to you, if you're finding it stimulating, you know what this means? You might be at risk. You might *be* a POSITIVE, or have the makings of one. If you are, let me warn you – keep away from the NEGATIVES.

NEGATIVE PEOPLE ARE LOSERS!
POSITIVE PEOPLE ARE WINNERS!

Throughout this book I'm going to quote other people who are much wiser than I am. First quote coming up. Our hero, a young man, heir to a vast family fortune and business, is talking to his beloved.

In Africa, there is a beautiful and fierce animal called the Sable Antelope. They run together in herds of up to a hundred, but when one of them is hurt – wounded by a hunter or mauled by a lion – the lead bulls turn upon him and drive him from the herd.

I remember my father telling me about that. He would say that if you want to be a winner then you must avoid the company of the losers – FOR THEIR DESPAIR IS CONTAGIOUS.

Wilbur Smith, *Eagle in the Sky* (Heinemann, London)

It's a bit early for stuff like that, maybe, but *I* know it is true, having been through the fire. Most really successful people in business know that it is true, also.

I worry about **negatives** a lot, because there are so many of them. I worry about where they are going. But more than that, I worry about how many of us **positives** they are going to take with them. We are outnumbered 10 to 1.

**Hey!** I wanted to sell you something. I think you said you *were* interested.

It's a truly fantastic product. It'll really turn you on.

It's called **success**.

But it's only for **positives**.

**Positives Have the Edge. Here's Why.**

If you are selling, managing the sales operation, marketing or steering the entire business ship, you don't need me to tell you that, with few exceptions, it's a **buyer's market**.

There are too many suppliers with too much capacity and not enough customers to go round.

It's likely to stay that way for a very long time – maybe for ever!

What does that mean? It means for most of us that whatever we're selling, wherever we're selling it, we're likely to be up against strong competition.

Times ain't wot they used to be. Times is 'ard!

But there *is* business out there. Oh yes! I know it. You know it. A lot harder to get it may be, but it's there all right.

This book is about **getting it**! It's written for people who **want** to get it.

In any buyer's market, depression, period of recession, call it what you like, there is strong motivation throughout Selling for the **negatives** to give up – to believe the gloom-mongers who keep saying 'There's no point in trying harder'.

The majority of **negatives** in selling have already, to some extent, given up. That's a fact, and it might include **you**!

For the purpose of this particular thesis, these people we shall call **sheep**.

Only the **positives** in Selling are wise enough (maybe they've been through a few buyers' markets before) to know different. These **positives** know what makes the Sellers and the buyers tick.

For the purpose of this thesis, these **positives** we shall call **wolves**.

Wolves understand and use to their own advantage the psychology of the **negative**, the **sheep**, in business. Sheep bleat a lot and do little else but follow those gloom-mongers. The psychology is very simple. It goes like this:

1 RECESSION BREEDS DEPRESSION.
2 DEPRESSION RESULTS IN FAILURE.

(Not all of the time – just **most** of the time!)
Wolves also know that when times are good, another series of actions and reactions take place.

1 BOOM TIMES INCREASE OPPORTUNITIES.
2 OPPORTUNITIES DEMAND POSITIVE ACTION.
3 POSITIVE ACTION GENERATES EXCITEMENT.
4 EXCITEMENT BREEDS ENTHUSIASM.
5 ENTHUSIASM BRINGS SUCCESS.

Wolves assume that in a buyer's market the world doesn't beat a path to anyone's door, so opportunities are scarce. They know they have to generate their own opportunities. They know they have to find ways to counteract the depression factor.

Wolves set out to provide for themselves those essential four ingredients for success which you should be able to pick out from the 'good times' actions and reactions – ingredients that good times provide automatically:

OPPORTUNITIES
POSITIVE ACTION
EXCITEMENT
ENTHUSIASM

and they set out to do this because they want to **win**.

'When the going gets tough the tough get going!'
Lee Trevino, Richard Nixon and about 10,000 other guys!

The fact that you are reading this, I am going to assume, means that **you** want to win. Okay, throughout this book I shall be showing you ways to make your own opportunities, ways to take effective and positive action, ways to generate excitement and ways to stimulate enthusiasm in your sales team and in yourself. I shall be showing you how to be a wolf, not a sheep. How to win the business battle. And I'm going to show you how **easy** it is!

### Generating Excitement

Take generating excitement. As a consultant, I have been retained by many managing directors to help them revive their struggling and despondent businesses. The situation is nearly always the same – the people in the business are mostly **negatives**, have given up, don't know which way to turn to improve things, are wondering how long the company can hang on, look miserable and sound miserable.

The first action I propose is nearly always the same. Warm things up. Get the molecules of the business moving faster. Generate some excitement. Get things buzzing again.

Then use the excitement's momentum to do all the other things that have to be done. To try to do these things while everyone in the business is cold and stagnant and miserable is a hundred times as difficult.

So my instructions to my managing director client are these: 'For the next month, everywhere you go in your place of business – offices, works, wherever – you **run**. You trot. You bustle. And you do it at all times with the corners of your mouth turned up –

with a **smile** on your face. Nothing else; just **run** everywhere and **smile**!'

Most of them do it. Two days later, a couple of colleagues on the board are in the managing director's office asking: 'What the hell's going on, George: you gone daft or something?' George swears them to secrecy, and tells them about this idiot consultant. Next thing, all three of them are running everywhere and smiling all the time. A few days later, the entire business is vibrating. Everyone is wondering what's going on. They don't know what it is – but it's faster and it's happy, so it must be good news.

That's the momentum. Everything else happens from there – and everyone in the business believes that everything that happens subsequently has been well thought out *before* the day the managing director began his happy marathon.

The guy who trained me, Joe Windsor, had a managing director once who point-blank refused to run everywhere, smiling. So Joe looked round for an alternative way to generate the necessary excitement. The company in question was in distribution. No factory, just a warehouse and a large sales office. Part of the way across the sales office was a partition wall that didn't seem to be serving any useful purpose. Joe asked the managing director – 'Would business suffer in any way if that wall wasn't there?' The managing director, puzzled, said 'No'. So Joe said, 'Okay, Monday morning, we're going to knock it down!'

'Why?' said the managing director.

'No reason,' replied Joe. 'Trust me, and see what happens.'

So Monday morning, the wall came down. And the vibrations started. Something was happening. The business woke up – and up it went.

That's how easy it is to generate excitement in a business.

And I bet *you* can come up with some better, or more original ideas than just knocking a wall down.

If you *don't* really want to **win** – if you don't care one way or the other – then there is no hope for you at all in Selling. Please get out of the profession and leave a bit more room for those of us who *do* want to win. You're getting in the way! You're a **negative**.

If you truly want to **win** – and if you work at winning during this 'buyer's market' era, then I promise you you'll become so strong that no competition will stand a hope of catching you up.

DO YOU ACCEPT *WINNING* AS OUR MAIN OBJECTIVE?

Do you accept the accolade **wolf**?

Are you willing to banish **all** negative thoughts and actions?

'There are only two ways of
getting on in this world:
by one's own industry, or
by the weaknesses of others.'
Jean de la Bruyère
1645–96


## YOU May Be Willing, but Is Your INNER Self?

There is one snag. Even when you really want to win, that
insidious negative thinking can creep into your subconscious and
screw it all up for you.

A sales manager I know who runs a large salesforce has a
one-off exercise aimed at changing a particular kind of subconscious negative thinking back to conscious positive thinking.
He calls it the 'I can't win with this guy' feeling. It comes to quite
a lot of Sellers after they've tried for an appointment, say, three
or four times and got a blunt 'No' each time. The occasion I
heard of when he exercised (or should it be exorcised) his salesforce went like this.

He called all fifty of his salesmen together for half a day, telling
them to bring all their customer and prospect records with them.
They were all seated around a big hollow square table, the sales
manager walking about most of the time. There was a bit of
general business to get through, which took the first hour – then
he gave his instructions:

'Sort out from your prospect record cards the six **worst** prospects you've
got; people who so far have said 'No' at least three times when you've
tried for an appointment; people who you **know** are good prospects, yet
with whom you haven't got even to first base.'

When each of his fifty salesmen had done this, he gave his next
instruction:

'Now, each of you pass the six cards you're holding to the person on your
immediate right.'

This they each did. Then the sales manager pointed to the
clock on the wall and shouted:

'Right, you have two hours to get out of here, every one of you, find a phone and get a firm appointment with those six prospects you're now holding in your hand. GO!'

All fifty salesmen sat dumbstruck. 'He can't be serious!' they were saying to themselves.

'GO!' the sales manager thundered. 'Two hours – no more.'

Gradually, initially a few at a time, then a rush which turned into a stampede, and the fifty salesmen were gone.

*Three* hours later, not two, they were all back in the room, once more seated around the square. Scores were totted up, and to everyone's amazement, the overall success rate was 160 appointments out of a possible 300. More than 50% success – much better than normal performance in the field. And these were the worst possible known prospects.

On the analysis, three key reasons for this success were established:

1 The salesmen had no preconceived failure complexes in their sub-conscious. The prospects they telephoned were unknown to them;

2 They had maximum enthusiasm for the task, because they took it as a personal challenge from a sales manager they respected (that's leadership!);

3 Most of the successful 160 were telephone calls where the name of the salesman who had passed on his six cards to the caller was used *by* the caller, as a third party reference.

'Your name has been given me by one of my colleagues, Joe Randolph. He reckons we've a deal coming up that could save you a fair bit of money. Could you spare me ten minutes, say, on Wednesday, for me to come over and talk to you about it?'

The 'deal' they invented. The objective was to secure the appointment. They discovered that the name of one of their own salesmen was almost as effective as the name of one of their customers. They had plenty of time to think about what best to say and do when they arrived face-to-face.

So much for the subconscious negative trap. Few of this particular salesforce ever suffered from it again – and, from time to time, some of the salesmen even continued swopping 'difficult' prospect cards.

So to stand out from your particular crowd and become a **positive**, don't believe what your conscious mind and your sub-conscious mind tell you. Keep an open . . . !

Two notices which might help . . .

# YES YOU CAN!

# Why not, why not?

Sir Barnes Wallis

. . . and one for all those negatives . . .

# If you're not part of the Solution You've got to be part of the Problem

# 2
# How to Develop the Killer Instinct

**He possessed all the attributes of a forged, razor-edged tool. The verve and confidence, the bright quick mind and adventurous spirit – but above all he possessed the aggressive attitude, the urge to compete, that is defined as the killer instinct.**

Wilbur Smith, *Eagle in the Sky*
(Heinemann, London)

The term 'Killer Instinct' might well put some people off. But it doesn't mean what you think it means.

"PATIENCE MY EYE—
I'M GONNA
KILL SOMEBODY!"

## Definition

'The Killer Instinct' is a term sometimes accorded by Sellers to other Sellers because those other Sellers have an uncanny knack of winning orders against seemingly impossible odds.

And that is what we are about!

But unfortunately, the killer instinct is *more* often accorded out of *jealousy* for another's success, rather than out of *respect* for another's success, by Sellers who are themselves **negatives**. Worse than this, it is a term used when talking about *the competition*. And that is commercial suicide.

**Negatives** spend a hell of a lot of their time talking **positives** *out* of doing anything positive. It's always been like that. 150 years ago in the wilds of America, where the competition was *very* fierce, it was like that. Read this film script of the action as it was then, and think about it in the context of business today.

## Film Script

(*Sounds of galloping horses, whooping Indians, rifles and six-shooters being fired*)

BIG JOHN     Well, Old Timer, looks like they got us pinned down like skunks in a tar barrel.
               (*whoop, gallop*)

OLD TIMER Yep, sure does, Big John – I ain't niver seen 'em so wild before – do yer reckon they been at the firewater?
               (*whoop*)

BIG JOHN     No, Old Timer, that ain't firewater fightin', they mean business and no mistakin'.
               (*arrows-thud, thud*)

OLD TIMER Time was when a man could come out to these parts 'n settle. Maybe raise a few head, do some prospectin', make a decent livin' fer himself – even take a woman.

BIG JOHN     Things've changed, Old Timer – these injuns are as cunning as coyotes and (*whoop, gallop, bang!*) meaner than starvin' grizzlies. They reckon they got more right to be out here than you'n me.
               (*whoop, gallop, arrow-thud*)

OLD TIMER   Look out, John – behind you! (*whoop, gallop, bang!*) Nice shooting, Big John, but there's plenty more where he came from. I'm down to ma last three slugs – I guess they've done fer us this time.

BIG JOHN   The hell they have! I'll be a fly on a mule's (*bang*) before I'll sit'n wait to have ma hair cut by a bunch of savages! Let's see what they say when I git on ma horse and give'm a taste of their own medicine.

OLD TIMER   Don't do it, Big John, you ain't gotta chance against that number of injuns!

BIG JOHN   Leave me be, Old Timer, I know yer mean kindly but there comes a time when a man's gotta do what . . . (*distant cavalry bugles*).

OLD TIMER   John – do yer hear that! (*cavalry noise louder*) It's the cavalry – we're saved.
(*cavalry noise louder and louder to close*).

If *you* were in that situation you just re-lived (did you see the film?) – what would you do?

Would you stay with the wagon train until your water and ammunition ran out? Would you hang on in the hope that the cavalry would rescue you?

No! Because in real life – in business life – the cavalry is just a figment of your imagination. You're kidding yourself. The *only* alternative to disaster is to get out and fight.

When you get determined to give the competition a taste of their own medicine, of sallying forth and tackling seemingly impossible odds – you've acquired the right kind of killer instinct.

If only these **negatives** who keep getting in the way of progress would take the trouble to learn how easy it is to develop the killer instinct for themselves.

It's a mixture, you see, of just two things:

## Confidence *and* determination

The development of Confidence is critical and fundamental to success in Selling. And there are three kinds of confidence at the top of the priority list:

Self-confidence;
Confidence in the products or services you sell;
Confidence in the company that employs you.

Without the second and third kind, it is very, very difficult to generate much of the first and most important kind – **self-confidence** (unless, of course, you work for yourself!)

Okay, I know what you're thinking. This is old hat. We've heard it all before. But what people do not seem to realize is that Confidence comes from just one place. Nowhere else.


## Confidence Comes from Knowledge

Think back. Remember that feeling you got when you were face-to-face with that potential customer (we've all had the feeling at some time or another) – that you reckoned you were imposing on his valuable time? That, in his eyes, you were a bit of a pain?

Well, you got that feeling because of a lack of confidence.

And the feeling shouldn't have been there. Because whenever you are face-to-face with a customer or a potential customer

**You are an expert.**
**You are *not* there to sell your products or services.**

You are there to show the customer how he can run his

business more efficiently or more profitably; how he can improve on a process; how he can make more money from every foot of his shelf space; how he can *save* money; how he can solve a problem, improve his working environment, provide for his retirement, reduce his own workload – even increase his own prospects for promotion and minimize the risk of *him* being blamed if things don't work out as planned – by **using** your products or services.

You know more about *your* products or services than any customer will *ever* know – about how they can be put to use – about the benefits customers derive from them. If this isn't true then, yes, you'll come over to the customer as a pain, and you'll get that 'imposing' feeling.

The customer will see you as the other kind of expert – spelt slightly differently:

**x** – an unknown quantity.
**spurt** – a drip under pressure.

The *right* kind of Selling expert knows a lot – in at least four areas:

1 **Everything** about the products or services; how they can be applied; how they can benefit the customers.
2 A lot about the *competitors'* products or services and how they compare with his own.
3 A lot about the customers and how they run *their* businesses.
4 A lot about business in general – especially trends in markets, and how *money* makes the wheels go round.

The right kind of Selling expert reads a lot – and not just fiction. Building on the knowledge every day. And knows how to **use** the knowledge – not as a know-all, a braggart, but as a confidant; who tries every way to help the customers – even if occasionally the help given doesn't result directly in business. Sowing the seeds that can be reaped later – but always with an eye on future business.

Once you have cracked this knowledge factor and can honestly call yourself an expert – I promise you, you'll never get that feeling of imposing yourself on a customer – of wasting his time – ever again.

This will bring you all the Confidence you need.

It never ceases to amaze me how many companies send their Sellers out to sell to customers without any more than a superficial injection of knowledge.

One week! Two at the most – of product training.

Nothing on the competitors. Nothing on the kind of customers they will be calling on. Nothing on business in general and what makes the wheels of industry go round.

Is it any wonder, therefore, that so many Sellers fail. It isn't their fault; it's the fault of the companies that employ them. There just isn't any substitute for knowledge.

At this point there are going to be umpteen sales directors throwing their hands in the air and shouting – 'That's all very well, but how do we find the time to do all this knowledge training, and where does the money come from to allow us to make it happen?'

Valid point. In the real world there is never enough time to do everything you need to do. But hold on, remember that old saying:

**There's never time to do it right,
but there's always time to do it again!**

We are talking here about *losing business* because of not doing it right. There may not be *an opportunity* to do it again. Where does *that* stand in your priority list?

I know of only one way to shorten the knowledge learning curve and inject the required amount of product, application, benefit, competition, customer and business knowledge into a salesforce **faster** and at much less cost. This is what I call it.

## A Day's Worth of USP

USP stands for **Unique Selling Point**. It was all the rage before someone invented the word 'Marketing' and fudged everything.

USP is the difference – the edge – you've got over your competitors. It's likely to be different for each product or service, against each competitor. If you don't know – in fine detail – what your USP is, then you can't sell successfully against competition.

Finding out what your USP is, if you are a sales manager, also gives your salesforce all that essential knowledge they need, from which they build their confidence.

Let's assume you *are* a sales manager. Call a meeting. Take a room for a day – big enough for your entire salesforce – new recruits, trainees and all the old hands. Cover the walls of the room with blank flip charts. You'll need at least ten. Twenty would be better.

You've told your salesforce to be there at 9.00am sharp for the meeting, but you haven't told them why. Introductions over, you start the ball rolling:

'Okay team, we're going to spend the entire morning answering in fine detail just one question. The answer we're going to write on these flip charts around the walls – and I expect to fill every single one. The question is: **why do people buy from us?**'

The first ten minutes will be easy. All the old chestnuts will come out. 'We're best.' 'We're oldest established.' 'The customers know us.' 'They know the product's a proven seller.' Lists begin

to develop on the flip charts, but the answers at this early stage will be rather too superficial, too broad, lacking depth. So you begin to question each answer, using that very useful key word – why?

And gradually, the superficial answers will grow roots and the *real* reasons will be uncovered. Then you begin separating each product and each type of customer or application – and your team begins to see that a certain USP for one product does not apply to another. And certain types of customers appreciate certain aspects of certain products, while for other customers those aspects are irrelevant.

The pace of the meeting will quicken, as the members of your team get the hang of it and realize what's going on. The old hands contribute the most, of course, and the new recruits learn things they wouldn't learn in a month of Sundays out in the field.

By lunchtime, every flip chart is filled.

After a good lunch (but not too good!) the team reconvenes. During the lunch break, all the used flip charts have been replaced with fresh blank ones. The used ones lie on the floor all round the room.

You lead off again:

'Right team, this afternoon we are again going to devote entirely to answering just one question, in the same kind of fine detail as this morning. The question this time is: why do people buy from our competitors?'

The team sets off at a much brisker pace. The usual chestnuts again come out first: 'Their prices are lower.' 'Their delivery is shorter.' 'They spend more on booze and entertainment than we do.' 'Their advertising is more effective.'

Again you question the superficial chestnuts. 'Do *all* our competitors have lower prices than ours?' Of course they don't. So you separate those that do from those that don't. 'Can all our competitors deliver quicker, or does this only apply to certain areas at certain times?'

'How important is the entertainment factor, compared with the tangible cost-saving benefits?' 'Which of our competitors truly beat us on advertising and which do we beat?'

Separate lists grow and grow. And as they do, one thing becomes all too clear – most of the answers in the afternoon look pretty much the same as the answers in the morning's session. So about tea time the morning's flip charts come up again off the floor to be matched against the afternoon's and any identical answers are cancelled out by striking a line through them.

By the end of the day, the *true* USP – your **true selling edge** – will have been established for at least your three main products or services, when sold to your three main types of customer, when up against your three main competitors. That will be $3 \times 3 \times 3 = 27$ variations of USP – and you won't win all 27. For some you'll clearly see that your competition has the edge. But you'll also see clearly what you have to do to *improve* your USP and get back on the winning side. (We deal with this many times in this book.)

Every member of your team, old hands as well as new recruits, will leave that room with more product, customer and competition knowledge than you'll ever inject through the usual style of product training sessions. And after that first day, you'll arrange other days, probably once a month, because most of you have a lot *more* than three main products, types of customers and competitors. If you have *six* of each, your possible variations of USP are $6 \times 6 \times 6 = 216$. So that's your monthly sales meetings sorted out for at least the next year. But it won't take a whole day after the first meeting. They know what to expect and will prepare accordingly. Two hours should get you another 27 variations each month.

Now, all you individual Sellers out there – don't wait for your sales manager to call the meeting. Get cracking yourself. The meeting might never happen, and that's a hell of a lousy reason to stay ignorant!

Let's recap.

We are looking at how to develop the killer instinct and we've now covered the first of the two key factors: **confidence which comes from knowledge.**

So let's look at the second key factor.

## Determination

The easiest way to get to grips with the development of determination is never to forget what I see as the first law of Selling:

**There are no prizes for the seller who comes second.**

You won't last long in this business if you see yourself as a kind of benevolent consultant, keen to offer advice and help, but without an eye, an ear and a nose for *business*. Determination means that once you are in there – an expert who has found a need and is working hard at fulfilling it with *your* product or service – you don't give up when the customer says: 'I'm not really interested,' or 'It's too much trouble to change all that.'

Even if a customer gives you a direct 'No', with determination you don't take **no** for an answer unless you are sure of his reasons for saying **no** and, even then, only if they are *valid* reasons. (Remember what you could do when you were five?)

Perhaps your knowledge of the situation gives you the feeling that he's putting you off – that there is something behind his resistance that he's not coming clean about. You get determined to find out what that something is – after all, he's got no right to mess you about after you've spent all that time trying to help

him. You've got a right to some kind of return, or at least the satisfaction of knowing the **real** reason why you failed – so that you can avoid making the same mistake again.

But you *do not* get aggressive. You don't get annoyed with the customer.

You keep your cool and you **probe**. You ask the customer questions like: 'When you say you're not interested, does that mean you've found a better way of doing it than we can give you?' If the customer says 'No', which he almost certainly will, you follow up with: 'Well, if you haven't found a better way, what do you mean?' And for the too-much trouble situation: 'When you say it's too-much-trouble, do you mean the savings won't cover the costs of changing over?'

This will leave him speechless and rubbing his chin, so you follow up with: 'Well, okay then, let's establish the break-even point and see if we can improve things'.

Here's a dilly for when the hold up is just *him*: 'Is there anyone else in your company likely to put obstacles in the way of progress, for purely selfish reasons, if you go ahead? Are you saying no because of this?'

He'll think of everyone who might conceivably point the finger at him and his 'political' resistance will quite often disappear.

Or you can look the customer straight in the eye and say: 'We've established that there are real savings if you use this equipment, so how can you give me a straight **no**? I'd appreciate knowing your reasons for turning me down.'

That's **determination**. And when you have determination backed by Confidence and Knowledge, if you come upon a situation where you establish that you *cannot* be of help to a customer, he doesn't have to tell *you* that – you tell *him*!

But be warned. If you try to push **determination** *before* you've put in the work to learn how to handle the Knowledge and Confidence bit, the customer will see you as just another pushy, pain in the ass, high pressure Seller.

There are no short cuts that I know of, other than the day's worth of USP. If you don't know what you are selling and why people will buy it, you won't develop the killer instinct, you'll develop the *suicide* instinct, and likely as not you'll finish up down the pan!

# 3
# How to Find New Customers Before Your Competitors Find Them

**There's new business out there, no matter how depressed the market.**

**All we've got to do is find it – and find it first!**

As I said at the beginning – there is business out there.

Not as much as in times of boom economy, but still some. It's more difficult to find, but it's *made* much *more* difficult than it should be by the Sellers' natural and **negative** feelings about actually *looking* for new business.

They don't like doing it!

In fact, it would be true to say that the majority of Sellers only voluntarily look for new customers on **warm, sunny days**. *Never* in drizzle, ice or snow.

With this kind of attitude prevailing at the sharp end, is it any wonder that the growth potential of many businesses is so sadly under-developed?

And looking for new customers – 'prospecting' – is so **easy**! Once you have developed a nose for it. You need to enjoy playing detective – that's all.

## Detectives and Carrots

Good detectives succeed because they are inquisitive, because they employ method and because they have a purpose – to prevent crime and to catch criminals.

Good Sellers find new customers by being inquisitive, by employing method and with just as strong a purpose – to achieve and surpass target. To win more business than their competitors win.

The method couldn't be easier. All that has to be established is:

**Where to go**
**Who to see**
**What to do and say**

and from the knowledge they're building up, good Sellers know before they start the *kind* of people or the kind of business *most likely* to be prospects. So they know where to start looking.

They also know they have to be inquisitive enough to dig up what we call a **carrot** – a reason for making the first call.

That's what prospecting research is for – not just finding the 'suspect' and pin-pointing who the key decision-maker is – but digging up a carrot; a problem the suspect is encountering; a project he's starting where your product or service might help; a big contract he's just won; something that will indicate the *possibility* that what you sell may be of use to him. When you've found your carrot, the suspect becomes a prospect.

Once you have the carrot, you know what to say when you telephone for the first appointment. *And* you know what to say when you get face-to-face for the first time. Exactly the same words in both cases.

You've offered to discuss just the *possibility* that you might be of value to the prospect in one specific area – and that possibility seems reasonable enough for the prospect to say to himself: 'Okay, I'll give this person ten minutes and see what he has to say.'

That is your **objective** – nothing more, nothing less.

You might find your carrot is no good after five minutes face-to-face. That 'possibility' area doesn't pan out after a few searching questions. No matter. By then you are asking questions in other directions and seeing quite clearly **other** possibilities and the best line to follow.

It *is* possible, of course, sometimes to succeed in winning a first interview **without** bothering to dig up a carrot to dangle – but it's certainly more difficult to win that way, and more risky. Why take the risk? All it does is increase your chances of coming **second**!

That carrot you need can often be pin-pointed with just a phone call to someone in a suspect's business, other than the person to whom you will subsequently want to sell.

The phone call goes something like this:

'I wonder if you can help me? I sell widgets. I'm hoping to sell some to your company, but I'm short of a bit of information. If I can bend your

ear for two minutes – what I need to know is – what sort of widgets do you use?'
(*Answer – LISTEN*)
'Where do you buy them from ?'
(*Answer – LISTEN*)
'Who do I need to talk to – the person who buys or specifies your widgets?'
(*Answer – LISTEN*)
'Do you know if there are any problems on widgets?'
(*Answer – LISTEN*)
'Is there anyone other than Mr – that I should talk to about this?'
(*Answer – LISTEN*)
'That's super. Thank you very much. Goodbye.'

Detectives can do it . . .

If you want to find new customers before your competitors find them – you've simply got to be a better detective than your competitors' Sellers are.

In a buyer's market, you should be looking for businesses that are doing well, expanding, taking on people.
Here are five methods of finding these kinds of new customers.

## Method 1: Local Job Advertisements

Consider the incredible amount of detailed information local job advertisements contain. What the company is doing. What equipment it has. Why it wants the people for whom it is advertising. The key contacts.

Here are a few lines from advertisements I've found in my own local newspapers:

'. . . is entering a phase of planned expansion which will double manufacturing capacity.'

'The successful applicant will be responsible to the Cash and Carry Depot manager for the total floor operation.'

'An important secretarial appointment. Secretary to the Chief Engineer. The job will include the supervision of the department's secretarial throughput.'

'For varied and interesting work in our new factory.'

Did *you* know they were building a new factory? How much of that double manufacturing capacity at . . . gives *you* scope for selling? What kind of things will that chief engineer's secretary be buying in a couple of months time? It's all there – in these kinds of advertisements.

Any advertisement that's looking for more than one person – if in doubt – assume expansion.

If there's a box number so you can't tell which company it is, apply for the job. A very short letter from your home address: 'Reference your advertisement, please send me an application form.' They'll write back: 'Haven't got an application form, please send your CV' or they'll send you an application form. Either way you've got what you wanted – their letterhead, names of directors, etc. Now you can telephone.

The most important job advertisements are those advertising for the key decision-makers themselves – directors, senior managers, purchasing managers and buyers. For these kinds of advertisements, you need a card index filing system. You give each advertisement a card, maybe sellotape the advertisement to the back of the card. The cards are filed in date order.

Four weeks or so *after* the advertisement appeared in the local newspaper, you refer to the card and telephone the company that

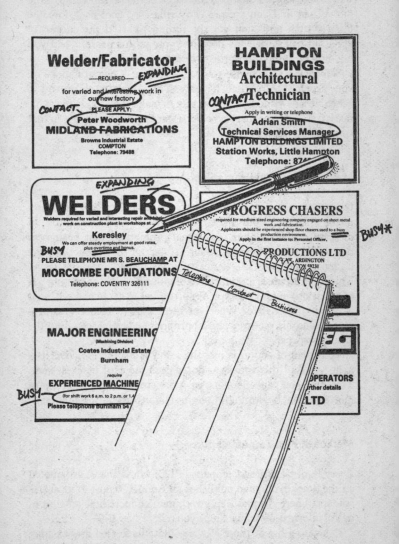

was advertising, to establish the name of the person who got the job. If you find you are too early, the card goes back into the filing system until you get the timing right. If the successful applicant has started his new job, you get his name. Then you can either telephone or write to *him*.

Whichever you choose to do, you begin: 'Congratulations on your new job'. After that, it's easy. You're starting clean, and so is he. He's new and will be wanting to make changes; to make his mark fast. And you've maybe been wanting to see changes in that company for years!

## Method 2: Internal Promotions

Okay, in times of recession, there are fewer local job advertisements than in boom times. But this is compensated by an increase in the number of internal promotions that businesses make. They have to shed labour maybe. Or they cannot pay the necessary increases in salaries so some people decide to leave. This is not necessarily indicative of a business that is coming out of recession, but it gives you opportunities to get in and sell, so it is of key importance. Whatever the reason, someone gets promoted, and his picture, plus appropriate editorial, gets into the local newspaper.

Your plan of action is just the same as for the job advertisements, except this time you don't need the card index system. This time you can telephone or write straight away to the promoted person, beginning: 'Congratulations on your promotion'.

## Method 3: PLC Annual Reports

Every Public Limited Company (PLC) whose shares are quoted on the Stock Exchange publishes an Annual Report to its shareholders. These Annual Reports contain an incredible amount of useful information which helps you sell.

Draw up a list of those PLCs you are interested in – existing customers as well as prospects – establish the date of their financial year end and at the appropriate time (about three months after the end of their financial year) write to the Company Secretary at the registered office of the PLC and ask for a copy of the Annual Report. Personal letter, not from your company. You'll get the Report by return, plus a lot of other bumph. The Company Secretary has to assume you are a prospective shareholder.

Apart from the balance sheet and accounts (which you *must* learn how to interpret, because these tell you how much money has been put aside for development and expansion or modernization) you have in a PLC's Annual Report the Chairman's statement. This can be your most valuable selling tool. Let me quote from a few Chairman's Statements to show you why:

'Obviously a setback of £5m off our profit budget is a very big handicap but we have decided none the less to go flat out for our original budgets. Despite this financial penalty, and to demonstrate our confidence in the future, we plan to invest approximately £230m in total over the next three years in public houses, catering and production facilities.'

'Plans for the modernization of the . . . division, including a move to a new single-storey building where production, warehousing and office functions will be integrated, are well advanced.'

'Operations by . . . in handicraft kits and rug-making accessories have now been discontinued and the premises used for this purpose are being converted to more profitable use by the group.'

'We will not allow short-term cyclical movements in the economy to influence unduly our long-term strategic thinking. We have substantial unused financial facilities and will continue to implement our planned programme of expansion.'

There is your **carrot**, dug up and on a plate. And just imagine being face-to-face with an executive of the PLC with 'substantial unused financial facilities' with his Chairman's statement in your briefcase, hearing the executive saying to you 'We can't afford it.'

'What?', you'll say, showing surprise and pulling the Annual Report out of your bag. 'But your Chairman says here . . .'

It's truly incredible how much you can broaden the discussions you have with PLC customers, just from what you learn about their businesses by reading their Annual Reports. Remember the Confidence from Knowledge factor?

## Method 4: District Council Planning Registers

Every application for planning permission to build something, or extend something, or change the use of a building, must, by law, be entered in the appropriate District Council's Planning Register.

There are 400 such registers in the UK, and they are all open for inspection by the general public (that's you!) during normal business hours.

'You'll get everything you need in the register – developer, user, client, architect, contractor, project, surveyor, and the Council's decision.

You may not be concerned about buildings and building services – but you **will** be concerned about what goes on in, and around, the project when it is finished – be it boilers, toilet rolls, copiers, computers, cars, insurance, fire extinguishers, vending machines, paper, packaging, or whatever.

This is **advance** prospecting, and well worth the time of

getting yourself down to every Council office in your area once every month to find out what's in the register – before your competitors get there. If you want to WIN, that is!

## Method 5: End of Call Questions

More commonly called 'referrals'.

How many calls do you make in a year? 1,000? 1,500? 2,000?

However many, on every single one of these calls you make there is the opportunity, at the end or somewhere during the call, to ask: 'By the way, do you know of anyone who might be able to use our kind of equipment?'

Or, for retailers: 'I know things are pretty competitive in your business, but do you know of anyone else who it would be worth me calling on while I'm in this area?'

And for large companies: 'While I'm here, do you know of any other departments who might be able to use our services?'

And on regular, repeat calls: 'I know I ask you this every week,

Charlie, but anyone worth me calling on, this time round?'

Ask the question religiously, every call (and it doesn't matter what *kind* of call it is, *or* the status of the person you're asking) and some of your regular customers will begin feeding you names *before you ask*.

And whenever you get a name – even if it is one of your customers – you don't stop, you keep on going with *more* questions.

Chances are he'll know a lot more than you do about people and businesses in his own locale.

'What do they do?'
'What kind of widgets do they use?'
'Where do they buy them from?'
and you dig for that carrot:
'Do they have any problem?'

Give anyone an opportunity to talk about *someone else's* problems (not his – he'll shut up on his!) and the roof will blow off. You'll have trouble keeping up. It's the national Sport!

You probe for contacts:

'Who's your opposite number over there?'
or
'Do you know the name of their chief buyer?'
and for friendships. or the opposite:
'Do you know him well?'
and you finish with:
'Well, thanks. Do you mind if I mention your name when I ring for an appointment?'

But if you're really good and he obviously knows well the person he's been talking about – you finish like this:

'I wonder, would you mind giving him a ring for me while I'm here – to see if he could see me today, while I'm in the area?'

Oh yes, they *will* do it. More than 60% of them will do it. If you don't believe me, try it for yourself and see.

But before you can try that finish, you've got to remember to start the ball rolling – to ask the **first** question. The incredible thing about Sellers is that most of them *don't remember* to ask the first question. They throw away probably 500 opportunities to get face-to-face with new prospects every year (if you make 1,500 calls a year, that's a 1 in 3 ratio of positive results from asking the question, batting average for most people who **do** remember).

One sales director I know got so annoyed with his salesmen forgetting something this good – and this basic – he fitted their briefcases with special handles which had engraved in them the words: '**Ask the question**'. When they picked up their briefcases to leave the customer, they had to see those words. And I bet a few of his salesmen looked down at the words and said to themselves: 'What question?'

I tailor-made this referral technique not long ago to fit a small company that sells showers, door to door. The company had a team of five young lady 'canvassers' and some installers. The canvassers weren't very good at canvassing, but they *were* good at getting orders – they were closing on average 20 orders a week total.

Only advertising and direct mail was generating new business enquiries, but this the company's managing director considered to be far too expensive.

'How do I get my team of young lady housewives to use referral techniques?' was the problem he posed to me. 'Probably you don't,' I replied. 'What do you want to see your sales increase to?'

'I'd be happy with 50 orders a week,' he told me. 'After that I'll have problems with installation and delivery.' 'Okay,' said I, 'forget your canvassers. You do it. Are you prepared to make 20 calls a week yourself, on the customers who had your showers installed, say two/three weeks ago? – and in the evenings?'

'No problem,' he replied.

'Right,' said I, 'just knock on their doors in the evening, out of the blue, no appointment, hand whoever opens the door your business card, introduce yourself and tell them you've just popped round to make sure everything is okay with the shower (and hope that everything is okay!).'

'They'll be so surprised, and delighted, they'll invite you in for a cup of tea. They'll even turn off the TV. (Only managing directors have that much charisma!) And when they've finished telling you how nice the shower is, you say:

"Before I go, I wonder if you'd be kind enough to give me a bit of help. My job is to find people like you for my girls to talk to (not sell to) about showers. You're happy with yours. Can you give me the names and addresses of anyone else you know who you feel might be just as happy as you if they had one?'

'And off you go. You should average three names and addresses per call. Your girls will crack 50 orders a week within a month of your starting to make *your* calls. And don't come back to me with your delivery and installation problems; that's not my field.'

It's that easy to create your own opportunities for successful Selling – to take positive action and win. So will you use these five methods for finding new customers? Will you adapt the end of Call Questions technique to work for you – as I adapted it for the shower company?

## The Five Card Trick – the Ultimate Referral Technique

The word 'trick' should not be in the professional Seller's vocabulary, but with such a title as 'The Five Card Trick' it is irresistible.

This is the ultimate Referral technique; developed by J. Douglas Edwards and used by many Million Dollar Round Table members to keep themselves well over their MDRT qualifying target. The technique is not restricted to use only in the life insurance business, however. It can be, and is, used very successfully in other kinds of direct selling and in selling to industry.

The Five Card Trick is more than a technique, it is a game – a game played between Seller and customer. It is the customer's natural curiosity to find out what happens next that helps make the technique successful.

The objective? To walk away from a call with **five**, yes, **five**, new and fully researched prospects given you by the customer you have just called upon, and for whom firm appointments have already been made on your behalf **by the customer**. (That's why this technique is the ultimate! But it is not, repeat not, for the novice Sellers.)

The **five** Card Trick is **only** used when the situation is right for it. The customer is happy with what the Seller has done for him. The customer is relaxed and not in a hurry to get on with something else – he has a few minutes to spare after the business with the Seller has been satisfactorily completed. If all these conditions are 'go', the Seller says:

'Before I go, I wonder if you'd be kind enough to spend ten minutes giving me a hand with how I have to do *my* business?'

If the situation is really 'go', the customer's reply will be 'Sure. What do you want to know?' or something like that. The seller then takes out of his jacket pocket five blank cards, each about 15cm×10cm, and lays them out in a line on the desk in front of the customer. While he's doing this, he doesn't say a word.

Then he begins asking questions. The questions he asks are ones he knows, from his knowledge of this customer, will be pertinent to the customer.

'You've lived/worked in this area for some years now, haven't you? Is there anyone else you can think of who also lives/works around here who, you feel, might benefit from our product/services the way you have/are going to?'

The Seller is searching for names. When he gets one, he writes it down on one of the five cards. If he gets two or three names as a result of his question, he writes one name only on each of two or three cards. His target is five names, one on each of his five cards. He keeps asking questions until he has achieved this target. No more, no less. Stop at five – always.

'Are you a member of any trade association? Last time you attended a meeting of the association, was there anyone there who, you reckon, could benefit from this the way you're doing?'

'Do you play any sports – golf or tennis or anything? Last time you were down at the club, was there anyone there who, you feel, might be able to use this?'

'Has anyone you know gained promotion recently? Gone up in the world so that his/her requirements may have changed and so will give us an opportunity?'

Each of the questions is designed to get the customer thinking about a relatively *small* number of people. This achieves the best results. Few people will provide you with names if they are trying to find one person out of 100,000 packing Wembley Stadium (metaphorically speaking!).

When each of the five cards bears a name, the Seller thanks the customer and moves to stage two:

'Have you got your telephone directory handy? Could we together dig out the addresses and the telephone numbers of these people, just to make sure I have the correct ones?'

'Sure. Why not?'

The request seems reasonable to the customer. After all, there are probably fifty Charlie Browns in the telephone book. And, by this time, the customer's natual curiosity will have taken hold. No way is he going to stop until he finds out what's going to happen to those five cards. So together, Seller and customer dig out addresses and telephone numbers, which are written on each of the five cards.

This completed, the Seller silently re-aligns the five cards into a neat line, studies them for a few seconds, and then asks:

'If you were me, which one of these five cards would you call on first? Which one do you think would be the **best** customer for me?'

After a few seconds rubbing his chin, the customer will select one of the cards. 'This one.'

'Why did you pick that one?' the Seller then asks. 'What makes him better than the other four?'

And the customer explains why he chose that person as number one. The Seller notes the relevant data on the card. One fully researched, fully qualified prospect.

'Which one would you see as second best?'
'Which one is third best?'
'Which one is fourth?'
'Which makes this one last? Why is he not as good as the other four?'

Five fully researched, fully qualified prospects, lying there in a row. The feeling of elation could be forgiven any Seller who gets this far. But the hardest part is yet to come. Not hard meaning difficult, but hard meaning having the guts to **do it**.

The Seller picks up the number one card, offers it to the customer and says:

'One last favour. Would you ring Mr . . . for me, while I'm here, and ask him if he can spare the time to see me sometime during the next few days?'

You won't believe it until you try it yourself, but more than 60% of customers who are asked to telephone that number one prospect **do it**. And they do it with enthusiasm. And of course they give the Seller the best possible impartial plug when they are talking to the prospect – they can't do anything else.

'You've got to see this guy, Charlie. He's got something that must be just up your street. He's here with me now. Wants to know if you can fit him in for half an hour, tomorrow or the day after. Or this afternoon, if that's not too soon for you. What? Yes, I've bought some. They look great.'

Better than this, every customer who telephones that number one prospect will also go on and telephone the other four. The Seller's only uncontrollable risk is that the prospect doesn't answer when the customer rings.

For the less than 40% of customers who say 'I'd rather not' in reply to the first offered card and the request for them to telephone on the Seller's behalf, the Seller says:

'Okay. Do you mind if I mention your name when *I* ring for an appointment?'

100% of customers who turn down the Seller on his first request, say 'Yes, of course' to his second request. No one can say 'No' twice running in this technique. And that's why the **guts to do it** are necessary.

So the jackpot is five firm appointments made on your behalf by a satisfied customer. The consolation prize is five fully researched, fully qualified prospects and the okay to use the customer's name when *you* telephone for an appointment.

Not bad for ten minutes sheer professional enjoyment? That's really Selling!

## Be an Entrepreneur

Be different. Stand out from the crowd. Do things that the average Seller wouldn't even think of doing. That's the way to sell successfully against competition.

How different? Let's take a few examples for finding new customers.

## The Cocktail Party

Clive Holmes began his sales career selling carpets off the back of a van. Now he's the acknowledged king of the British Life Insurance business – a life member of the Million Dollar Round Table (to get that accolade you make the million dollar target in ten consecutive years) and founder president of the Life Insurance Association. A very high FLIA indeed.

Very early on in his life insurance career, he discovered that if you tell a stranger you sell life insurance, the stranger disappears, almost in a puff of smoke. He found this particularly so at cocktail parties, which he frequented avidly, knowing that in the life insurance business, if you run out of people to sell to, you're out of business.

So he perfected a subtle change in technique for his cocktail party prospecting which went like this:

| | |
|---|---|
| STRANGER (*G & T in hand*) | 'What do *you* do for a living?' |
| CLIVE | 'I buy life insurance.' |
| STRANGER (*puzzled*) | 'What do you mean, you **buy** life insurance?' |

CLIVE                              'I buy life insurance for people at the
                                   lowest possible cost for the maximum
                                   possible benefits. Would you like me to
                                   buy *you* some?'

It worked like a dream – even when the prospect twigged it and
laughed.


## Car Spotting

I've spent a fair amount of my time over the years, trying to get
car salesmen to stop sitting on their bottoms in their showrooms,
waiting for the world to beat a path to their doors. Taking the
demonstration car round the area, knocking on people's front
doors and saying, 'Let me take you for a ride?' would be better
than that, but gives problems with lady customers if you don't
get the words right!

A really switched-on car salesman, determined to beat his
many local competitors, also has an eye for where his profit
comes from. Two places: from the sales of his new and A1
guaranteed nearly-new cars, and from the sale of cars he has to
accept in part-exchange from his customers – most of these
vehicles being passed on 'through the trade'.

He knows that if he sits in his showroom and waits for customers to come to him, he has absolutely no control over the kind
of cars he has to take in part-exchange. If he refuses to accept a
part-exchange, he loses a sale. If he offers a silly price, same thing
happens. Yet he knows that some cars hold their value better
than others and are easier to sell on. So he goes out into his area –
**looking for these kinds of cars.**

He goes out armed with a bundle of specially designed letters,
lists of the new and A1 guaranteed nearly-new cars he has for
sale, plain manilla envelopes and his confidential copy of *Glass's
Guide* (the trade price book for car dealers). He finds suitable cars
parked all over his area.

He examines the exterior appearance and bodywork of a likely
looking parked car. He checks the tyres. He can even test the
shock absorbers if he's careful, by pressing gently down on a
couple of corners. He can see the interior of the car and he can

normally tell whether the car is privately owned or a company car, by its contents. (He's looking for 'privates', not company owned.)

He can see the mileage on the speedometer and knows the age of the car from the registration number. So he has everything he needs to decide a conditional price for that car.

He fills in the details on one of his specially designed letters. It reads like this:

*'Hello,*
*Your car, registration number . . . is worth a lot more than you probably think. If the mechanical condition is as good as the body condition and if the mileage shown on the speedometer (. . .) is genuine, we would offer you £. . . for your car in part-exchange for any of the new or A1 guaranteed cars you'll see on the attached stock list.*

*Why don't you and your family drop in to our showroom this weekend and let us give you a demonstration drive. No obligation.*

*And hire purchase facilities have never been easier to arrange.*

*We look forward to seeing you.'*

The letter and stock list go into a manilla envelope and the envelope goes on the windscreen, under the wiper blade. A good

car spotting salesman should be able to find and 'process' about thirty profitable part-exchanges a day.

The owner of the car comes back to his vehicle, sees the envelope on the screen and thinks: 'Hell, I've got a parking ticket'. He gets into his car, opens the envelope in high dudgeon and finds it is **not** a parking ticket. His mood switches instantly from anger to pleasure. Just right for impulse-buy decisions. Some of them are down at the showroom within the hour.

Maximum prospects, maximum sales, maximum profit. Yet you don't see many car salesmen doing it, do you? Most of them are too busy thinking up reasons for *not* doing it!

## Early Risers

It's the early bird that catches the worm! Never as true as in selling against competition. The entrepreneurial fork lift truck salesman, for example, gets up very early a couple of times a month so that he can be down at the British Rail National Carriers Goods Depot before 8.00 am, while the van drivers are still sorting parcels and loading vans.

He's armed with a couple of packets of cigarettes and his A4 size survey pad (you can't sell successfully with anything smaller). At 8.00 am in the morning he has no trouble persuading half a dozen van drivers to stop work for a few minutes and join him for a fag.

'Please can you give me a bit of help?' he asks them. 'I sell fork lift trucks in this area. Most of my trucks are used by companies for loading and unloading vans like yours. Do you know of any companies that you deliver to and collect from that don't have a decent truck, or don't have anything at all to help you load and unload the heavy stuff?'

Wow! Free fags and an opportunity to have a free moan at someone else's expense. The national sport again. The survey pad is full in minutes. A salesman who does this kind of thing regularly will find such people waiting for him to come back, with their own lists of prospects for him. Some will ask for a sales brochure to give to one of the companies they deliver to, and will do some selling on the salesman's behalf.

You see, deep down, people *love* to be helpful. Provided they are *asked* for help correctly. There are very few truly 'nasty bastards' around.

Transport cafes serve the same purpose as goods depots, except the prospects found tend to be national instead of local. Astute salesmen will lunch at transport cafes, get into conversation with a couple of lorry drivers and use exactly the same technique. Across the whole salesforce, leads gained from such sources would be fed into a central co-ordinator for redistribution to the territory concerned.

## Minders!

A guy I met on holiday in the West Indies has a lovely idea for getting acquainted with new prospects. He sells time-sharing for a beachfront estate in Antigua. Some days he quits the estate office and takes himself along the beach or on one of the tourist 'pirate cruises', dressed only in bathing trunks and flip-flops. Being a smoker, he carries a packet of cigarettes and a lighter in his hand.

He has an eye for likely prospects – couples who look like they've lived long enough to be able to afford what he's selling. When he finds a couple, he smiles down on them and says:

'Hey, I wonder, would you do me a great favour? I want to swim. Would you look after my cigarettes and lighter while I'm in the water?'

After the swim, getting into more meaningful conversation and inviting the couple to come and see his time-sharing units is a piece of cake.

If he's on board a cruise boat, the patter goes:

'Hey, I wonder, would you do me a great favour? I'm going to swim ashore, rather than take the dingy. Would you take my cigarettes and lighter ashore with you?'

*The Star Prize*

The most glorious example of being different, the one to whom I give my star prize, I came upon in 1978. It's never been surpassed.

The company in question had found that within its list of good prospective customers there were several hundred that were refusing even to grant its salesmen the opportunity to get face-to-face. 'Not interested', was the message even though research had proved that the company could improve those prospective customers' businesses no end.

The powers-that-be decided that something must be done about it. All that business going to waste just because the salesforce couldn't get in to start selling. But no one could crack the problem.

Then the publicity manager came up with what everyone considered was a really wild, mad idea. If it hadn't been so much business at stake, if the research hadn't been as thorough, it's doubtful if the idea would ever have got off the ground.

But it was, so it did.

The best 100 'not interested' prospective customers were selected. An order was placed with a top manufacturing jeweller for 100 specially designed gold medals, in velvet lined presentation boxes. A calligrapher was commissioned to design and produce

100 parchment certificates, which were then framed – non-reflective glass and all. Total cost around £4,000.

With a suitable prestigious covering letter from the company's chairman, a gold medal and framed certificate were sent by Securicor to each of the 100 top prospects. The certificate contained these words:

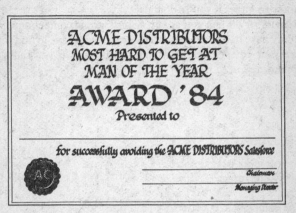

This is really high-psychology. The framed certificates by themselves would have got up most people's noses. It was the solid gold medals that did the trick. No one would go to that much trouble and expense if they were not sincere. There weren't many of the hundred certificates that weren't hung in prospective customers' offices immediately. Such people would consider the award a very high honour indeed. After all, they were all founder members of the 'We hate salesmen' club. The gold medals had pride of place on their office desks.

Now for the results of the exercise. The salesforce didn't stop trying to get in, of course. In face, they renewed their efforts with increased vigour. And this time they succeeded. Within three months of the presentations, 77 out of the 100 had been cracked.

Think about it. To whom else but the representative of the company that had presented the award could those 100 prospects properly show their appreciation, and demonstrate that the award was being displayed in their office for all to see?

A very fruitful investment, the powers-that-be decided on review – but no one has done it since. Maybe the spiralling price of gold has put this kind of 'being different' beyond reach.

So be different. Go on. You can do it if you put your mind to it. And it will demoralize your competitors dreadfully when they get to know about what you're doing.

Remember – when you are up against strong competition, you not only have to find more new customers, you have to find them *before* your competitors find them. So it helps if you can slow them down.

# 4
# How to Make 'Cold Canvassing' Productive

The managing director of the pump manufacturing company stands up and addresses his salesforce.

*'All you've got to do,'* he tells them, *'is get out there and look for chimneys. Wherever there's a chimney, there's going to be a pump underneath it.'*

The novice salesman, one month into his new job, has been let out to call on a few customers 'to get his feet wet' after a couple of weeks in the sales office and the works, learning about the products. He encounters this huge sign at the entrance to a large industrial estate.

'*Wow,*' he thinks, '*a whole day's work with only ten miles on the expense account. That'll please my manager.*' And he parks his car, loads his briefcase with literature and proceeds to knock on doors.

The sales director has been examining his salesforce's call reports and expenses claims. His boardroom colleague in accounts bent his ear yesterday about the spiralling costs of telephone calls. Face-to-face selling time is 70% of what it was this time last year. The salesforce spends on average 1½ days every week at home, making appointments, preparing proposals and planning ahead. He decides that a change of policy is required. He pens a memo to his salesforce.

'Far too much selling time is being spent at home, instead of with customers and prospective customers. Starting Monday, I want to see the number of sales calls made increasing by 20% minimum. YCSSOYA!'

The customer's purchasing committee is holding its monthly meeting. All the executives with divisional and departmental buying responsibilities are present. the subject under discussion is **time**. The time the members of the purchasing committee spend talking to representatives of suppliers and potential suppliers.

'I had seventeen salesmen asking to see me last week,' says one executive. 'None of them had an appointment and, out of the five I actually saw, only one knew anything about our business and what I was responsible for buying.'

'I can beat that,' says another executive. 'My secretary's been keeping a record since our last meeting. In the last month, we've had ninety-four representatives try to get to us, without a prior appointment, twenty-six attempts to secure an appointment by suppliers we don't do business with, eighteen attempts to sell over the telephone and twelve visits from people we **do** business with.'

Each of the members of the purchasing committee has similar figures. Each agrees that, in order to be effective as an executive with buying responsibilities, some suppliers' representatives **must** be seen. One must keep up-to-date with what's available and make regular checks on prices, quality, delivery, etc.

But the time available for talking to suppliers' representatives is strictly limited, and must be even more strictly limited in future. Everyone agrees.

Thus, the purchasing committee decides that a notice shall be displayed in the main reception hall . . .

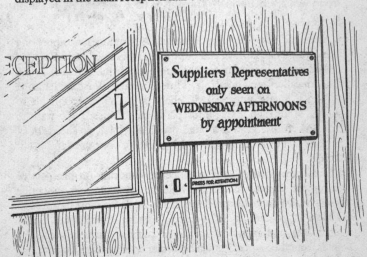

. . . and the reception hall staff are briefed on how to handle people from the pump manufacturer, novice salesmen and those discouraged by their companies from using their telephones to make appointments.

More and more 'By Appointment Only' notices are appearing in reception halls. More and more customers are **demanding** that Sellers make appointments and are point-blank refusing to see random callers – on principle. Time is money. Wasting that time talking to inept, unprepared Sellers is no longer acceptable to anyone other than inept, unprepared customers. If you want to plan your future growth around people like that, go ahead, but I bet you don't make the end of this book, or your sales and profit targets.

**Cold canvassing** – the practice of knocking on prospective customers' doors, out of the blue, no appointment, no prior research, isn't a viable proposition any more for most businesses. Which is something of a pity, because every good Seller sometimes underruns on a planned call and finds himself fifty miles from the nearest known customer with an hour to spare.

The logical thing to do with that spare hour is to talk to a few receptionists about what their companies do, what they buy and who's responsible for the buying or the specifying. Prospecting research; detective work as discussed in the previous chapter, to pave the way for an effective, by appointment, call the **next** time you are in that section of your territory.

But wouldn't it be satisfying if, with the appropriate degree of professionalism and original thinking, the Cold Canvass call **could** be made viable again. Think how a few extra orders secured this way could bring you over target with no additional selling costs.

Here are a few ideas to get you thinking about how **you** could crack this problem. There is but one proviso – the prospective customers on whom you Cold Canvass **must** be businesses that should be able to use your products or services. This much research has to be done in all cases.

(To put you out of your misery, YCSSOYA stands for 'You can't sell sitting on your . . .')

## Business Cards with a Difference

Let's assume there are no 'By Appointment Only' notices to hold up progress. The average novice Seller walks into the reception hall for a Cold Canvass call, presents his business card to the receptionist and asks to see the person who is responsible for buying or specifying, let's say widgets.

The receptionist takes the business card, rings through to the person responsible and says something like this:

'There's a Mr John Fenton here to see you.'

The reaction of the person responsible will, more often than not, be – 'What's he want?'

The receptionist, more often than not, will then take the line of least resistance. She has the Seller's business card in her hand, so she simply reads it to the person responsible.

'It says here "Universal Widget Corporation – area representative".'

What an incredibly powerful carrot with which to hit the person responsible between the eyes. Awe-inspiring. He's so impressed, all he can think of saying is – 'Tell him I'm too busy. Get him to leave some literature.'

The receptionist looks up at the Seller and says – 'He's too busy at the moment but if you'd like to leave some literature he'll be happy to look through it when he's got time.'

There's nowhere else to go. Leave the literature and say goodbye. Another abortive call. Yes it is; he'll *never* get round to reading the literature, even if it ever gets as far as his office.

Okay – if you reckon I'm being a touch over-dramatic, dig out your own business card, put yourself in the shoes of that person responsible and read it to yourself as if it were the receptionist reading it. Bet you don't get face-to-face with yourself!

So the first rule for Cold Canvass calls is – don't use your business card unless it says something that will clearly come over as a dangled carrot. Just be yourself.

'My name's John Fenton, from Universal Widget Corporation. I'm after the person responsible for buying or specifying widgets in your company. Could you tell me who that is?' She tells you. 'Will you find out from him if he can spare me ten minutes, please?'

She contacts the person responsible. He still asks 'What's he want?' But now she can't take the line of least resistance. She has to turn to you and say – 'He wants to know what you want.'

So you say – 'Well, it's a bit complicated. Can I borrow your 'phone and explain to him myself? It'll be much easier.'

Now you're at exactly the same point where you would have been, had you telephoned in advance for an appointment. So dangle the carrot and close – 'It'll only take you ten minutes for us to establish whether we can give you a better deal or not. Can I see you now, or would you prefer me to call back later this morning, say, in an hour from now? I've got to see one of our customers just down the road, anyway.'

If you are very, very good, then on that one in a thousand Cold Canvass call you might find a straight personal challenge will get you face-to-face and further.

Stuart sells racking and shelving. One Friday afternoon approaching 5 pm (there's a novelty!) he made a Cold Canvass call on a division of Walls Ice-Cream. He didn't use his business card and swiftly found himself holding the receptionist's telephone and speaking to the works manager. After a few minutes of carrot dangling, the works manager said to Stuart – 'We're quite happy with our present suppliers and have been for the past 10 years.'

Stuart, quick on his feet, straight away replied – 'I've been eating Lyons Maid Ice-Cream with complete satisfaction for the past 25 years, but I'm willing to change if someone convinces me there's a better ice-cream.'

The works manager couldn't help laughing. 'All right you so and so,' he said, 'come up and talk to me.'

Stuart has since supplied several thousand pounds worth of racking and shelving to Walls, at no great difference in price or quality compared with the supplier the works manager said he's been happy with for the past 10 years.

Now wouldn't it be better if your business card dangled the carrot for you?

Consider the fun you could get – and the business you could get – from your Cold Canvass calls if you used a card like this.

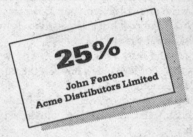

25%

John Fenton
Acme Distributors Limited

You walk into reception, ask for the name of the person responsible, hand the receptionist your card and say 'Could Mr Green spare me ten minutes?'

She rings through to Mr Green, gives your name and company and he says, 'What's he want?' She takes the line of least resistance and reads the card. 'It just says 25%!'

Mr Green, maybe a touch irritably, asks 'What's *that* mean?' The receptionist turns to you and says, 'He wants to know what the 25% means.'

You simply reply, 'Well, that's the average amount we save our customers on warehousing costs if they use our products.'

'Oh,' she says, and goes back to Mr Green. 'He says it's what they usually save people who use their products – on warehousing costs.'

Now consider Mr Green's position. If he says to his company's receptionist, 'Tell him I'm too busy' he's declaring to a lesser employee that he doesn't care much about saving his company 25% off anything. Is he likely to put himself in that position? No, he's not.

The worst that can happen to you is that you get face-to-face with Mr Green and he tells you to close the door quietly on the way out – in private!

The 25% business card has another, equally powerful use. Note it does not have a telephone number.

Say you have compiled a list of suspects or prospects and you are approaching the stage of first contact. Icy cold will be the usual reception when you telephone for an appointment – you can't use the 25% gambit on the telephone. But you still know that an appointment is more professional than just dropping in, even with ammunition like the 25% card.

So you address small envelopes to each name on your suspect/prospect list, write on the back of your 25% cards – 'Please ring me on 0926 37621' and post just a 25% card to each person, in the envelope, on its own, by itself!

Curiosity does the rest. 99% response. And when they ring *you*, they're warm, not icy cold. They ask the question direct – 'What's this 25% mean?' and off you go.

Think of the economics as well as the fun – you've spent money on a stamp and an envelope, but **he's** paying for the telephone call.

If you're selling to retailers and department stores, consider this second example which you could hand to a counter assistant to take to the manager or department buyer.

The four top priority objectives for any retailer. Profit, throughput, quality and price competitiveness. How could any store manager given this card by one of his assistants send back a message via that assistant 'Tell him I'm too busy' without risking the word going round that he didn't care any more?

## Titles

Still on the subject of business cards, a very effective force for getting in on a Cold Canvass call is to carry the highest possible title. If you are a managing director, this title on your card will get you face-to-face with just about anyone, with or without an appointment. But how many managing directors make Cold Canvass calls?

One London-based wholesaler, fed up with the number of times its five salesmen were turned away by its retailer prospective customers, decided to trade in the salesmen's Minis and replace them with Jaguars and gave them business cards carrying the title 'Sales Director'.

As a direct result, sales ten-folded in two years.

## Put Yourself in the Customer's Shoes

That's a very important thing to be able to do if you want to be a successful Seller in a competitive market-place, but in the context of successful Cold Canvassing, I use it to mean – assume the role of a customer when you walk into that prospective customer's reception hall. When prospective customers walk into suppliers' premises out of the blue, they get a totally different reception from that given to Sellers who walk in out of the blue, don't they?

Don't they?

Back in 1976, I set up a 'Customer's Shoes' cold canvassing technique for a machine tool company. The company sold very expensive computerized turning machines with very high production rates and component quality.

The first objective for the company's sales engineers was to find out what kind of components a prospective customer was producing, in what quantity, at what level of quality and on what kind of machines. The most effective way to establish all this essential information was to get into the prospective customer's machine shop and see it happening. But getting the prospective customer's works manager to let them into the factory was something the sales engineers found somewhat difficult.

So we drew up an A4-sized card on which was printed sectional drawings of a representative selection of the kind of components that the company's turning machines were best at producing.

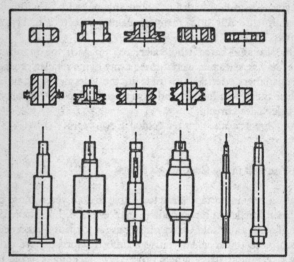

The sales engineer walks into the prospective customer's reception hall. He has the components' card in his hand and his survey pad. No briefcase. A briefcase at this stage would be a dead giveaway. He bids the receptionist good morning.

'Could you ask your works manager if he could spare me ten minutes. My name is John Fenton. I want to find out if you make anything like these.'

The receptionist looks at the card and doesn't know if its owner is selling or buying. If she asks 'Are you buying or selling?' the sales engineer replies, 'I hope to be instrumental in increasing your business quite substantially.'

She rings through to the works manager. He comes out to reception and the sales engineer shows him the components card. 'Do you make anything that looks remotely like any of these?'

The works manager is immediately locked in on the card. He can't help himself. 'Er, well, we do something like that, and like that, and a few now and again like that,' he says, pointing to the appropriate sectional drawings on the card.

'What material do you make them in? Do you have to put them through a grinding operation to get the necessary surface finish? What sizes of batches? What kind of machines do you produce them on? Do you use numerical control or computerized numerical control at all?'

The picture which the sales engineer builds from the answers to these questions very quickly takes shape. 'Wow,' he says, 'I might be wrong, but I reckon we could cut your machine shop production and labour costs as far as turning and grinding is concerned by probably 50%, **and** double your capacity if you're looking for more work. Could I take another ten minutes of your time and get you to let me have a look at your machine shop?'

More often than not, the works manager, his curiosity and appetite aroused, says, 'Don't see why not – follow me,' and off they go.

Late in 1983, I was guest speaker at a sales conference held by TNT Overnite – the express parcels delivery service. For a bit of fun, I built a fairly large parcel, wrapped round with metres of TNT Overnite tape. Inside the parcel was a small cassette tape recorder, and I'd put into the cassette a recording of a very loud, very tinny, ticking alarm clock.

Amplified by the tape recorder, the ticking sounded pretty urgent!

Thus, I made my entrance and did my thing. The ticking parcel achieved a resounding ovation, and my opening words, 'If you walked into a prospective customer's premises, out of the blue, carrying one of these, and asked to speak to the Despatch Manager, what would be the reaction of the receptionist?' were developed into ten minutes of highly productive discussion.

'Forget the ticking clock,' the conference decided. 'What would be the reaction if you just walked in with an urgent parcel? You wouldn't look like a sales person any more, you'd look like a customer. Almost certainly, you'd get face-to-face with the Despatch Manager – cold canvass – in minimum elapsed time.'

I left the conference deliberating on how to disguise all the salesforce's briefcases as TNT Overnite parcels!


## The Jekyll and Hyde Technique

There are some areas of Selling where teamwork pays better dividends than the lone approach, especially from the Cold Canvassing aspects. Two Sellers working in partnership, can break down barriers that the single Seller often finds insurmountable.

Take Double Glazing and Replacement Windows, sold direct to householders by Sellers on commission only. Arthur and George decide to team up. On one particular day, they Cold Canvass a particular housing estate. They tackle a street at a time, Arthur knocking on doors on one side, George the other side.

'Good morning,' says Arthur to the lady of the house. 'I'm from UWC Double Glazing. We're conducting a market survey of houses on this estate, to find out how many of them are already fitted with double glazing or secondary glazing. Can I ask you a few questions about your house?'

A few questions further on and Arthur figures this particular house is a good prospect. But he also knows that, having started with the Market Survey technique, he cannot now switch over and start selling. To do so would send the prospective customer shrieking into the night.

This is where the teamwork comes in.

'If I might make a suggestion,' says Arthur, 'we've produced a video film of what we've been doing in this and other areas to make houses like yours a lot more comfortable to live in at very little expense, especially in noisy districts. I know my colleague George Ratcliffe is in this district next Tuesday evening. If Tuesday is a convenient evening for both you and your husband, I could get in touch with Mr Ratcliffe and have him bring over the video film to show you. It only takes about twenty minutes. He's got a video player, if you haven't got one yourself. You'll probably enjoy seeing how easy it is to play video through your tele as much as seeing our film. What would be the best time on Tuesday evening – around 7.30 or would you prefer a bit later?'

George Ratcliffe is busy on the other side of the street, checking out houses and making appointments for Arthur for next Tuesday evening. On Tuesday, they're both back, but on opposite sides of the street.

This Jekyll and Hyde technique can be applied to any reasonably compact area and used for office equipment, microcomputers, vending machines, carpet cleaning, cars, in fact any product or service where a market survey can be credibly conducted.

## Cold Canvassing by Telephone

So far, we've looked at the kind of productive Cold Canvassing that comes from face-to-face calls. Many businesses, however, find that the Cold Canvass element is best tackled by well-trained office-based people, whose job is to conduct a telephone market survey and, if the suspect turns into a prospect by the end of the survey, to fix appointments on behalf of the field salesforce.

This kind of Cold Canvassing is a systematic, full-time job, where the suspect lists are derived from directories or computer bureau print-outs. The telephone surveyors sit at specially constructed desks with accoustic panels all around them, the panels bearing check lists of the best things to say to prospects who show resistance, without upsetting the prospect and to achieve the objective in spite of the resistance.

Such telephone survey teams run daily, weekly and monthly competitions for those who book the most appointments, with penalty points for any that subsequently prove useless by the time the field salesman has visited the prospect. In this way, morale within the tele-team and between the tele-team and the field salesforce is maintained at a very high level, as are results.

If you're wondering why you're in a business that doesn't have any directories or computer print-outs that can be used for activities like this, I can put your mind at rest. There are directories, guides, year books, trade association membership lists, professional body membership lists, specialist bureaux and computer print-outs for **every** kind of business. You just haven't found one for yours yet.

Keep looking. There are over 2,000 different directories published each year in the UK alone. Two of them are directories of **directories**, published by CBD Research Ltd of Beckenham, Kent, and British Rate and Data, MacLean Hunter Ltd, London. Two more are directories of available mailing lists, published by Gower Press Ltd (*The Direct Mail Databook*) and Benn Brothers (*Benn's Direct Marketing Services Directory*).

To whet your appetite with a few specific examples – if you are looking for scrap merchants there is the *European Scrap Directory*. If you are after property developers, there is the *Property Directory*. If you sell welding rods for strange materials, maybe the *Stainless Steel Fabricators Directory* will do you some good. If you cater for coal mines, *The Guide to the Coal Fields* gives you everything in the UK, even maps. If you want to sell rubber truncheons, *The Police and Constabulary Almanac* is a must.

## Once in a Lifetime – Yorick from Warwick!

Once in a lifetime, you get the opportunity to develop something that really is unbeatable. It happened to me in 1982, and it happened by chance. My wife bought me a somewhat unusual birthday present – a human skull, about 150 years old, mounted on a plinth, with the cranium neatly cut all round and hinged, so that the brain cavity could be inspected. Obviously it had been in the hands of a medical student at some time in the past.

Being born of Stratford-upon-Avon and resident eight miles away in Warwick, my skull was christened **Yorick** – from Warwick. I was tempted to spring-load the jaw bone so that I could ask it 'What do you think of it so far?' But I resisted the temptation. Instead, Yorick became potentially the most powerful Selling Tool ever invented, capable, in the right hands, of increasing both face-to-face selling time **and** orders by 1,000%, on Cold Canvass calls.

Yorick has appeared many times on television and has been put through his paces (the skull *is* a 'he'!) in front of more than 20,000 Sellers. I have personally tested his effectiveness in six different real-life situations and he has a 100% success record – so far.

Yorick performs best when he's selling the latest kind of pocket calculator; one that, when you push the buttons, actually **speaks** what you have pushed – 'Nine zero four divided by two zero equals four five point two.' The calculator, in its leather case, fits snugly into Yorick's brain cavity.

So picture the real-life selling situation. A crowded retail shop, the kind that sells calculators, cameras, stationery and what have you. A dozen or so customers. The manager and his assistants all busy serving. The kind of situation where, if you were selling into that type of retail shop, you have to wait patiently until the customers have been served before you stand a hope of getting five minutes of the manager's time – and where, as customers go

out, more keep coming in. You could be stuck there waiting for an hour.

But now you have Yorick to help you. He's under your right arm as you walk into the shop. Your briefcase is in your left hand. You stop in the centre of the shop. You just stand there, saying nothing. All conversation stops in three seconds flat. Deathly silence. All eyes are focused on Yorick. The manager of the shop is the first to speak.

He says, 'Excuse me for a moment,' to the customer he is serving, walks up to you and commits the cardinal sin of retail or exhibition selling. He says 'Can I help you, sir?'

You put your briefcase down, pat Yorick on the top of his head and say, 'In here, is the nearest thing to the human brain that's so far been developed. Let me show you.'

You walk to the nearest counter, set Yorick down and open his cranium. If you're unlucky, the oldest customer will faint. You take out your Speaking Pocket Calculator, making sure the volume control is turned up to maximum, and proceed to demonstrate. 'Eight five two divided by three multiplied by one six equals four five four four.'

'That's fantastic, how much is it?' one of the customers in the shop is certain to say, because of course you've demonstrated your calculator to everyone in the shop. 'Ooo, just what I need for my nephew's birthday,' is a strong possibility, if the audience has recovered.

'It retails at £49.50, including the leather case, batteries and full instructions,' you explain to the customer. Then you turn to the manager and say casually, 'I've got three in my briefcase and some more in my car down the road. How many would you like for stock?'

That's **really** productive Cold Canvassing.

My big problem now is that I've got to find something even better than Yorick. The unbeatable must be beaten. That's the kind of challenge I like.

# 5
# How to Stop Competitors Stealing Your Customers

> Psst. It's all changed!
> No good just sitting there.
> Okay, so you hate change.
> Just remember, it's the
> only thing in life (other
> than death) that's permanent.
> Sit there much longer,
> and your competitors will
> have it all. They've been
> changing for quite some time now.
> Get off your bottom!

Consider this notice, seen more in restaurants than anywhere else.

IF YOU ARE SATISFIED
PLEASE TELL YOUR FRIENDS
... IF NOT, TELL US!

Such notices are tributes to a belief in the power of word-of-mouth communication and referral. But few people realize just how powerful word-of-mouth communication really is – or realize how much it can damage, or build, a business.

In 1982, Coca-Cola commissioned some research in the USA to try to measure this power. The firm that conducted the research, Technical Assistance Research Programs Inc. of Washington, talked to 1,717 Coca-Cola customers (the stores, not the drinkers!) and found that:

Customers who had complained and who felt their complaints had *not* been satisfactorily resolved, talked about their complaint to between nine and ten other people.

Customers who had complained and who were *completely satisfied* with the response to their complaint, talked about their complaint to between four and five other people.

Think about these statistics. Think about how susceptible these customers are to the overtures and advances of your competitors. That your business is different from Coca-Cola's doesn't matter much. Don't kid yourself this doesn't apply to you. Surely it would be less expensive to prevent migration by resolving the complaints of existing customers than to win new customers? But how about doing **both**? That's *really* winning! Especially against competition.

The Coca-Cola research also covered **enquiries** as well as complaints, and discovered:

Customers who had made enquiries and felt they had *not* received satisfactory answers, talked about it to between four and five other people.

Customers who had made enquiries and were *satisfied* with the answers, talked about it to between three and four other people.

Proof again that bad news travels fastest and furthest.

Consider how much *more* difficult it would be to sell to a newly found prospect if he happened to be one of those nine and ten, or four and five other people. Don't neglect this critical and very grey area of your business.

Robert Townsend, while chief executive of Avis-Rent-A-Car, suggested the best way I know of tackling the complaints problem. He passed it on to all in his fantastically successful book *Up the Organization* (Michael Joseph, 1970).

With his and his publishers' permission (but you should **still** buy his book) I pass his words on to you.

## Chairman of the Executive Committee

Most companies are doing it all wrong. They're wasting this title and others like it on retired brass. These titles can be very useful.

A certain national Institute was created recently. It has a young director with a good deal of experience in the field, but not much experience in managing an organization. He had his objectives clearly thought out and budgets prepared showing how and where he hoped to reach them and what it would mean to the industry. But it was already clear that one of his problems was going to be visits and phone calls from international visiting firemen and from people in the industry wanting to talk to the boss.

He had no room in his budget for an assistant and besides people won't be pushed off on an assistant. He *did* have a substantial expense account for entertainment. So he called up an old friend who was retired and said, 'I can't pay you a salary, but if you'll come and take all these phone calls and lunches and dinners off my back, I'll make you Chairman of the Executive Committee. You can have some fun and meet some interesting people and I can spend all my time getting the Institute going.'

The key is in the title. Nobody knows what it means. It can mean much or nothing. But nobody ever gets mad when the boss says, 'Let me switch you to the Chairman of our Executive Committee – this is the kind of thing he takes charge of.'

I've seen this work in an area like customer complaints. People who write or call with complaints want someone to listen, sympathize, apologize and, if indicated, correct the matter. And the higher up their complaint is handled the quicker their fire goes out.

But companies still insist on having these complaints handled by 'customer services departments' or 'complaints departments'. If I'm switched to one of these, I'm twice as mad as when I called. But I'm docile as a lamb if I hear, 'Let me transfer you to the Chairman of the Executive Committee. One of his people will take care of you. He likes to hear about all the complaints.'

I could be talking to the same clerk in the same department (except now he is speaking for the Chairman of the Executive Committee). And the letter of apology on that glorious letterhead not only rubs out my grievance, it retains me as a customer and gives me something to brag about to your other prospects.

## Complaints Handling

There is a tried and tested method for dealing properly with customer complaints whether or not you are blessed with a 'Chairman of the Executive Committee'. It goes like this:

1 When a customer complains about something, *don't ever* side with him against your company. (However you do this, whether you switch from 'we' to 'they' or from 'us' to 'them', you'll be suggesting to this customer that this sort of thing is always happening and that if he was a bit brighter he would deal elsewhere.)
2 Never, never, never take the complaint personally. It's not *you* he's having a go at, it's the product, the service or the company. Stay cool.
3 Thank the customer for bringing the problem to your notice and for giving you the opportunity to put things right. (But don't ever patronize.)
4 Tell the customer you are sorry he's been upset. (But *don't* apologize on behalf of your company at this stage for having done something wrong. You don't even know whose fault it *is*, yet!)
5 Get the full story down on paper. (If the customer gets everything off his chest in one go, you'll have a much easier time.)
6 Never interrupt, or argue, or justify. (But you can ask a few questions to clarify any areas of doubt.)
7 Tell the customer what action you are going to take. Get him to agree to it. **Then take it**. (And keep him informed.)

## The Ostrich Complex

A lot of complaints' mountains grow out of mole hills right across Selling because of the Ostrich Complex – the practice of burying one's head in the sand until the problem has gone away. But, of course, the problem never does go away.

A lot of these kinds of complaints are caused by late deliveries. (If your company suffers regularly from this problem, get hold of a book by Sydney Paulden entitled *How to Deliver on Time*,

Gower Press, 1977). If a delivery is going to be late, the Seller has a plain, simple duty to the customer to tell him **fast**. Give the customer as much notice as possible, so that he can change his own schedules or arrangements.

# The Ostrich Complex

You will still get a rocket which will turn both your ears red, but that is far, far better than to say absolutely nothing and then have your customer telephone a few days **after** the scheduled delivery date to enquire 'Where the hell is it . . .?' and have to say 'Oh, er . . . I'm sorry, but, er . . . it's going to be another six weeks.'

A Seller who does that doesn't deserve customers, and certainly isn't going to win *this* business battle.


## The Odds

Never underestimate the Competition. Most Sellers are up against very poor odds. No bookmaker would take money on their chances of success – whether it's retaining existing customers or winning new customers.

If ten suppliers are sharing a particular market, then for every

Seller trying to keep and protect a particular customer, there are nine other Sellers trying to steal that customer away. Most prospects are someone else's customer. So every Seller to whom this is being done is, at the same time, doing this to someone else.

The late Douglas McGregor conducted some experiments many years ago. He took a number of 'representative samples' of people, several bunches of students of similar mix, and communicated to them some ideas which they accepted. Then, after a couple of days, he subjected the same representative sample bunches to another person, who communicated to them some entirely different ideas on the same subject.

80% of the people in the representative samples changed their minds and opted for the second set of ideas.

McGregor then took a similar number of completely new 'representative samples', although the people were the same kind of people. He conducted the entire exercise again, but this time, at the end of his first communication, he added something. He told each bunch that in a couple of days, another person would come to see them, would give them some entirely different ideas and would try to make them change their minds.

The other person duly did his thing, but this time, only 20% changed their minds.

The ramifications of McGregor's tests are mind-bending! It is obviously possible to build mental barriers in people's minds which reject advances from competitors. A natural resistance to change – something that your existing customers should all have to a very advanced degree, but that your prospective customers and you yourself should **never** suffer from.

How do you build such mental barriers and resistance in a Selling situation? Well, you don't *knock* the competition, that's for sure. Do that and you're back in the crowd.

You sell the Difference – the USP – and you reinforce the difference at every opportunity, reminding your customers of all the benefits they're getting by buying from you.

'You can get this product cheaper, of course, but then you wouldn't be getting the extra reliability and longer life, or our design service.'

'Bloggs make very good pumps, but you're getting some very

important extras from us that you wouldn't get from Bloggs. Our multiflexible couple, for example. How would your chaps cope without that? And our automatic declogger.'

You can even quote generalities like: 'There's nothing in the world that can't be made just a little cheaper – and just a little worse.'

Or ask questions like:

'If you were an astronaut, about to blast off for the Moon, and you learnt that the million components making up your space capsule had all been bought on the basis of the lowest price, how would you feel?'

## Rumours

Way back in the days before mini- and micro-computers, there were only about five major main-frame computer manufacturers competing for the very big business, the highly specialized business, at the top end of the market.

The market itself, in Britain, totalled only about thirty key decision-makers.

A rumour was spread, no one knows whether deliberately or not, to the effect that one of the big five computer manufacturers was planning to pull out of the UK market, due to a fall-off in demand and insufficient profits.

Within days, all thirty of the key decision-makers had got wind of the rumour. As a result, that manufacturer didn't get one enquiry from the market for almost a year. No one was prepared to take the risk.

A true story about a totally untrue rumour.

Do your competitors spread rumours about you and your company? If they do, what action do you take?

Here's another true story which shows you what action you *could* take.

A company in the materials handling industry was based at Grays, in Essex, the flat bit of the Thames estuary. One summer evening, half the county of Essex was subjected to a sudden and incredibly savage cloudburst. Three hours of the heaviest rain anyone had ever seen. The drains and sewers couldn't take it. Manholes blew everywhere. Roads were washed away. Landslides and widespread flooding.

A day later, only the debris was left. The water had gone.

A month later, a rumour began to spread about the materials handling company at Grays. Competitors' salesmen were saying to customers and prospective customers: 'Hey, you want to be careful if you do business with . . . their factory gets flooded out pretty regularly and you know what water does to this kind of equipment.'

The management of the Grays company happened to be fast on its feet. A light aircraft was hired for a day and a photographer sent up to take pictures of the factory and the surrounding area. The most suitable picture was selected and prints run off for each of the salesmen.

A meeting was held to brief the salesmen on how to use the pictures. They were told to talk about the rumour, the flood and show the picture, on every single call they made, **at the beginning of the call**. A fly on the wall probably heard this:

'You know, Mr Jones, it's incredible the lengths our competitors go to, to try to discredit us. There's a rumour they're spreading now that our factory floods every month. Actually, it got flooded out in that cloudburst a few weeks back, along with just about every other factory in Essex, but look at this.'

(*Salesman brings out aerial photo of factory.*)

'Here's our factory. Here's the river Thames, half a mile away. And, look, running all the way from Dagenham to Southend, unbroken, is this railway embankment. Now I ask you, how the hell could our factory get flooded?'

End of story; beginning of business discussion.

If you're still a fly on the wall of Mr Jones' office a few days later, when one of the competitors tries spreading the rumour, you'd see Mr Jones lean back in his chair, fold his arms and wait for the salesman to finish his knocking. Then you'd hear Mr Jones ask:

'Have you ever seen that factory down at Grays?'

'Er, no. Why do you ask?'

'Because it's half a mile from the river Thames and there's a bloody great railway embankment running continuously between the two. So how do you reckon their factory gets flooded?'

The salesman goes bright red from neck to forehead, and the rest of the visit is a disaster – for him.

Two months of the Grays' salesforce using the aerial photograph on every call they made and not only did the rumour disappear, the company was stronger, compared with its competitors, than it had ever been.

Hoisted with own petard, I call that. And a lot of fun while you're doing it.

## Taking Advantage

Be careful not to give your competitors an opportunity to steal your existing customers.

Here's an example from the printing industry. One of the major suppliers of lithographic printing plates found it had a strike on its hands and saw fit to inform its customers. A letter duly went out.

*Dear Sirs,*
*As you may be aware, employees engaged in the manufacture of lithographic printing plates and chemicals are in membership of the National Graphical Association.*

*Regrettably, I have to advise you that the NGA have given us notice of their intention to support a withdrawal of labour with effect from Monday, 29 June.*

*This stoppage is particularly disturbing since the company's offer had previously been recommended for acceptance by the National Executive Council of the NGA who are now giving official backing to industrial action in pursuit of the wage claim.*

*Whilst we can appreciate an individual's aspirations, in these matters the cumulative effect of excessive wage settlements cannot be in the interests of the industry, or those whom it employs; one would have hoped that the events of the last year would have been evidence enough.*

*As a British company, and a major supplier to the UK printing industry, we believe that we have a responsibility to provide satisfying, rewarding jobs for those in our employ; we also believe that we have no less a responsibility to the industry to play our part in maintaining a reliable product, dependable service and stable prices, and it must be borne in mind that the offer in dispute is in line with the settlements recently concluded in the printing industry. So whilst we apologize for any temporary inconvenience or interrruption of supply, we trust that you will bear with us and we hope we can resume normal service as quickly as possible.*

*If, in the meantime you require assistance or advice please contact your local depot.*

*Yours faithfully*

Two days later, one of the company's major competitors sent out a letter to all the relevant printers, offering to provide plates during the strike.

*Dear Sir,*

<u>Presensitized aluminium offset litho plates</u>

*I understand that one of our competitors has circularized the printing industry concerning their inability to supply offset plates due to industrial action.*

*Whilst I have no particular enthusiasm for capitalizing on another's misfortune, I am very conscious of the fact that you will need a supply of plates if you are to keep your presses running, otherwise more print work will go overseas. I am also concerned that you continue to use plates manufactured in Britain as your alternative source.*

*As the largest supplier of positive working offset plates to the UK market may I reassure you that we will be able to satisfy your requirements whatever the size. Also there is little likelihood of us being unable to supply due to industrial action.*

*You may recall that we have recently installed a new production line, which is generally regarded as being the most sophisticated plate manufacturing unit in the Western world. As well as improving the quality of our products this new line also gave us a significant increase in capacity.*

*We may also be able to supply negative plates in limited sizes and quantities but positive working plates are definitely our lead products.*

*The . . . range of positive plates is fully described by the enclosed literature.*

*All three plates are compatible with most brands of positive developer although best results are obtained using . . . Positive Developer.*

*So, if you are worried about the continuity of your plate supplies, just give us a call at Head Office or any of our Branches.*

*Yours faithfully*

As a result, the competitor acquired a considerable slice of the strike-bound company's business – and kept quite a bit of it long after the strike had ended.

There are lessons to be learned here!

# 6
# How to Organize Yourself for Chasing Business, Not Just Customers

> We've got strengths and
> we've got weaknesses – but
> so have our competitors.
> If we sell our strengths
> against their weaknesses,
> we'll win.

Most calls made by most Sellers are not *effective* calls because they lack an **objective** – a reason for the call which the customer or prospective customer himself sees as worth his time. We've been through this for first-ever calls on new prospects – the reason for the call, the objective, will come straight from the carrot you dig up.

But for repeat calls on existing customers, or repeat calls on prospects, a call without an objective is the 'dreaded lurgie' of Selling. Such a call (especially if it is made out of the blue without a prior appointment) is called a **courtesy call** – and it often drives the customer mad.

The simplest kind of courtesy call goes like this:

'Morning George; how're things? Everything okay? Fine – see you next month, then. Bye!'

No research. No advance thought. No questions to probe for things new. No offer to tell the customer any news you've picked up which might be useful to him. Just routine – the old rut.

An interesting thing to remember if you *have* an objective is that *then* you are **chasing business, not chasing customers.**

If you ever look at trends in Selling – and I probably look at a lot more than most – you'll find that the more experienced Sellers get, the more they tend to throw away the Selling manual and play things off the seat of their pants.

Their **egos** take over and convince them that they don't need to do research, dig up carrots and make appointments any more, that their experience will carry them through. **It doesn't work.**

The result of this **ego** trip is that they probably stay just average Sellers, earning average money, never getting promoted.

Two epigrams fit this situation:

'Experience is not what happens to you – it's what you *do* with what happens to you.'
Aldous Huxley

'We judge ourselves by what we feel capable of doing, while others judge us by what we have already done.'
Henry Wadsworth Longfellow

Putting it into my words – **ego** is screwing up the will to WIN.

There is a second criteria for an effective call – a 'chasing business' call – you must get face-to-face with the right **man** – the key decision-maker who, to qualify for that title, must have three things going for him:

Money
Authority
Need.

If the key decision-maker is a woman, it goes:

Wherewithal
or
Money
Authority
Need.

I find it incredible the number of Sellers I meet who don't know the customers and prospective customers on which to concentrate – those due for a 'chasing business with an objective' call – and which customers can be put aside for a while without risk. Both kinds are bundled together – literally.

Invariably this tells me that the Sellers in question are not properly organized. Also they're not doing enough research.

They obviously don't really want to win, and they're hardly likely to win against any kind of professional competition.

Being properly organized, so as to make 100% effective calls, is, in fact, much **easier** than playing things off the seat of your pants. You see, effective calls derive from only five places:

Customer records and prospective customer records
Suspect lists
Outstanding proposals lists
Enquiries from advertising
Customers who holler!

If you operate a record system that includes the first three of these five, plus facilities for dealing with the other two, you'll not only maximize your effective calls, you'll find it very easy indeed to put together a really meaningful weekly call plan – and that will please your sales manager no end. (Remember the Longfellow epigram?) And remember this – 'Any Sellers who don't keep their records religiously up-to-date and in apple-pie order are reducing their effectiveness and therefore are declaring themselves losers'.


## Customer and Prospective Customer Records

The best kind of Record is a foolscap size manilla **file**, not a card. With a file, for repeat business and prospective customers alike, all correspondence, copy action reports, quotations, drawings, can be kept safely **inside** the file. Everything in the one place.

A properly designed Record file, as illustrated on the next two pages, properly used, brings many benefits to the successful competitive Seller.

For example:

1 It facilitates efficient and longer-term planning of territory coverage (maximum calls, minimum miles).
2 It increases the number of hours available for face-to-face selling (the selling day is **not** steadily getting shorter – this is only a myth, much promoted by bleating sheep).
3 It banishes Courtesy calls for ever (every call made has a clearly defined, prior agreed objective).

Customer

Address

| Business | KEY CONTACTS (circle code letter of main decision makers) | | | | |
|---|---|---|---|---|---|
| Industry Code | | Full Name and Initials | Job Title | Best Day and Time | Lunch Habits | Agreed call frequency |
| Owned by/Owns | P | | | | | |
| No. of Employees | Q | | | | | |
| | R | | | | | |
| Turnover | S | | | | | |
| Other Locations | T | | | | | |
| | U | | | | | |
| | V | | | | | |
| Terms of Payment | W | | | | | |
| Credit Limit | Customer's Opening Hours | | | | | |

OPEN ⌊ ⌋ ⌊ ⌋
Works  Office                                    Start  LUNCH

| | | Calls on each key contact | | | | | | | | | Total Calls | Total Business | Jan-Mar | Business Spread Apr-Jun |
|---|---|---|---|---|---|---|---|---|---|---|---|---|---|---|
| | | P | O | R | S | T | U | V | W | | | | | |
| FORECAST 19 | | | | | | | | | | | | | | |
| ACTUAL 19 | | | | | | | | | | | | | | |
| FORECAST 19 | | | | | | | | | | | | | | |
| ACTUAL 19 | | | | | | | | | | | | | | |
| FORECAST 19 | | | | | | | | | | | | | | |
| ACTUAL 19 | | | | | | | | | | | | | | |

CALL RECORD

| Date of Call | Face to Face / Telephone | Contact | What happened during the call | Action to be taken as a result of the call | THIS CALL Order Value Secured |
|---|---|---|---|---|---|
| | | | | | |
| | | | | | |
| | | | | | |
| | | | | | |
| | | | | | |
| | | | | | |
| | | | | | |
| | | | | | |
| | | | | | |
| | | | | | |
| | | | | | |
| | | | | | |

| | Telephone | | Area Code |
|---|---|---|---|
| stal Code | Telex | | |

| | | Nearest other customers | | |
|---|---|---|---|---|
| Appointment preferences | | Name | Location | Best Day and Time for main-decision makers |
| | | | | |
| | | | | |
| | | | | |
| | | | | |
| | | | | |
| | | | | |

| Finish | Works | Offices | CLOSE Works |
|---|---|---|---|

| d by time Jul-Sep | Oct-Dec | Business Spread by Product Code 0 1 2 3 4 5 6 7 8 9 | Competing Suppliers | Percentage Bus. 19 19 19 |
|---|---|---|---|---|
| | | | | |
| | | | | |
| | | | | |
| | | | | |
| | | | | |

NEXT CALL

| Main Objectives Agreed for the NEXT call | Contacts | Date of Call | Time of Call | Appointment |
|---|---|---|---|---|
| | | | | |
| | | | | |
| | | | | |
| | | | | |
| | | | | |
| | | | | |
| | | | | |
| | | | | |
| | | | | |
| | | | | |
| | | | | |

4 It minimizes abortive calls (best day and time, appointment preferences, lunch habits, agreed call frequencies, etc.).
5 It gains the Seller advance commitment of a kind almost impossible to achieve by other methods (the 'Sales forecast' section).
6 It enables the Seller to use local third party references during the sales presentation (the 'nearest other customers' section).
7 The way the record file is filed away in the Seller's system provides **automatic** sorting of which customers are due for a call at any point in time.

## Maximizing Calls – Minimizing Mileage

The more the Seller knows about his customers' and prospective customers' habits, the easier it is to achieve this objective. Consider the 'Key Contacts' section in the record file on pp. 96–7. There is provision for eight key contacts, coded P to W. There is provision for circling the code letters of the most important contacts. There is provision for listing the full name, initials and job title of each contact.

Following this there is detailed provision for listing each contact's habits. Best day and time for a visit. Is he normally out on Mondays and in on Thursdays? Is he clear of clog before 10am because the post hasn't yet reached him? Does he work on after normal closing time? If so, will he see *you* after closing time (I assume, of course, you'll see *him*!) Lunch habits. Does he go out, go home or eat sandwiches at his desk? If sandwiches, can you bring yours and join him during lunchtime to discuss that outstanding project?

Agreed call frequency. How often do you need to call on each contact to be as certain as you can of securing the business that's available? Can you alternate a visit with a telephone call? Appointment preferences. Does he insist on firm appointments every time, some of the time, or is he happy that you 'drop in' on the preferred day, at the preferred time and at the preferred frequency, without an appointment?

Once you have all this 'habit' information agreed and documented on your record file, it is incredibly simple to maximize 'chasing business' calls and to minimize mileage. How do you get all the information? Well, dummy, you just **ask the contacts themselves**. Face-to-face, with that record file in your hot sticky hand. You write down the answers you get to your questions and you let them see clearly what you are doing.

Do you get the feeling you'll offend anyone? Of course not. You'll just come over to them as a more thorough, more professional Seller. And that's what we're about!

### Face-to-Face Selling Time

The average face-to-face Selling time for Sellers who take their products or services to the customers is probably running at less than two hours per day. That's no good at all. You must aim to double this if you want to win – to sell successfully against competition. We're half-way there already, with the 'Key Contacts' information. To crack the other half, all we need to do is to make the Selling day longer.

In respect of the record file on pp. 96–7, this process begins with the defining of each customer's opening and closing times and the start and finish of his lunch break. You will see a special section on the file labelled 'Customer's Opening Hours' which is for this purpose. Without this fundamental information you don't really know where to begin. After that, it's entirely up to you. It's that Positive/Negative attitude thing again.

If you plan to get out of the metropolis before 3.30 pm so as to avoid getting snarled up in the traffic, then, for you, the time you have for face-to-face Selling will be less, not more. Your success will follow the same trend.

If you don't use records like our example and you're prepared to be convinced that no customer will see you before 10 am or after 4.30 pm or between 12 noon and 2.30 pm or on Friday afternoons, then there isn't much hope for you.

If you don't like getting up early, or if you get stuck with the school-kids' delivery and collection service, you've got big problems in this Selling business.

If you do **anything** deliberately to lower the number of days or hours you have available for Selling or for planning for Selling, you won't get far in this profession – and, worse than that, you're **stealing** from your employer. Time is money!

A true story: I know a sales manager with a great sense of humour who had a salesman suffering from a work problem – he didn't like it! This salesman was having one day off every two weeks with a migraine. Consistently. Too consistently!

The sales manager decided that the time had come to sort the salesman out. But he didn't want to demotivate him. No big sticks. No official warning letters. He simply called the salesman into his office one morning, sat him down across his desk and asked him to hold his hand out on the desk. Then he took a very large glass jar of paracetamol tablets out of his desk drawer,

unscrewed the top, poured about a hundred tablets into the salesman's outstretched hand, put the jar down, closed the salesman's fingers round the tablets like a fist, held the fistful tightly, looked the salesman straight in the eye from one foot away and said:

'George, I don't care if you take these one at a time or all at once, you're not having a day off every two weeks with a migraine. Do I make myself clear?'

George muttered.

'Er, yes, I think so.'

'Off you go then,' said the sales manager, releasing the fistful of tablets. And off George went.

*It cured* his migraines. Don't know which way, but it cured 'em! And that's *brilliant* sales management.

## Banish Courtesy Calls For Ever

If you use the kind of record file we're discussing, then during every call you make on a customer or prospective customer you define and agree the objective for the **next** call.

That's why, in our example on pp. 96–7 each line of the 'Call Record' is divided into two parts – 'This Call' and 'Next Call'.

And again, to maximize effectiveness and impact on the customers, both parts should be filled in while the Seller is face-to-face with the customer, **not** back in the car.

## Advance Commitment

This is the only bit of this book that deals with the much neglected art of sales forecasting. You may produce weekly, or monthly or quarterly forecasts, best-bets lists, long range predictions, market feels or whatever. It doesn't matter; the most important forecast is still the **annual** one.

But, if I may direct this next bit firmly towards management, the annual sales forecast, to be any use whatsoever, **must** be produced mainly by the people closest to the customers. The people at the sharp end, the Sellers. And a good annual sales forecast will take probably three months to produce. (If you give the Sellers three days, all you'll get is a wet thumb in the air!)

I say three months because this is the probable time it takes for a Seller to get round each and every one of the customers and known prospective customers in the territory – the Cycle Time. If your cycle time is different, substitute for the three months.

During this three months, the Seller is going about the normal worthwhile tasks, chasing business, making effective, non-courtesy calls. But during every call in this period, with the record file open at the ready, a couple of questions are added:

'I've been asked by my company to prepare a forecast of probable business for next year, Mr Jones. I wonder, could you give me any idea of what you are likely to be ordering from us in the next twelve months?' And referring to the record file, 'How does this relate to the business we've done so far this year and what we did last year?'

Consider carefully the very detailed kind of forecast you could produce by using the 'Forecast' section of our example record file on pp. 96–7. Not just total business in money terms. Also the spread over the year and broken down by product. Total calls required and how these are divided among the key contacts. An analysis of the competitors you are up against in respect of this customer and how you are performing in relation to them.

Several hundred such precise forecasts, added together, produce the most accurate forecast any Seller can arrive at. The most accurate because most of the data was provided **by the customers.** Some of these several hundred will be estimates made by the Seller, of course; not every customer will co-operate fully – but even these estimates will be much more precise than that previous 'wet thumb in the air' single guess.

Consider now what such a detailed forecast, contained as it is within the record file, means to the Seller as the year of the forecast unfolds. Every time the Seller pays a visit, he is monitoring the forecast given by the customer himself. If business falls behind the forecast, the Seller can ask why, and will get a straight answer.

**New Business Forecasts** – the part of a Seller's turnover which must come from prospective customers not even found at the time the forecast is produced – should be calculated jointly by management and the Seller and be based on the Seller's performance over the last three months and the new business target hoped for by the Company. For capital equipment Sellers, this might be as much as 80% of the total forecast.

Here is an example:

New business target – £400,000
Average order/account value in first year – £50,000
Number of new accounts required to achieve target:

$$\frac{400,000}{50,000} = 8$$

Personal performance over past year (count the types of calls – new business prospects only)
For every 5 first-ever-calls made, 1 proposal is submitted.
For every 5 proposals submitted on new prospects, 1 order is secured.

Thus, the number of first-ever-calls (new prospects) required to achieve new business target is:

$$8 \times 5 \times 5 = 200$$

Assume there are 10 working months per year – that's 20 first-ever-calls per month.

Too many for comfort?

Okay, do something to improve your performance. That's what this book is all about. Say you could reduce those two ratios to 3 to 1 and 4 to 1. How many new prospects would you need to find then?

$$8 \times 3 \times 4 = 96 \text{ or only 10 per month.}$$

## Local Third Party References

Back to our example record file again and the section headed 'Nearest Other Customers'. This is important to the Seller because, when he is establishing 'Best Day and Time' and 'Call Frequency' with any key contact, he also needs to remember which of his customers are nearby and on which days and at what times he calls on these customers. Then he can knit together the most effective day's work from the point of view of maximizing calls and minimizing mileage.

While doing this, he can show a prospective customer the list of nearby customers with whom he is doing business. A highly effective way of applying 'Joneses Principle' techniques.

**Automatic Sorting**

Because every 'Next Call' has a definite date and time (and failing this, an approximate date will do), with this kind of record file the normal method of filing away is **according to the date of the next call.**

The process is on-going. Every customer and prospective customer due for a call, say, in September will be there in the September slot, waiting for you when September arrives. Or you can file by day, week or by month, whatever your business dictates. Self-adhesive colour codes are normally used at the top right hand corner of the record files (Area Code) to indicate the geographical location of the customer or prospective customer.

I have belaboured this customer and prospective customer file, not because one of my companies designed it, but because it is the single most important, most powerful weapon in the professional Seller's armoury. Learn to use it well, and success against the severest competition will be assured.

**How One Seller Chases Repeat Business**

Remember that car salesman who went out car spotting several days a week, sticking envelopes on windscreens? He's also the guy who tries as hard as he can to *retain* his domestic customers once they've bought a car from him. He knows that, apart from fleet customers, he's unlikely to see a customer more than once every two years, unless something goes wrong, so the kind of customer record we've described is likely to be a trifle superfluous for his domestic customers. A simple card record is all he needs, on which he records date of sale, type of vehicle, requirements of customer and family, and, most important of all, **the date the hire purchase is due to be paid off,** if HP is involved.

In chronological order, the salesman does three things to try to retain his customer:

1 At the time of delivery of the sold car, he writes the **ignition key number** on the back of his business card, hands the card to the new owner and says: 'Keep this card safe in your wallet/purse. I've written

your ignition key number on the back, so if you ever lose your key, you'll be able to get another one without much bother.'

So, his business card stays with the new owner for the life of the vehicle, more often than not.

2  Three weeks **after** the new owner has taken delivery of the vehicle, and at six monthly intervals thereafter, the salesman telephones the customer, just to make sure everything is all right. Best time for this call is in the evening – the impression it makes is worth **extra** business, the customers tell their friends.

3  Two months **before** the hire purchase payments are completed, the salesman telephones the customer to establish what plans the customer has to dispose of the vehicle and acquire something new. The salesman has a demonstration ride all lined up, ready to offer. Then the cycle begins again.

It's so simple, why don't 99% of dealer salesmen do it?
Here's a letter used by Buick Motors, USA, in dealership sales training.

*Dear Salesman:*

*I was surprised when you didn't see me a week or two after you delivered my new car that morning, not so many years ago, for I like you and your company. I was planning on introducing you to some of my friends. I confess, I was a little disappointed when you didn't come. A good many times in the past years, especially for those first two when it was hard to find the payments on the car you sold me, I wished that you would come and tell me again about the values of it, and make me as enthusiastic about it as I was on the day when I bought it . . . BUT YOU DIDN'T COME.*

*I was a little flattered when you persisted in seeing me, before I bought it. It made me feel worthwhile. I thought perhaps you liked me for my own sake as well as for the sake of my business. I thought you judged me an interesting fellow; but I guess I was mistaken, for you have never come back.*

*Every year I think, well perhaps I should trade for a new car now, but then I spend more money on the old one and keep driving it. I have often wondered why you didn't come back to see me and save me that money . . . but you never came back. The man who sold me my first insurance policy likes me, and enough to come in to see me, even though he knows I don't need more insurance. The result is that I have been buying insurance from him all my life. I have spent a lot of money with your company . . . more than I have buying insurance . . . BUT YOU NEVER CAME BACK.*

*Of course, I have bought lots and lots of cars from many different salesmen, each time thinking, 'I liked this man and will let him be my automobile*

salesman,' but my life has been a continuous procession of strange salesmen
. . . *because THE OLD ONES NEVER CAME BACK.*
  Sincerely,
NEW CAR BUYER

It says it all, doesn't it?


## Suspect/Prospect Lists

The traditional way for Sellers to note down suspects and prospects as they come across them is on the back of cigarette packets
or business cards. The snag is, half the notes are lost well before
action can be taken on them. A more disciplined approach to
self-generated and to company-generated prospecting is called
for if you want to win – like this example suspect list.

A 'Suspect' is someone, or some company, who just *might* be
needing your products or services. A nibble, a name worth
checking out. Detective fashion.

A 'Prospect' is a Suspect who's *been* checked out, and has come
up positive. A carrot has been established. A potential has been
estimated. The best line of attack and the reason for this line has
been thought out and documented. The decision-maker has been
pin-pointed. Everything is ready for the telephone call to make
the first appointment.

The Suspect List illustrated is designed to take both self-
generated suspects and suspects picked up by your company's
advertising and sales promotion efforts. Some suspects also pop
up out of the blue, telephoning your office and asking about
something. The space labelled 'Source' is to indicate where the
suspect came from.

The tick boxes labelled 'Card', 'File' and 'Dead' are for resultant action – you have made out a record card for this prospect
(you don't consider he's worth a file yet!) or a record file (he looks
very promising!) or you've written him off as useless.

If you completely filled one of these Suspect Lists each month,
and fully researched every new suspect to establish 'Best Line of
Action and Reason' (the carrot!) before attempting to make the
first appointment, you'd be well on the way to achieving a new

REF: SL/S1268

| "SUSPECT" LIST | AREA **W. MIDLANDS** | SALESMAN **J. WATSON** |

| COMPANY NAME & ADDRESS | DECISION MAKER | POTENTIAL | BEST LINE OF ACTION & REASON |
|---|---|---|---|
| Date **13/7** Source **FACTORY EQUIP. NEWS** I. B. E. BIRMINGHAM 33 Tel. No. **021- 998-7061** | R. J. JUSEM WORKS MANAGER | 500 HBV UNITS. | DEMO 478 MODEL. Card ✓ File Dead |
| Date **3/7** Source **F.E.N.** SMITH DAVIDSON LTD BIRMINGHAM 6 Tel. No. **021-978-8181** | B. JONES DIRECTOR | BUYING 100 AJS FROM B&B PER YEAR. | TRY 478 FOR COMPARISON. Card ✓ File Dead |
| Date **7/8** Source **REFERRAL** MALTBY & PALMER COVENTRY Tel. No. **0203-781880** | | QUOTING FOR SEWAGE WORKS. | CHECK PLANNING REGISTER FOR WORKS DETAILS. Card File ✓ Dead |
| Date **18/8** Source **LOCAL AD. IN TIMES.** VICTORIA FORGE BINLEY WOODS COVENTRY Tel. No. **0203- 347221** | J. BRIDE BUYER | USE SNOOKS | HAVE DELIVERY PROBLEMS. Card File ✓ Dead |
| Date **20/8** Source **REFERRAL** TAYLOR & FLETCHER SMETHWICK Tel. No. **021-493-4281** | F. HARRISON PROD" MGR. | MAKE M.O.D. COMPONENTS | CHECK SPEC-V-U840 FOR BETTER DEAL Card ✓ File Dead |
| Date **27/8** Source **ENGINEER DIGEST** TENSILE STEEL CO. CASTLE HILL DUDLEY Tel. No. **0384 - 92631** | H. WATKINS DEV. ENG | | DESIGNING NEW PRESSURE SYSTEM Card ✓ File Dead |
| Date **28/8** Source **CHAMBER OF COMM.** C & F TOOLS LTD. BIRMINGHAM 10 Tel. No. **021- 776-3234** | F. COCHRANE MAN. DIR. | HAS A RUSSIAN CONTRACT FOR 24 M/CS | FIND OUT HYDRAULIC SPEC Card File ✓ Dead |
| Date Source Tel. No. | | | Card File Dead |
| Date Source Tel. No. | | | Card File Dead |
| Date Source Tel. No. | | | Card File Dead |

SALES CONTROL & RECORD SYSTEMS LTD. CONCORDE HOUSE, 24 WARWICK NEW ROAD, ROYAL LEAMINGTON SPA CV32 5JH business target based on 10 first-ever-calls each month. If your success rate of telephone calls to appointments secured is 2 to 1, you'd need 2 such lists per month.

After your Suspect/Prospect lists have been completed and you have no further action to take on any name listed, you **never** throw them away. They either go back to head office for analysis of the sources of the names (how effective is your company's sales promotion, advertising and direct mail activity?) or you keep them yourself in an 'In Memorium' file (dead but not forgotten).

Why? Because you may get promoted next year and find yourself supervising a novice Seller who is doing the job you used to do. Do you want him to waste half his time chasing the **same** suspects you've already written off?

And . . . what might be a dead suspect today might be a live prospect next year if your company brings out a new product.

## Outstanding Proposals List

If you use the record files I've described, you'll rarely lose sight of an outstanding proposal that needs following up. The copy proposal is *in* the record file and the file is in the correct slot for your follow-up, if this is the most imminent action in respect of this customer.

If you use record *cards* instead of files, you cannot be this efficient. Your copy proposals need to be stored elsewhere, and with so little room on the record card to write anything really meaningful, there is always the danger of mislaying or overlooking a follow-up and losing the business to a competitor. The 'Outstanding Proposals' sheet illustrated is an effective way to solve this problem. It has two sections, one for existing customers, the other for prospects, three columns in each section for dates of follow-up calls, and is designed to be used like a cash book i.e. ongoing entries as they happen. Proposals that result in orders or that you lose to competitors are struck out. Likewise, if you are asked by a customer to re-submit because of changes, the original proposal line is struck out, 're-submit' entered in the result column, and the re-submitted proposal itself becomes a new entry further down.

**OUTSTANDING PROPOSALS**  SALESMAN **J. WATSON**

E = EXISTING CUSTOMERS  P = PROSPECT

| DATE REQUESTED | DATE ISSUED | E OR P | QUOTE NO. | VALUE | COMPANY | PRODUCT GROUPS | FOLLOW UP 1 | 2 | 3 | 4 | 5 | RESULT |
|---|---|---|---|---|---|---|---|---|---|---|---|---|
| 2.8.82 | 4.8.82 | E | 7251 | 368 | SIEMENS | 9 + 10 | 4/8 | | | | | O |
| 2.8.82 | 6.8.82 | E | 7255 | 1021 | JONES & STER. | 1 + 6 | 2/8 28/8 8/9 | | | | | L |
| 5.8.82 | 11.8.82 | E | 7259 | 481 | POTTERSBY & CO | 2 | 6/9 7/9 | | | | | |
| 20.8.82 | 24.8.82 | E | 7301 | 1671 | EKEL VENTS | 9 + 10 | 9/9 | | | | | |
| 20.8.82 | 26.8.82 | E | 7310 | 896 | ASH & CO LTD | 3 | 21/9 | | | | | |
| 25.1.82 | 26.8.82 | E | 7311 | 184 | ABRAHAMS | 4 | 14/9 3/10 | | | | | |
| 2.9.82 | 3.9.82 | E | 7320 | 267 | BREEDON SMITH | 1 | | | | | | O |
| 7.9.82 | 15.9.82 | E | 7351 | 900 | P.K. VALVES | 6 | 21/9 13/10 | | | | | |
| 9.9.82 | 16.9.82 | E | 7363 | 1021 | C & S | 9 + 10 | 24/9 | | | | | |
| 21.9.82 | 29.9.82 | E | 7400 | 860 | BLOGGS PUMPS | 3 | 13/10 | | | | | |
| 30.9.82 | 2.10.82 | E | 7401 | 290 | NORTONS | 4 | 10/10 | | | | | |
| 15.10.82 | 26.10.82 | E | 7410 | 765 | P.K. VALVES | 9 | | | | | | |
| | | | | | | | | | | | | |
| | | | | | | | | | | | | |
| | | | | | | | | | | | | |
| 2.8.82 | 4.8.82 | P | 7253 | 496 | E. GRAY & CO. | 3 | 11/8 | | | | | L |
| 2.8.82 | 5.8.82 | P | 7254 | 870 | ASTON HYD. | 9 | 18/8 | | | | | O |
| 4.8.82 | 7.8.82 | P | 7256 | 488 | A.P.T. LTD. | 2 | 14/9 7/9 | | | | | |
| 11.8.82 | 20.8.82 | P | 7271 | 1066 | DROP FORGES | 1 | 9/9 | | | | | O |
| 20.8.82 | 21.8.82 | P | 7273 | 1290 | DROP FORGES | 1 + 6 | 9/9 9/9 9/10 | | | | | |
| 3.9.82 | 9.9.82 | P | 7333 | 440 | HEREFORDS | 4 | 21/9 | | | | | O |
| 6.9.82 | 10.9.82 | P | 7326 | 600 | C. RIGBY | 9 | 13/10 | | | | | |
| 12.9.82 | 18.9.82 | P | 7391 | 550 | T. STEEL & CO. | 1 + 3 | 8/10 | | | | | |
| 1.10.82 | 6.10.82 | P | 7402 | 413 | SNOOKS ENG. | 4 | 14/10 | | | | | |
| 7.10.82 | 8.10.82 | P | 7403 | 1030 | ARNOLDS | 4 | | | | | | |
| 8.10.82 | 8.10.82 | P | 7409 | 460 | WILD BROS. | 3 | | | | | | |

REF. OP/S1315

© SALES CONTROL & RECORD SYSTEMS LTD, CONCORDE HOUSE, 24 WARWICK NEW ROAD, ROYAL LEAMINGTON SPA CV32 5JH

The 'Outstanding Proposals' list is also superb as a 'Best Bets' list for short-term forecasting, as it tells you the total business you've got in the pipeline at any point in time. Some Sellers who use the list for this purpose use the follow-up columns to note important future dates – such as 'one week before decision day' or 'expected order placing day'.

## Following up Advertising Enquiries

Any enquiry generated by your company's advertising and sales promotion campaigns **must** be immediately followed up **by tele-**

---

# Enquiry Follow-up by Telephone

1. Identify you are speaking to the Enquirer.
   *"IS THAT MR. SMITH?"*

2. Tell him who you are.
   *"GOOD MORNING. MY NAME IS _____ OF _____ ."*

3. Set the scene for him to tell you why he enquired in the first place – and make sure you get the words EXACTLY right.
   *"THANK YOU FOR ENQUIRING ABOUT OUR _____ ."*
   (or *"thank you for sending in the coupon from our advertisement in _____ .)*
   *I'VE GOT A LOT OF INFORMATION I CAN SEND YOU, BUT JUST TO MAKE SURE I SEND YOU EXACTLY WHAT YOU WANT... TELL ME... WHAT MADE YOU ENQUIRE?"*

4. Shut up – and write down here what he says.
   _____
   _____
   _____

5. Now all you have to do is ask him a few questions, relevant to the above reason for his enquiry – questions which will help you quickly decide if he is worth visiting or not; and questions which will also keep him turned on and impressed by your professionalism. Questions like:-
   *"WHERE DO YOU BUY YOUR _____ FROM AT PRESENT?"*
   _____
   *"WHAT ARE YOU PAYING FOR _____ AT PRESENT?"*
   _____
   *"HOW MUCH OF IT DO YOU USE?"*
   _____
   *"WHAT HAVE YOU DONE SO FAR TO COPE WITH THIS?"*
   _____
   *"WHO ELSE ARE YOU IN TOUCH WITH?"*
   _____

6. If you decide from this that a visit is warranted, finish like this:-
   *"WELL, I CERTAINLY THINK WE CAN HELP YOU. LOOK, I'VE GOT SOME SAMPLES AND INFO ON A COUPLE OF OTHER COMPANIES LIKE YOURS WHICH I'D LIKE YOU TO SEE. I'M IN YOUR AREA... LET'S SEE... (consult diary)... NEXT _____ ; CAN YOU SPARE ME HALF AN HOUR SAY, AT _____ , OR WOULD _____ BE MORE CONVENIENT?"*
   Appointment booked for _____

7. If you decide he's not worth a visit – send him something by post, and staple your business card to the top. It won't need a covering letter; just say:-
   *"WILL IT BE OKAY IF I SEND YOU THE INFORMATION WITH MY BUSINESS CARD, RATHER THAN WITH A COVERING LETTER? I CAN GET IT TO YOU A BIT QUICKER THAT WAY."*

**phone**. Don't send literature and a covering letter. If you do, when you follow up later, in the majority of cases all you'll get will be 'Ah, yes, we've received your literature. Nothing's going to happen for quite a while yet. When it does, we'll let you know.' You won't even find out the most important thing of all – **why he took the trouble to respond to your advertisement**. Without knowing this, you can't start selling.

Telephone first, preferably at the sharp end. If this is not practical for some reason, use someone competent at head office or regional office. And **always** use a check list. There is absolutely no excuse for getting anything wrong with this kind of telephone call. An example check list is illustrated left – Section 3 is the most critical. You have to get that bit **exactly** right, or it won't work and you'll lose probably 30% of the appointments you go for.

## Making Appointments

With your customer record files, your suspect/prospect lists, your outstanding proposals list and your enquiry follow-up check lists, you have organized nearly everything you need for success. Nearly everything. You're still short of a mounted map of your territory, on which the precise position of each of your customers and known prospective customers is clearly indicated with a coloured map pin. And you need a decent sized diary. (You think I'm being just a touch too basic? Even patronizing? You'll never convince me. I'm the guy who regularly addresses 2,000 Sellers for a day and finds 400 of them have turned up without anything to write with, let alone anything to write on. Mounted maps and pins are just about unknown. Diaries not quite so bad.)

Assuming you have organized your map, pin-pointing all your known customers and prospective customers, you could still do with one more thing before you begin making appointments and building your weekly call plan – a piece of thin string.

So you know already the actual customers you want to call on next Wednesday. You know there are six of them. You know where they are situated. You know your start and finish point for

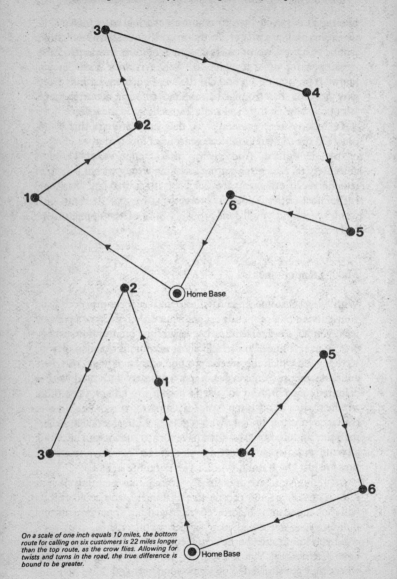

On a scale of one inch equals 10 miles, the bottom route for calling on six customers is 22 miles longer than the top route, as the crow flies. Allowing for twists and turns in the road, the true difference is bound to be greater.

the day. But, do you know the most economical order in which to call on these six customers? The route from one to the next through the day which will result in the minimum of miles travelled? That's where the piece of string comes in. From home base, round the six pins denoting the six customers you want to call on, back to home base. Both ends held firmly in left and right hands. Off the pins on to a straight scale. Then try again another way round the six pins. And again. The shortest distance wins, and you have two chances of achieving the shortest distance, clockwise or anti-clockwise.

**Now** you are ready to pick up the telephone and make some appointments. And just in case your ego is telling you not to bother with that daft idea with the piece of string, let me confirm that you'll still get the same number of appointments without it, more or less, but you'll finish the year having travelled maybe 5,000 miles further than you need have done and you'll have deprived yourself of the opportunity to use that travelling time to make maybe 250 extra calls. It's that simple!

## Priority is for Prospects

Because first impressions count for a hell of a lot in this business, **all** your first-ever calls should be by appointment. Whether the prospective customer is self-generated or came by way of the advertising and sales promotion campaign, your initial research will have indicated the probable likely carrot to dangle. So hit him as professionally and as confidently as you can.

Don't ever aim your first appointment of the day for mid-morning or mid-afternoon. The most effective aiming sequence for a full day's appointment making is:

First Appointment: 8.50 am
Second Appointment: 4.50 pm (or 5.50)
Third Appointment: 11.50 am
Fourth Appointment: 1.50 pm
Fifth Appointment: 9.50 am
Sixth Appointment: 10.50 am
Seventh Appointment: 2.50 pm
Eighth Appointment: 3.50 pm

If you make less calls a day, knock out the fifth to eighth. Keep the first to fourth.

Why the ten minutes to the hour timing? It's an interesting piece of applied psychology.

Most prospective customers who are telephoned by Sellers have a subconscious clock which tells them how much of their valuable time the Seller is likely to need. Prospective customers' secretaries also have this sub-conscious clock.

If a Seller telephones and suggests 'How about 11.00 am?' the subconscious clock journeys round from 11 to the next 12 o'clock and a voice in his brain tells the prospective customer; 'Hey, this Seller is going to need an hour of my time'. That's too much of his time so he says 'No'.

Subconscious clocks all travel round to the next 12 o'clock. So an appointment suggested for 10.30 gets a half an hour reading. That's why appointments should be made at **ten to the hour**. Then they get a 10 minute reading and you have the best chance of getting a 'Yes'.

On 6 October 1982, I led a Road Show at Southampton, at which I explained this bit of psychology. On 8 October I received a letter from a Mrs Raie Balloqui, a director of a company selling business machines and electronic typewriters. She had been present at the Road Show. The letter read:

*Dear Mr Fenton,*
*I simply had to write and tell you . . . from seven phone calls made this morning, I have six appointments booked for next week, all at ten minutes to the hour!*

Proof of the pudding . . . ?


## Writing or Telephoning 'Cold' for an Appointment

Prospects whom you find yourself are known as 'Cold' – the prospect himself has no idea you are about to descend upon him, and (you must assume) knows little or nothing about your company or your products or services. (Don't get this mixed up with Cold Canvass – that's something different.)

You may have dug up a suitable carrot, but this still has to be effectively dangled in front of the decision-maker's nose before he grants you the opportunity to get face-to-face.

You can dangle the carrot either by telephone or by letter.

Whether you choose to telephone or write, always remember that your objective is simply to secure an appointment – **not** to get involved in a detailed explanation of what you want to talk to him about *when* you get face-to-face. To avoid this problem, many good Sellers send a letter first and then follow up with a telephone call a few days later, aiming to reach the decision-maker's secretary who should know about the letter and be more receptive to the telephone call.

Here is an example letter for a fairly technical selling situation, designed to be sent to the managing director or the production director of a prospect company.

*Dear Mr Jones*
*Technological advancement within your particular Industry is constantly bringing pressure to bear on companies, making them advance in step with technology or risk losing their share of the market.*

*An additional problem is that the economic state of industry in general this year does not encourage companies to invest in the necessary new plant, yet to stay competitive they must do something.*

*This is a problem on which my company has done a great deal of research and development. As a result, we have produced equipment which, for an extremely low capital investment, can increase automatic component production by something like 20 per cent over conventional methods.*

*If you can spare me an hour of your time, I would very much like to show you exactly what we have done at other firms similar in size to your own and discuss how our equipment might be of benefit to you.*

*May I telephone your secretary on Friday to fix a definite appointment?*
*Yours sincerely*
*John Fenton*
*Midlands Representative*

The carrot you want to dangle must come over loud and clear. There are two carrots in this example letter:

1 Increase the prospective customer's component production by 20%.
2 Show the prospective customer what you have done for other firms – maybe competitors, providing you do not betray any confidences.

Carrot 2 will be more powerful than carrot 1.

The managing director's curiosity will win the day almost every time.

Here are a few more choice phrases which are good for these kinds of letters:

'. . . you will save around 15% of your monthly distributing costs.'

'. . . in less than ten minutes I can show you five ways for you to reduce your transport costs.'

'. . . you can improve your productivity by at least 15% – with less demands on men and machinery.'

'. . . the enclosed article from Sludge Shifters Monthly explains what I am suggesting we can do for you.'

'. . . why not telephone Mr Andrews of Bloggs Pumps Ltd and ask what he thinks about us?'

'. . . your neighbours, Snooks Engineering Ltd, have been using our model 47B very successfully for two years now . . .'

Next, here is an example from the Insurance Industry, where it is probably more difficult to get face-to-face 'cold' than anywhere else.

The stamped addressed envelope **must** have a stamp, not be a printed reply-paid format. And, of course, the detailed information is not sent; the Seller or the managing director (who will undoubtedly still be selling hard in this business) will telephone Mr Rowbottom immediately on receipt of the returned letter and ask for an appointment, because there are a number of questions he still needs to ask and he's got some data on how other executives have done very well out of this new plan, which he feels Mr Rowbottom should see.

*WEST YORKSHIRE INSURANCE LTD*
*Incorporated insurance brokers and investment consultants*

*Halifax House*
*12 Bridge Road*
*Leeds, 4, Yorks*
*Tel: 0532 678855*

*Mr G. H. Rowbottom*
*Managing Director*
*Asquith & Smith Ltd*
*Morgans Wharf*
*Huddersfield*
*West Yorkshire*

*Dear Mr Rowbottom*
*Would you mind letting me have your date of birth below so that I can provide you with detailed information on a new executive protection plan which, due to its low cost and high benefits, is probably the most talked-about policy in the insurance world today.*
   *A stamped addressed envelope is enclosed for your convenience.*
   *Very truly yours*

*John Fenton*
*Managing Director*

*Name*_____

*Address*_____

_____

*Telephone Number*_____   *Date of Birth*_____

## Going for the Very Top

The best example of writing for an appointment I have ever seen happened early in 1983, and may well go down in selling history as a classic for maximum 'knock-on' effect. The selling company in question was selling strong to many executives in many branches of the prospect company for many months, on the strength of just two letters they received in reply. With the permission of the perpetrator, here is the example in detail.

The company wrote, enclosing a sample of the product, to the Chairman of the British Steel Corporation. The covering letter read:

Mr I. MacGregor                                         7 January 1983
Chairman
British Steel Corporation
9 Albert Embankment
London, SE1


Dear Mr MacGregor
Please accept a small aid to productivity.
    It is a spray nozzle which mounts and aligns in one movement. No screwing. No Spanners. Repeated very often, and multiplied by thousands as sprays on big installations need cleaning or replacing, its simplicity could save a lot of maintenance time for the Steel Industry and safeguard product quality by making a necessary service task less liable to neglect.
    The concept is new and unique and because we believe that it really can contribute to productivity at British Steel, we decided to be brave and go to the top. Anyone you referred us to would have our instant attention.
    Yours sincerely

The reply from Ian MacGregor was dated 10 January 1983.

Dear Mr —
Thank you for sending me a sample of your development of a new type of two-piece nozzle installation with a bayonet connection.
    I have passed the sample on to Dr Fitzgerald, who heads our Technical and Engineering function, with a request that he evaluates the potentialities of the product and communicates with you directly.
    Thank you for bringing this development to our attention.
    Sincerely,

The selling company promptly made contact with Dr Fitzgerald, to make sure he had safely received the sample spray nozzle from Mr MacGregor. They also sent Dr Fitzerald some technical information and performance data.

On 21 January 1983, a reply was sent to the selling company by Dr Fitzgerald.

Dear Mr —
Thank you for your letter of 17 January.
    I have passed the information you sent me to our engineers. As soon as I have some response we will get together and discuss opportunities.
    Yours sincerely

Now the very vastness of the British Steel Corporation hides layer upon layer of inter-departmental politics, a 'Parkinson's

Law' rivalry that creates incredible quantities of obstacles which get in the way of progress. A rather cruel joke on this subject goes – 'What's the difference between the British Steel Corporation and British Rail? Answer – the British Steel Corporation carries more passengers!'

The new and unique spray nozzle, if sold to the maintenance engineering department of, say, Port Talbot works, might be tried out and a few dozen subsequently ordered, but that would be as far as things would go. The last thing likely to happen would be for someone to recommend the nozzle to another British Steel works.

By starting at the very top, this selling company had bypassed the politics, but in such a way that, from then on, the normal obstacles at works level were replaced with politically-motivated enthusiasm. The salesforce of the selling company were busy all over the UK, at all levels of BSC. Wherever they went, whoever they talked to, copies of the two letters from Ian MacGregor and Frank Fitzgerald went with them. Maintenance engineers, works engineers, plant managers, divisional directors competed frantically to make it known to the top brass that they supported this new development. Response was what Dr Fitzgerald had said he was waiting for. Response was certainly what he got.

### Wives . . . God Bless 'em!

A very effective way to secure a 'Cold' appointment by telephone is for a salesman to use his wife, or an office-based secretary, to make his appointments for him. If he uses his wife, the kids and all domestic background noises must be banished. This is absolutely essential. The wife, when she telephones prospects, is **never** the salesman's wife – she is always his secretary. The call goes like this:

'My boss, Mr Andrews, has asked me to telephone you to arrange for him to come and see you – hopefully some time next week. I think it is in connection with improvements in your widget crushing plant. Could you spare Mr Andrews ten minutes, er, on Tuesday next, say at 9.50, or would the afternoon be better for you, say ten minutes to three?'

Often the prospect plays hard to get and asks for more information. This is where having a secretary who telephones is a winner:

'I'm terribly sorry, but I don't know any more. Mr Andrews just asked me to make the appointment. Look, if Tuesday is not convenient for you, would Wednesday be better?'

Alternative choice of date and times, always.

Lady Sellers take on a dual role for appointment-making. They become their own secretaries.

The most difficult people to get face-to-face with 'Cold' are people like architects. They tend to hate salesmen. They don't like sales literature much either. So unless they have a specific need for something, the answer nine times out of ten is 'No, go away!'

One company I know cracked this problem with ease. They harnessed the one factor that **did** turn architects on – **innovation**. Architects are designers, first and last. They yearn to create something that will make a name for themselves, win a building prize, enable them, if they work for a large firm, to set up in practice for themselves.

So whereas architects dislike sales literature, they simply **love** design manuals. This company therefore took their standard brochure on the products, which happened to be a range of mechanical and hydraulic dock levellers for warehouse loading bays, added some extra pages at the front on how to design loading bays which used their dock levellers, and retitled the brochure '**Modern Loading Bay Design**'.

The company's salesmen then telephoned architects and said:

'We've brought out a new design manual for loading bays. I'm in your area next Tuesday, can I drop you a copy in and show you the recent developments we've put into it?'

Success rate increased to six out of ten.

### Incoming Telephone Calls

You don't have to telephone every prospect. Sometimes they telephone **you**, but when they do, there is still your back-up to contend with.

Many a hot prospect has been lost because his telephone call was badly handled when he made the first contact, out of the blue. His requirements were not listened to or properly documented. The note made got lost before it could be sent to the Seller in the territory. The voice he heard irritated or depressed him.

No one can afford to lose business in this kind of way. Here's a specially designed Action Report for Incoming Telephone Calls.

---

## Incoming Telephone Call    Action Report

It's ringing... but before you pick up the phone

**SMILE!**
(go on, force yourself)

"**Good Morning Good Afternoon**

(say christian name and surname)

**Can I help you?**"

Person taking the call must fill in his/her name

Date of call _____  Time of call _____

Name and Initials of Caller _____
(ask him/her to spell name if in doubt)

Company (if relevant) _____

Address (if relevant) _____

_____  Post Code _____

Telephone Number (if relevant) _____  Extension _____

Reason for the Call _____

_____

_____

_____

_____

Action to be taken agreed with caller _____

_____

_____

_____

_____

The Institute of Sales & Marketing Management

---

There are two essential rules for the use of this form:

1 The person in your office who is going to pick up the telephone when it rings has a pad of these forms, and writes his/her christian name and surname on each sheet of the pad before business begins for the day.

   This simple action doesn't just make sure that the person taking the telephone call can be identified after the event – it also gets the person accustomed to using his/her christian name and surname when the phone rings – 'Good morning, Sally Haynes, how can I help you?' (It's incredible how reluctant people can be about using their own names.)

2 Before the ringing telephone is picked up, the corners of the person's mouth **must** be turned upwards – he/she **must** be smiling. A mirror on the desk helps. 'Think a smile' is a fundamental rule throughout Selling. It's a physiological fact that when your face is smiling your voice comes out happy. Even on black days when you feel like death warmed up, when you grit your teeth and force yourself to smile, your voice will still come out happy. The mirror on the desk is really for the black days. You grit your teeth, look in the mirror and force yourself to smile. It looks so darn stupid to you that you start laughing. So pick up the phone – 'Good morning, Sally Haynes, how can I help you?'

## Customers who Holler

The few customers who holler for you to go and see them, shouldn't be allowed to disrupt your plan. Don't drop everything unless it's a real emergency. Don't accept on face value the message passed to you by your office, either. Phone the customer back before you jump into your car. Make the visit on your terms – a day or two rarely makes any difference, it's just a misplaced sense of urgency building up in your mind. The better your planning, the easier it is to crack this problem.

## The Resulting Call Plan

From the foregoing you can really get your teeth into making effective appointments, beating your competitors to the business that's going, making the customers prefer to do business with you rather than with some less professional, less organized, competitor's Seller.

And from all this you'll be able to produce a proper, fully detailed call plan like the one illustrated on the next page.

One of the oldest formulae for success in Selling comes to mind here. It goes:

**Plan your work – work your plan**

| | TIME | APPT or COLD | COMPANY | CONTACT | TELEPHONE NUMBER | AIM OF CALL |
|---|---|---|---|---|---|---|
| | | | CALL PLAN WEEK NO. 14 | | SALESMAN J. WATSON | |
| MONDAY | 8.50 | A | PRESSED STEEL CO | J. BLACK | 021-328 1961 | GAIN ORDER |
| | 11.30 | C | POTTERSBY & CO | MAN DIR | | FACTORY EXT. PLANNED |
| | 2.00 | C | J & B ENGINEERS | E. JONES | | RE STOCK ORDER |
| | 3.45 | A | HEREFORD & CO | R. JUDSON | 021-888 6464 | NEG. CONTRACT RENEWAL FOR VALVES |
| TUESDAY | 8.50 | C | BAYTON ROAD, EXHALL – COLD CANVAS IND. ESTATE | | | |
| | 10.50 | A | FISHER & WADE | E. SAMSON | 0203-88771 | ENQ FOR PUMPS |
| | 2.00 | C | CONTINUE COLD CANVAS | | | |
| | 3.50 | A | EXHALL TOOLS | R. PRANKS | 0203-87651 | DISCUSS NEW VALVE |
| WEDNESDAY | 9.00 | A | MEET SALES MGR @ COVENTRY STATION | | | |
| | 9.50 | A | JONES & PLAT | N. SMYTHE | 0203-38221 | NEW CONTRACT FOR LINING |
| | 1.50 | A | DROP FORGES | J. HINKLEY | 0203-47652 | GAIN ORDER |
| | 2.50 | A | F. LACEY & CO | L. BRIGGS | 0203-43355 | DISCUSS NEW VALVE |
| | 3.50 | A | ARUNDEL DEVELOPMENTS | WORKS DIRECTOR | | BUILDING NEW WKS |
| THURSDAY | 8.30 | A | ALL DAY @ H.Q. PRODUCT TRAINING ON NEW VALVE. | | | |
| FRIDAY | 9.50 | A | B. S. C. | M. DALY | CORBY 57221 | COMM. NEW PLANT |
| | 11.50 | A | AQUASCUTUM | R. ROSS | CORBY 56652 | GAIN ORDER |
| | 2.00 | A | BRITISH SEALED BEAMS | D. DAVIES | CORBY 59241 | DISCUSS NEW VALVE |
| | 3.50 | A | GOLDEN WONDER | N. JENKS | CORBY 59911 | INCREASE STOCKS |

That's how to make sure you're always chasing business, not just chasing customers or will-o'-the-wisps. Common sense? Of course it is. But as I've said before common sense isn't practised all that often in Selling – unless you really want to win, that is!


**Break a Leg!**

The telephone is a most under-utilized Selling tool, except in businesses like Birds Eye, Ross Foods and Coca-Cola, where it gets 95% of total business when used by Tele-Sales teams.

Most Sellers traditionally believe that the customers much prefer the face-to-face approach. One salesman I know proved it was all different. He didn't set out to prove it – he just broke his leg in seven places, skiing, and wound up in traction for six months without the option.

Lying there, he began worrying about his customers, and about his job. (Wouldn't you?) So he resolved to do something about it. He got his wife to collect together all his customer records, files, cards, assorted paperwork and deliver it to his bed. Then he set about devising a plan for systematically telephoning every one of his customers and prospects, potential business

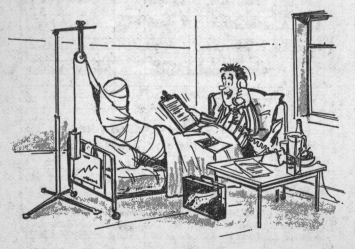

determining the frequency of the phone call. One of his colleagues handled any trouble-shooting necessary during the six months.

And what did he find?

Business didn't go down, it went **up**! Okay, during the first month he got a fair bit of sympathy business and, not being a dummy, he took advantage of this. But after the initial month, business still kept increasing. The salesman himself told me why, a few months after he'd recovered and gone back on the road.

'I found I was contacting every single one of my customers about four times as frequently as when I was making visits to them. And, you know, they didn't mind. They didn't bother that it was just a telephone call, not a visit. They were quite happy doing business over the phone. This was the shock I had to get over. Okay, I had no other options open to me so I probably did a much better job on my phone calls than I would have done normally. But, it showed me the true situation.

'Now I spend only half my total time on the road, most of it chasing new business, and the other half manning my own Tele-Sales Desk. And sales are still going up.'

Maybe your business is different – but is it *that* different?


## A Final Word on Paperwork

Most Sellers don't like it. Some positively hate it. Some go to great lengths to avoid it. One sales manager I know said this to me recently:

'One of my salesmen is allergic to NCR paper!'

Another Sales manager I know received a formal doctor's note from one of his salesmen which read:

'The forms and reports which Mr . . . is required to submit are creating unacceptable stress and must be reduced if his health is not to suffer further.'

If you feel any sympathy at all with these two salesmen, get out of Selling; it's not your kind of business. Paper work – the right kind of paperwork – is essential. Get organized to chase business, not just will-o'-the-wisps.

But don't computerize it all. That's *really* playing into the competition's hands. Computers and salesforces just don't go together. All the reasons would take another book. Until it's written you'll just have to take my word for it.

# 7
# How to Win Business from Your Competitors

**Most of our growth, next year, will have to come from business we take from our competitors.**

**We're not going to do it by cutting prices; we're going to do it by aggressive, confident, professional selling.**

If you want to win more business from your competitors then – in the eyes of their customers – you've got to come over **better** than your competitors; more professional than your competitors. And the difference has got to be significant, not marginal.

For example, consider that record file again, full of the paperwork appertaining to the customer with whom you are face-to-face. How would you come over to him if you were visibly armed with that kind of documentation about the relationship so far? Would he be impressed? Would he be *more* impressed than he is with the way your competitors do business (or than he is with the way *you* work now)?

There are many ways you can come over better. You can show a greater concern for the customer's time. You can get to the point faster, impress him with your efficiency. You can even get the customer to tell *you* how you can achieve your objective of winning business from the competitor he's buying from at present.

Let us assume you have done some research and found that a particular company uses widgets, but you haven't been able to dig up a carrot or establish any more tangible objective than 'I want to sell this company some widgets'. You make contact with the key decision-maker, preferably face-to-face, but by telephone will do, and you say:

'Good morning, Mr Jones, As I understand it, your company uses a lot of widgets. (*pause*) My company sells widgets. Very good ones. I'd very much like to see you using some of ours. Please may I ask you a very direct question?

'What do I need to do to get you to buy some of your widgets from us?'

The last line is what I call 'the most powerful question in Selling'. Learn to use it well, and your order book will always be full. But don't smile when you use it. You must come over to the customer with complete sincerity. You really want to know – it's the most important thing in your life.

In some cases, the final question in the sequence might be:

'What do we need to do to get on your list of approved suppliers?'

Whatever he suggests you do, you can add a bit of confirmation and commitment before you actually do it:

'Fair enough. If we can do that, will you place some of your business our way?'

You'll find, as you become more and more proficient at competitive selling, that those three little words: 'If we can . . .' unlock more doors than you thought possible.

You can also attempt to quantify the business:

'How much of your business would you be able to move to us?'
'How soon? What sizes?'

Now all you need to do is what he suggested you do. Do it to his complete satisfaction, and the business must be yours.

Do you suffer from little tin god customers who keep you all to themselves but don't buy much from you – they place most of their business with a competitor? The 'what do I have to do' technique is superb with those kind of people.

There is another problem, however. Those little tin gods keep you away from other important contacts you should be making in that company. Remember you're chasing business; you're not there just to keep little tin gods happy.

The average number of people who exert influence on a decision to buy something, or change a supplier, increases as the size of the customer increases. In small companies, most decisions will be taken by one person, the boss. In very large companies the trend is more and more towards buying by committee.

If you want to win more business than your competitors, you've got to make sure you talk to *more* decision-makers and influencers than they do. If you don't you'll come second again.

A survey some years ago produced these figures on decision influencers. The survey covered 1,100 British companies across a wide spread of industries.

| Size of company (Number of employees) | Average number of decision influencers | Average number of influencers who talk to Sellers |
| --- | --- | --- |
| less than 200 | 3.43 | 1.72 |
| 201 to 400 | 4.85 | 1.75 |
| 401 to 1,000 | 5.81 | 1.90 |
| more than 1,001 | 6.50 | 1.65 |
| *The trends* | *This average is steadily increasing* | *This average is static* |

If a little tin god gets in your way, you've got to find a way to gently, but firmly, move him to one side. Not easy, but here's one way to achieve this – **and** to continue the process of appearing *better* in the customer's eyes.

## The Purchasing Cycle Plan

You ask a question:

'By the way, do you have a copy of your purchasing cycle plan handy? I wonder if I could have a copy?'

Every company goes about its requisitioning and purchasing of goods and services in a certain way. More often than not, there is a standard procedure laid down. This standard procedure, if translated into diagram form, is the 'purchasing cycle plan'. But rarely *is* the standard procedure translated into diagram form, so the usual reaction to your question will be:

'What do you mean, purchasing cycle plan?'

Great! Just the reaction you wanted. The opportunity to explain:

'Just a chart, a picture, in flow diagram form, of how your company operates in respect of requisitioning and purchasing its supplies.

'I wanted it because we make a point of learning as much about how our customers operate as we can. That way, we can give the best possible service. Often, we can adjust our own standard procedures to dovetail exactly into a customer's standard procedures.'

Then you dive into your briefcase and pull out a couple of examples of purchasing cycle plans – one for your *own company's* purchasing department and the other for one of your better customers.

You explain how your own purchasing department operates, how it uses its disciplines and procedures to make sure customers are never let down on deliveries through hold-ups in the supply of components or materials. You explain how the cycle plan for your customer has helped you give that customer a *better* service and how it helped you pin-point an area where greater efficiency could be, and was, achieved.

And all the time, this guy you're talking to is saying to himself:

'This salesman's a lot different from the usual rubbish that I have to see. His company seems to appreciate customers, too. Hmmm! Maybe I should try them out. This plan idea's not bad, either. I could use one of them. Do me some good with the boss.'

At an appropriate time in your explanation, you say:

'Does your cycle plan look anything like these? If you haven't got one in this form, can we draw it out now, on my pad?'

And before you know it, you and he are building his purchasing cycle plan on your A4 size survey pad. (Again, a pocket notebook is useless!)

Now you can start asking questions about each bit of the plan as it develops. 'What does this do?', 'How does this bit operate?', and 'Who is involved in this section?', 'Who actually does the requisitioning?', 'Who actually signs the order?'.

With some adroit questions during the drawing up of his purchasing cycle plan, most of those hitherto hidden decision

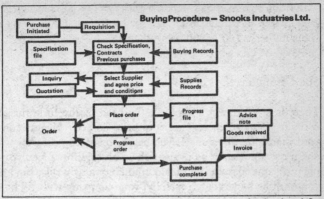

By the way, do you have a copy of your purchasing cycle plan handy?
I wonder if I could have a copy?

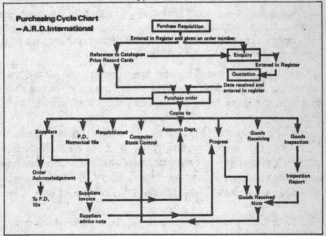

influencers can be uncovered, and your little tin god has very little
opportunity to object to your talking to them from that point.

When the plan is completed, you thank him, and go to put it in
your briefcase. What is guaranteed at this point is that he will say:
'Hang on, can I take a copy of that before you go away with it?'

That's competitive salesmanship!

But don't go mad and walk out with *just* the purchasing cycle plan instead of with an order. This is just the preliminary stage. Hang in there. You've still got work to do.

## Short-circuiting the Politics

There is another way to go over the head of the little tin god without giving offence. That is to bring in your biggest gun – your managing director. (If you have a managing director who doesn't see himself as a big gun to help his salesforce, you've got big problems all round and I don't think I or anyone else can help you until he moves on. Hopefully, your company will still be in business when he does.)

The opening goes like this:

'My managing director would like to come in and talk to your production director. He's asked me to fix a meeting. I think he has a few things up his sleeve which could save you a fair bit of money. Can we fix up a convenient date and time, and include you in the meeting?'

You'll be there too. This top brass gambit will always overcome the political problems, and such a meeting should always end with the order being secured, or a firm commitment for the future.

But the truly incredible thing about this business isn't the number of managing directors who won't back up their salesmen when it's necessary – it's the vast majority of salesmen who *won't call in the managing director when it's necessary. It's their ego again, screwing up yet another piece of business they could have won.*

Not long ago, I heard about a 'big gun' attack which won an order **after** a customer had placed the same order with a competitor **and** paid a deposit of £1,800 to the competitor.

The product was a piece of metal finishing machinery – a kind of rumbling barrel with knobs on.

Our hero, the salesman who had found that he had lost the order to the competitor, reported this calamity to his sales director.

The sales director said, 'Hang on a minute; we've got one of these in stock. What delivery are the competition offering on this?'

'Six weeks minimum,' replied the salesman. 'So all is definitely not lost,' said the sales director. 'Come on, let's go and talk to the customer.'

Face-to-face with the customer's works manager a short while later, the sales director was proving on paper that a reduction of four weeks in the time before the machinery ordered could be in production represented savings to the customer which amounted to a lot more than the £1,800 they'd paid as a deposit. 'Cancel the order and place it with us,' the sales director suggested.

'Can't really do that,' said the works manager, plainly worried. 'A deal is a deal. I doubt if our managing director would wear that.'

'Well, let's go and ask him,' said the sales director. 'There's a lot of money at stake, and you know you could do with this equipment ASAP.'

Upstairs to the managing director's office – all the way through the calculations again – and one final offer from the sales director – a discount on the ongoing consumables which went in the machinery, so that the customer could recoup his £1,800 deposit over his first twelve months purchases of the consumables. The deal was clinched – the first order cancelled. And the competitor was, of course, hopping mad. He tried everything, but the more he tried, the worse he made his position. In the end, his company was declared 'persona non grata' by the customer.

So when is an order really lost to the competition?

Being seen to be **better** than your competitors can come in all shapes and sizes. Here are some examples.

## Be Better by Being Different

Let's go back to 1936; to a survey of 1,000 salesmen's reports over a one year period. (Yes, they *did* have to submit reports in 1936.) The survey totted up the number of times common excuses for **not** selling appeared in those 1,000 reports.

| | |
|---|---|
| Due to slump (now they call it recession) | 86 |
| Workers on short time | 50 |
| Christmas holidays | 140 |
| Summer holidays | 70 |
| Easter holidays | 35 |
| Tax bill to pay | 176 |
| No budget until next financial year | 134 |
| No money | 93 |
| Weather conditions!! | 66 |

That's a total, out of 1,000, of       850

I bet if you analyse **your** excuses for not selling over the past year, you won't find much difference. You're not even being original! The same excuses have been used since selling began.

Your management, quite often, doesn't help you overcome the excuses barrier, because negative thinking prevails in management just as much as it does at the sharp end.

Sales managers are often heard saying things like this:

'The product can't be sold at certain times of the year.'
'The product can't be sold in certain districts.'
'Trade is only seasonal.'
'You can't make calls the day before bank holiday.'
'Buyers place few orders during the first week of the new year.'
'Our salesmen don't take orders.'
'It's no good calling before 10 am, or after 4.30 pm or on Friday afternoons; they won't see you.'
'Large companies will only see you by appointment.'
'You can't get orders on Saturday mornings.'

What utter rubbish. All of it. Yes you can. Who made the rules anyway? What rules? As Sir Barnes Wallis used to say:

'Why not, why not?'

To beat your competitors, do all the things the average Seller won't do, and, every day, do at least one thing you don't want to do (Alfred Tack).

Be different, and from the difference, come over better.

You can't get orders on Saturday mornings? Of course you can in retail and direct Selling. In industrial selling it is more difficult, certainly, because the customers don't normally work on

Saturdays any longer. But one saleswoman cracked the problem.

Her name is Flo Wright, and at the time of this story she was manager of a machine tool distributor's showroom in the centre of Bristol. Her showroom had its own large car park and was right next to the MFI warehouse and the main shopping centre. Parking a car in the centre of Bristol on a Saturday for shopping was murder.

So, Flo decided to open for business on Saturdays. She had printed a quantity of car park passes and sent them out with a covering letter to all her customers and prospective customers. The letter read:

'If you shop in Bristol on Saturdays, you know how difficult it is to park your car. We have a large car park right next to the main shopping centre, and we are making it available to selected regular customers on Saturdays. Enclosed is your car park pass. If you show this to the car park attendant he will let you in.'

Quite a number of Flo's customers **and** prospective customers took her up on the offer. Good relations very well cemented. But Flo didn't stop there. She knew how husbands quickly develop 'shopping legs' and fall over with fatigue on Saturdays when out with their wives.

Strategically, the shortest route from her car park to the shopping centre was straight through the machine tool showroom. So, Flo set up a tressle table in the middle of the showroom and served free coffee.

'Have a cup of coffee before you start your shopping, luv; black or white? How does your wife take it?'

And again, when they returned, loaded with shopping. A life saver, and **very hot**.

So there was a customer, knowledgeable about machine tools, fed up about shopping, sipping coffee, too hot to drink, in the middle of a machine tool showroom on a Saturday – with his wife.

What does he do? He shows off his knowledge of machine tools to his wife, who never really understood what he did for a living. He demonstrates to her the kind of machines he is responsible for in his job. He demonstrates to her the power and authority he has in his job.

He places orders on Saturday mornings – verbally, and confirms them in writing on the following Monday.

So be different – like Flo Wright.

## Wooden Legs

I knew a salesman some years ago who was blessed with a wooden leg. Now, not many people would reckon a wooden leg was anything to be blessed with, but, then, not many people could use a wooden leg to make as much money as this salesman made. He was in a very competitive market that generated regular repeat business. He and a dozen other competitor salesmen fought for the business. He got most of it because of his wooden leg.

Not sympathy business, although if he got any of that he happily took it. No: all he did was use his wooden leg as a Focuser. (More of that in Chapter 10 – How to Demonstrate Your Superiority.)

When he first met a new prospective customer, he sat with his wooden leg straight out to one side, so that the prospect could see

four inches of polished teak between his deliberately short sock and his trouser turn-up. He'd turned down the offer of switching from a polished teak stump to a skin-coloured lightweight aluminium contraption years before. He knew what he was doing.

The sight of that four inches of polished teak used to hypnotize the customers, he reckoned. They couldn't take their eyes off it.

Ten minutes maximum and the prospect couldn't help but say, 'Excuse me asking, but is that **really** wood?'

'Oh yes,' the salesman would reply, pulling his trouser leg up another six inches and giving the polished teak a rap with his pen. 'Copped a packet during the last war, in Normandy.'

A few minutes were then spent talking about the war, and whether the salesman suffered when the weather was damp, but the key factor thereafter was that he was never forgotten. Securing the first order was easy. And thereafter, every time the customer said to himself, 'I need to order some more widgets,' the first supplier who came into his mind was 'wooden leg'. So he got most of the on-going business.

I know another young salesman who, first time he walked into a new prospect's office, overlooked the fact that there were two steps down from the door and fell flat on his face, arms and legs spreadeagled, briefcase and presenter flying into opposite corners of the room. Luckily, he didn't do any damage, to himself or to the prospect's office, only to his pride. The prospect, of course, laughed his socks off.

Again, the first order was easy, if only in return for the entertainment provided. But that salesman gets all the repeat business too, in just as competitive a situation as the guy with the wooden leg.

Another classic mind jogger. Every time that customer says to himself, 'I must order some more sprunge brackets,' he remembers the guy who fell flat on his face the first time he came into his office.

The salesman still gets embarrassed and colours up when the customer says to him, laughing: 'Hey, do you remember the first visit you made here . . .?' but it doesn't stop him accepting all the business that's going.

It was different for the salesman who over-emphasized a key point with his fist on the glass topped desk of the chief buyer, and cracked the glass from front to back. He didn't get the business!

## What Would You Do?

A salesman I know in the life insurance business does a lot of work at domestic parlour level, talking to the husband and wife who've been together for seventeen years and have never bothered to take out any insurance except on their house, furniture and car. They don't believe in life insurance. It will never happen to them.

This salesman analysed the domestic Selling situation and pin-pointed his biggest problem. The turning point from total rejection to total reception was getting the couple to think seriously about what they would do if one of them was to go – dead like! Once they'd thought seriously about what they would do, and had realized how long it would take for the money to run out and the difficulties they would have on their own, making ends meet, selling them a policy to cover the situation was easy.

The snag was they didn't **want** to think about it. What the salesman had to do was find a way of **making** them think about it, whilst maintaining total ethics.

After a lot of thought and experimentation, he hit on a winning idea. He had made a beautiful, solid mahogany, brass fittings, about a foot long, miniature coffin. It lived vertically in one side of his briefcase.

In the front room, sitting opposite Gladys and Henry, he'd get to the point of needing both of them to think seriously about what they'd do when one of them bought the farm.

'Just for a couple of minutes,' the salesman would say to his prospect couple, 'I'd like to get you thinking about something deadly serious.'

He'd reach into his briefcase, bring out the miniature coffin, place it gently and carefully, almost reverently, in the centre of the coffee table between him and the couple, turn to the husband and say:

'God forbid, but let's imagine for a couple of minutes that you are in there.' He puts one finger on the coffin. Then he turns to the wife and asks, 'What would you do?'

There are two or three seconds of pregnant silence and then, **every time**, the *husband* starts talking. And the salesman turns back to him, puts his finger on his lips, points to the coffin and says, 'Shhhh. You're in there.'

Then he turns back to the wife and asks again, 'What would you do?'

After that, the salesman maintained, the miniature coffin could be put away and it was all plain sailing. A perfectly ethical way of jolting a couple of prospects out of their dream world and making them realize and accept their future problems and responsibilities.


## Two Kinds of People

One salesman who sells investments has a method of tickling his prospects' egos and getting them on to his side. Early on in his presentation, he says to his prospect:

'You know, going through life and meeting as many people as I do, I've found that when it comes to saving money, there are only two kinds of people.'

At this point, the salesman begins drawing on his A4 size pad. As he draws, he keeps talking. First he draws two circles, like a disjointed pair of spectacles. Then he points to the left-hand circle and says:

'One kind of people tend to spend their income on whatever they need or want to buy, and if they've any left over after that, they might think about saving it, or investing it.'

And while he's saying this, the salesman is writing '**spend**' in his left-hand circle and then shading in the bottom of the circle, as if it were a quarter full of liquid. Then he points to the right-hand circle and says:

'The other kind of people tend to put some money aside **before** they start spending, to save or invest.'

And while he's saying this, he shades in the top portion of the right-hand circle and writes '**then spend**' inside the unshaded part of the circle.

Then the salesman draws an arrow from the bottom of the left-hand circle to the bottom of the right-hand circle and, while he's drawing the arrow, he says:

'And the funny thing is – these kind of people (the left-hand circle) always seem to finish up working for these kind (the right-hand circle).'

## Be Better by Being Thorough

Being different is good and is fun. Add being thorough to being different and you have the winning combination.

I'm a great believer in the use of check lists. Why strain the memory or risk forgetting something important. It goes back to 1962 and my second selling job. I was designing and estimating equipment for polishing the edges of glass mirrors. Automated, sixty feet long, very expensive. My company sent me down from Rugby, where I was based, to East London, to measure up for a big one. A whole day of measuring in the prospective customer's works, discussing the project with two of the directors. Everything went very well. I returned to Rugby with sheets of sketches, dimensions, figures, specifications. But no check list.

Next day I was at my drawing board, laying out the job to scale. Sixty feet is a long piece of tackle to fit into an existing factory, already full of plant and people. Then, as the day and the drawing progressed, I began having this vision. I could see this dirty great vertical stancheon sticking up, floor to roof, in the middle of the factory. Yet I hadn't a single reference to it in my notes and sketches. No, I must be imagining things. I tried to convince myself. It's in some other factory I've visited recently.

But the vision kept coming back. I began sweating. If I carried on in normal sales office estimating fashion, working to the edict, 'If in doubt, guess!' I knew, with my luck, the sixty feet long machine I was responsible for would run straight through the bit of the factory where stood the stancheon. Thank heavens for one thing. I may have been a novice salesman at that time, but I wasn't a bad engineer, and the edict for engineers is different from the edict for sales office estimating. The edict for engineers is 'If in doubt, **ask**!'

So I plucked up the courage and telephoned one of the directors I'd spoken with the day before in East London.

'Er, sorry to bother you, but I need to ask you a question. Have you got a stancheon in the middle of the factory?'

I was really sweating. It sounded such a stupid thing to ask anyone.

'Yes,' the director replied cautiously. 'Why do you ask?'

'Well, I seem to have missed it on the notes I took yesterday. Er, have you got a tape measure handy?'

'I might be able to find one.' The director was even more cautious. 'Why?'

'I wonder, would you mind measuring how far your stancheon is from the sides of your factory?'

There was silence for a good twenty seconds. I could hear him breathing. Heavily! Then, 'Ring me back in half an hour!' and he slammed the 'phone down.

For the next half hour I was convincing myself I should have made the 100 mile journey to London again, instead of telephoning. Looking back, it's clear that all I really needed to have had for my visit was a well-thought-out check list, one of the questions being, 'Is anything likely to get in the way?'

I'm not alone in my misery. I know a salesman who relied on a discussion across a desk, rather than taking the trouble to see for himself. He was selling a rather tall piece of equipment. Fourteen feet high, in fact. So he asked the obvious question – 'What's the roof height in your factory?'

'Nineteen feet' came back the answer without hesitation.

But when the equipment was delivered, the choice he had was either to dig a hole in the concrete floor or bash a hole in the roof, because the roof was pitched and the nineteen feet was the height at the apex. The salesman's equipment went up against one of the side walls, and there the roof height was only eleven feet.

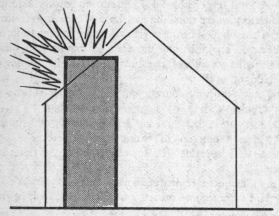

It didn't do the slightest bit of good, blaming the customer for the error.

Being thorough comes in all shapes and sizes.

My favourite check list of all is the one which covers the customer's objectives. I developed the example below for a materials handling company, back in 1974.

A company salesman used this check list to broaden the mind of his prospective customer – to open up for him a whole new world. He did this by showing his prospect the Objectives List at an appropriate and early stage in his presentation and saying:

'Our products usually enable our customers to achieve seven objectives which to them are pretty important. Most of the seven objectives involve saving the customer a considerable amount of money.

'I've got the seven objectives listed on this sheet. Can I ask you – which of them are relevant in your case? Which of these seven would **your** company like to achieve?'

# OBJECTIVES

Customer _____

Date _____

**What does the Customer want to do – and why does he want to do it?**

| Detailed objectives that this Customer wants to achieve (Strike out the sections which do not apply) | Order of Priority |
|---|---|
| INCREASE PRODUCTION/THROUGHPUT/VEHICLE TURNROUND | |
| REDUCE HANDLING TIME | |
| REDUCE LABOUR REQUIREMENT | |
| REDUCE MAINTENANCE COSTS | |
| BETTER UTILISATION OF EQUIPMENT | |
| BETTER UTILISATION OF SPACE | |
| IMPROVE LABOUR RELATIONS/SAFETY (Union attitude, accident rate, absenteeism, fatigue) | |
| OTHER FACTORS? | |

The prospect looked down the list. He'd probably been worrying for some time about how to reduce his non-productive handling time and how to cut his labour costs. He indicated as much to the salesman.

But he'd probably never even thought of reducing maintenance costs, gaining space, improving labour relations, throughput, safety or vehicle turnround times. And he'd certainly not ever considered achieving **all seven** objectives with one piece of equipment.

Was he going to be interested? You bet.

The minimum number of relevant objectives for each prospective customer, achieved by the Salesman who used this particular objectives list, was four. Often, it rose to six. Once the relevant objective had been identified, the Salesman went on to define more precisely what this particular prospective customer wanted to achieve for each relevant section. The precise objectives were written in the spaces provided under each heading.

Then the Salesman asked his prospect to put the relevant, precisely defined, objectives into priority order. 'Which of these four do you reckon is the most important to you? Which is number one? I'd like to get them in order of priority if you don't mind?'

After that, the selling, and the justification for the purchase, was easy. We'll meet this objective list again in Chapter 9 – How to Present Your Proposals, because it forms an integral part of the production of the most successful Proposal format I know of for selling against competition.

How thorough should you be? Well, if you were selling medium to large computers or similar capital equipment where board level sanction and budgets were required, consider this sales checklist from the Japanese Facom Computers organization. I came across it in Australia, and there Facom were beating all comers.

This checklist, headed 'Profile of a Sale', lists the eleven key stages a Facom Salesman is required to go through from the beginning to the end of one potential sale.

## PROFILE OF A SALE

1 **Research Prospect**
Annual report
Company structure
Cross directorships

**2 Establish Contacts**
Plan objectives for each call
Top down or bottom up?
**3 Meet Decision-maker and Recommender**
**4 Establish Needs and Wants with Decision-maker**
Probe for company 5 year plans with decision-maker
What are the key business decisions of the prospect?
Who makes these decisions?
**5 Basis of Decision**
Unique to FACOM?
Relevant to decision-maker
Written down?
Can FACOM satisfy all points?
Favourable cost/benefit ratio?
**6 Facom Review**
Review Basis of Decision with Manager and assess % chance of obtaining
the order
**7 Resource Allocation for Survey**
**8 Survey**
Review finding with prospect middle management
Have you established all objections?
**9 Presentation**
Plan and rehearse
**10 Proposal**
Document only what you have sold
Does it satisfy all the points in the Basis of Decision?
Sense of Urgency?
**11 Close**
Close quickly or find out why not?
Have you followed the Profile?

That's what I call being thorough.

## Using Survey Check Lists

How does a really good Seller get all the information and data he
needs to build an effective sales presentation for a customer?

By asking the customer for it. (But not the way I did back in
1962!)

The secret is in **how** the Seller asks and what information and
data he asks for.

Really good Sellers think it all out beforehand – and they **don't** rely on their memory. They use properly designed and properly printed check lists which fit into their A4 size survey pads. (You'll eventually learn to love A4 size survey pads as I do!)

Here are two examples of well thought out survey check lists – one for a problem-solving situation involving capital equipment or specialist services; the other for establishing what competition the user is up against.

**Survey Check List – Problem Solving**

1 What specifically
do you want to achieve?

2 What is the
problem
costing you?

3 How are you
thinking of
solving it?

4 Who else is involved
in this problem or in
finding a solution to it?

5 What would happen
if you did
nothing?

6 How much money
has been allocated
to solving this
problem?

7 How did you reach
this particular
figure?

8 When will this money
be available?

9 If we can produce
a significantly better solution
for slightly more than your
budget figure, will you consider it?

## Survey Check List – Competitors

| | |
|---|---|
| 1 | Which other suppliers are you discussing this equipment with? |
| 2 | Have you used any of these suppliers before? |
| 3 | When are the other quotations due? |
| 4 | Who decides which supplier gets the order? |
| 5 | Which supplier do you favour at this stage? |
| 6 | Why? |
| 7 | Does it give you a problem, the fact that you haven't done business with us before? |

## Be Better by Being Faster

There are some businesses where the first Seller in, following up an enquiry, gets the order because time is the essence and there is no advantage to the customer in delaying the decision until he's seen another couple of Sellers.

Quite often, customers in this situation send out enquiries to several suppliers, all at the same time. Thus, the fastest response gets the business. Half an hour could lose it and I know Sellers who have seen, literally seen, a competitor pick up an order which would have been theirs had they been able to find somewhere to park the car.

The answer to being **fastest**, if this is your business, is – **install a radio telephone or a radio pager**.

The cost is rubbish if it enables you to pick up orders that otherwise a more agile, in closer communication with his office, Seller would win. Radio pagers, which tell you to ring your office fast, can be hired for as little as £2 per month.

Alternatively, if your area is small and compact and parking your car is your biggest problem, use a bicycle, moped, motorbike or a taxi and ring in to your office every hour on the hour to keep tabs on those enquiries.

## No Reason to Change

The thorniest barrier to progress in Selling! The prospective customer comes out to reception to talk to the Seller. The Seller leaps to his feet and extends greetings and thanks for a few minutes of the customer's time. The customer holds up his hands like a traffic cop and says:

'We've been doing business quite satisfactorily with Apex Distributors for seven years now and see absolutely no reason to change – but if you'd like to leave your literature, I'll put it in our suppliers' file.'

The door quite firmly shut – unless, with determination and technique, the Seller can open it again.

'When you started to use Apex seven years ago, Mr Arnold, what made you choose them as your supplier?'

Mr Arnold has to come up with something. Just hope he remembers! If he mentions two or three factors which caused them to pick Apex, or to switch to Apex from another supplier:

'Are these factors still the same ones today?'

If Mr Arnold says Yes; great. If he says No:

'How have they changed? What is your criteria for ordering for the foreseeable future? Can I get it down on my survey pad?'

Then the Seller plays his ace:

'It's a fact the world over, Mr Arnold, that 92% of all the products in use today have been invented, introduced or refined into their present form **within** the last ten years.

'So if you're still using something that you started using seven years ago, you may be perfectly happy with it, but there's a good chance that by now there will be something better available. Certainly, in our particular business there have been a considerable number of developments these past few years.

'Shouldn't you take ten minutes to find out for sure that you're still getting best value for your money, because quite frankly, I don't think you can be?'

## Be Better by Being Honest

A rich businessman accosted a beautiful blonde at a cocktail party. 'For a thousand pounds will you sleep with me tonight?'

'You bet,' she replied, looking him straight in the eye.

'For five pounds will you sleep with me tonight?'

'What!' she exclaimed. 'You must be joking. What kind of a girl do you think I am?'

'We've established what kind of girl you are, my dear,' the businessman smiled. 'All we have to do is decide the price.'

The very mention of bribery and corruption in business, and of over-lavish entertainment and company yachts or grouse shoots, invariably sends shudders through any organization since John Poulson and Watergate and Lockheed blew the *status quo* through the roof.

But, there is still a lot of it about and it comes in all shapes and sizes. The average Seller probably comes up against it every day. Maybe he doesn't recognize the fact but it's there all the same. The funny story preceding this paragraph illustrates the basic factor in bribery and corruption. It takes **two** people to make it happen. Two basically dishonest people – a Buyer and a Seller. And either one can start the ball rolling.

Let's consider a typical situation when a dishonest Buyer and a dishonest Seller get together. The Buyer encourages and accepts a gift from the Seller for favours above and beyond his duty of getting the best deal for his company. In other words, in exchange for the gift which might be cash in the back pocket, membership of some exotic club, a free holiday, his house painted, a car at a bargain price or a thousand other things – he buys from a supplier who does **not** give him best value for money.

Having accepted the gift and placed the order, this Buyer is stuck with this Seller. He buys again and again. He has to. He cannot stop doing business with the Seller for fear that his indiscretion will be leaked to his management – or worse, to the local newspapers.

The cleverest dishonest Buyers manage, however, to cover themselves by still making sure they get the best deals for their companies. The dishonest Seller's competitor comes up with a lower price. The buyer contacts his supplier straight away and says: 'George, Apex Distributors have offered me grade B widgets at five per cent less than your current price. You'll have to match it, or my directors will soon find out.'

So the dishonest Seller either drops his price and keeps the business, or lets the dishonest buyer off the hook. If he aims to keep the business at all costs, two years of these tactics and he'll be lucky if he has any profit left at all. And this is business he is *buying!*

Of course, the dishonest Buyer's directors will soon find out if he doesn't make sure he keeps on getting the best possible deals for his company. The dishonest Seller's competitors will do their very best to bring the problem to the directors' attention. What they'd like to see is the dishonest Buyer replaced by someone with whom **they** can do business.

Faced with this, the less astute dishonest Buyers don't last very long. But most of them leave before they're pushed.


## Tactics for Beating the Bribers

If the deal you have to offer is the same or only marginally better than the deal the dishonest buyer is getting from the competitor he is buying from, you are going to have big problems. Let's face it, you're going to have big problems with *honest* Buyers if you've nothing extra to offer.

You've got **you**, of course. You'll look after him better. You'll see that he gets the best possible attention from your company's service engineers. You give him your home telephone number and tell him he can contact you at any time, any evening, over the weekend if he needs anything.

And you've got Second Source. He's got all his eggs in one basket. Dumb dishonest buyers invariably have.

'What would happen, Mr Thick, if Apex Distributors had a fire, or a strike, or went bust, and suddenly, without warning, couldn't supply you?

'How long would it take you to open an account with another supplier and to get things back to normal supply levels? Even two weeks would give you big problems, wouldn't it?

'If you were already buying, say, 20% of your widgets from a second source supplier, it would be so much easier for you to pick up the phone and get the second supplier to increase supplies fast, wouldn't it?

'And 20% wouldn't hurt your relationship with your main supplier, would it? You're only taking out some insurance and they must understand the wisdom and the logic of that.'

Help him get himself just a little bit off the hook, and once you've established a toe-hold . . .

If you **do** have a significantly better deal to offer a customer who is currently buying from one of your competitors and you come up against inexplicable obstacles which make you wonder if you are up against a dishonest Buyer – test the water with the most powerful question in Selling:

'Mr Thin, it seems to me that the deal we are offering you is significantly better than you're getting now from Dodgers in at least four ways, including price and quality.

'Can I ask you a straight question?' Just what do we have to do to get you to buy from us?'

If he's really dumb, he might suggest that you double what he's getting from Dodgers. Then you just pass the problem up the line to your directors and let them deal with it. More likely, he'll break out in a sweat, keep hedging and avoid committing himself. If he does this, you can be 99% certain you've got one of them.

You now have two courses of action, either of which you can take, or both, one after the other.

Course One: You brief your sales director on the situation. You establish with the dishonest Buyer or with someone else in his company some days when it is certain he **won't** be in his office. Your sales director pays a visit, out of the blue, without an appointment. He asks for a few mintues of the dishonest Buyer's time. He's told the Buyer is not in today. He asks to see the Buyer's *superior*. Because he's a sales director, he stands a good chance of getting face-to-face. In ten minutes, the significantly better deal and the inexplicable obstructions have been discussed. 'How do we get your business?' your sales director asks.

The day the dishonest Buyer gets back to his office, your phone rings. 'What the hell's going on?' the Buyer rants. 'Your sales director's been in to see my boss, behind my back. I take a bloody dim view of that!'

'Good heavens,' you exclaim. 'I don't know anything about this. Look, give me half an hour to find out what's going on and I'll ring you back.'

You make yourself useful doing other things for half an hour, then you ring the dishonest Buyer back.

'I've spoken to my sales director. Given him quite a rocket, actually. It's all quite innocent, really. He was in your area yesterday, and found he had an hour to spare because another meeting ran shorter than scheduled. He knew we had a deal under discussion so he popped in to see you. When he found you were out he asked if anyone else was available and your boss was, so they had a chat.

'He's ever so choked at annoying you so much. He's asked me to fix a date and time with you for him to call in to see you, so that he can apologize personally. Can you give me a couple of convenient dates in the next week?'

If that doesn't prise the business loose, then try Course Two.

The problem, the action taken so far, the suspicions, the details of the better deal, are all passed upstairs to your managing director.

Your managing director telephones the dishonest Buyer's managing director and invites him to lunch. Over lunch, the better deal is explained. Your managing director is puzzled why his guest's company is apparently not interested. His suspicions are discussed.

His guest assures him he will look into the matter as soon as he gets back to the fort. They relax over coffee and brandy.

A few days later, you will either be asked by a very frigid Buyer to call and discuss future supplies, or you will continue making regular, but more fruitful, calls, on the **new** Buyer.

But only managing directors can carry through Course Two.


## Plot and Counter-plot

A company in the business equipment field, let's call it Snooks, was seeking to interest a public corporation in a new system for processing mail. The company had one competitor and this competitor was also seeking to interest the public corporation in a similar mail processing system. We'll call the competitor Bloggs.

The Political and Union hierarchy of the public corporation dictated that the corporation's own design and development department should issue drawings and specifications for any new scheme intended for the corporation, and thus, drawings and specifications were duly issued to both Snooks and Bloggs for prototype equipment so that the viability and efficiency of the proposed system could be thoroughly tested before the big commitment was made. The prototypes were to be supplied at the supplier's cost – to be recovered in the subsequent big order.

Snooks, on examining the corporation's drawings and specifications, was alarmed to find that the design was identical to the Bloggs standard equipment. Obviously, someone had gained an inside advantage.

Snooks, knowing that its equipment was superior to Bloggs in a number of respects, devised a plan to deal with this unfair advantage. It knew that when it came to the maintenance of the new system, the public corporation would spend far more money operating the Bloggs equipment than it would operating the Snooks equipment.

Comparison figures, case histories from other customers,

graphs, photographs and proposals were put together fast and Snooks' sales team fixed an appointment to talk to the public corporation's maintenance department. Snooks knew that it was highly unlikely that maintenance was ever consulted about new systems until after the installations were completed. That kind of corporation operated on the 'warring tribes' concept.

Snooks' team pointed out to the maintenance people how a few minor changes to the corporations's designs and specifications could radically improve maintenance's part in the future operation of the system. The team was thanked profusely for bringing the matter to maintenance's attention. Yes, they'd certainly take immediate action to get the designs amended. (It wasn't every day they found such a golden opportunity to make the design and development boys suffer!)

Within a few days, Snooks received a letter from the purchasing department of the corporation, asking for all work to stop on the prototype, as changes had to be made and new drawings and specifications were on their way.

Phase one completed. At least the new drawings and specifications gave Snooks a sporting chance. But the advantage still had to be with Bloggs, because of the obvious close ties they had with someone in the corporation, and because, like most such public corporations, when it came to the tender for the big system, the order would probably still go to the lowest bidder. So Snooks set up a subtle trap.

The Snooks prototype was duly delivered. The usual delivery note accompanied the equipment but unfortunately someone made the mistake of typing on to the delivery note the price of the equipment. The very next day, one of Snooks' salesmen was calling at the corporation's goods inwards depot rather sheepishly explaining to the clerk that yesterday's delivery note for the prototype equipment had been sent in error and could he exchange it for the correct one.

Two hours and several departments later, the salesman emerged triumphant, clutching the first delivery note to his breast. But not before, Snooks figured, it had been photocopied a few times and had reached the corporation executive who was in close touch with Bloggs.

The Snooks and the Bloggs prototype equipment both passed all their tests. Formal tenders were submitted in sealed envelopes, in accordance with the corporation's tendering rules, for several hundred of the production versions of the prototype.

Several weeks after Snooks won the order, they established that the price tendered by Bloggs was exactly £100 per unit less than the price that had been typed in error on their prototype's delivery note.

But, of course, the delivery note price had absolutely nothing to do with Snooks' tender price. In fact, the price on the delivery note was considerably higher.


## Big Mouth!

There is a well-known quality restaurant frequented by most of the South Midlands business community. Lunchtimes in particular, it's normally always full of pairs, trios and quartets, busy discussing business.

Through 1981–2, a small local engineering firm rose rapidly in prominence servicing the motor manufacturers in the Coventry area. It became busier and busier, took on more and more staff, and its monthly account at the well-known quality restaurant grew in direct proportion.

Almost every lunchtime, and quite a few evenings, the principal director of the engineering firm was at the restaurant, entertaining customers and potential customers. The booze element of the daily bill often exceeded the food element.

The principal director wasn't very bright. He had a rather loud voice which became even louder when lubricated. He was also something of a braggart. Other customers in the restaurant had no difficulty listening to his business discussions, even from across the room. The one where he was offering the all-expenses-paid holiday in Italy was particularly interesting. It didn't take long for every regular customer of the restaurant to know in detail how the engineering firm was getting its business.

What the director hadn't bothered to consider (I've said he wasn't very bright) was that the customers of that restaurant ranged all the way up the business hierarchy of the motor industry; the chief executive of one manufacturer was a regular diner; the directors and senior executives of most major component suppliers; accountants, solicitors, estate agents. Socially or through business contacts, the word of what was going on filtered through to the powers-that-be.

Nothing drastic was done, either to the director of the engineering firm or to his main customer contacts. The customer contacts were simply moved to other responsibilities within the motor manufacturers, and 80% of the business going in the direction of the engineering firm stopped overnight.

That the moves were planned is not in any doubt. The restaurant was warned six weeks before to make sure the engineering firm paid all its outstanding accounts by the end of the month, and not to extend any credit whatsoever thereafter.

# 8
# How to Sell Quality and Your Higher Price

**We're never going to be the biggest, so we're going to be the best.**

Once upon a time there was a Seller's Market.

Customers clamoured to buy. Supply could not satisfy demand. Manufacturers developed mass production techniques, mechanization, automation, to try to cope with the demand for hitherto hand-made products. Craftmanship was sacrificed at the altar of volume.

It was called The Industrial Revolution.

It began 150 years ago. It was held back a few times by economic catastrophes like The Great Depression. It was stimulated by a few wars. It finally died in the mid-nineteen seventies when the Middle East marmalized Western Civilization by wopping up the price of oil.

Since then, we have been witnessing a fundamental change in people's buying habits. No longer do people buy what they can get. No longer do they buy just on price – the cheapest price they can find. (And if you don't believe this, just ask a few people what car they drive, and see how many have bought the lowest-priced car that would do the job they needed it to do.)

We have entered the **second** Industrial Revolution.

The first was based on **quantity**. The second Industrial Revolution is based on **quality**. That's what people will be buying from now on. I don't think the Seller's Market will be back in our lifetime. We've grown too intelligent!

**Selling the Best is the Easiest**

In Selling, the maximum job satisfaction, the maximum fun and the maximum rewards come from selling the **best** product or service at the **highest** price. It is also **easiest** when selling at this level, if the selling is done properly and if you are aiming for maximum profit, not maximum volume. In other words, you don't want to be the biggest supplier in your particular market, just the best.

No one will ever convince me that this is not so, because I've personally tested the theory and proved it fact, time and time again.

Okay, only one supplier in any market can hold the Quality number one spot. The rest have to make do with second, third, fourth best, down to worst. The higher you can get in the Quality league table, however, the better – and climbing up this league table is much easier and much less expensive than most businesses think.

There is no substitute for a really good product or a really good service, of course, but at the same time there is no point in making the product or service **too** good, if the market does not require anything better than is currently available. Thus, several suppliers can climb the Quality league table and, on product or service, performance, reliability and all the other 'tangibles', find themselves all at exactly the same level, if their market dictates terms in this way.

If this is your problem, a more intangible form of quality comes into play, known as **perceived value**.


**Perceived Value**

Roughly translated, Perceived Value means 'If the product and its trappings **look, feel, smell or taste** more expensive than those of other suppliers, then the customers are likely to be happy to pay slightly more for them, or be less demanding on discounts'.

By 'trappings', I mean everything that goes to make up the supplier's Corporate Image. Consider the 'trappings' shown as

pieces of a jigsaw puzzle. Each piece is an essential part of the complete picture – the Corporate Image. If one or two pieces don't fit, then the complete picture falls asunder. So it is with a supplier's Corporate Image. All the pieces must be made to fit the picture which you want to portray to your customers.

It's question of Aesthetics. The overall impression of you and your company – as a better supplier – that is seen by the customer; that is *perceived* by the customer. The dictionary definition of the word Aesthetics is 'the perception of the beautiful'. As long as you don't put it in the context of conning people, the old saying 'What you believe is more important than the truth' might fit the bill.

Everyone in the world is looking for something better at no extra cost. Maybe you are seeking, as a business, to *maintain* your prices while your competitors are cutting theirs. To do this, you have to sell the intangible form of Quality. You have to make the customers *believe* they are getting something better – getting more for their money if they buy from you.

In periods of stiff recession, Selling Quality can be the key to survival while the competitors go down the tubes.

Let's examine what might be done to improve the pieces of this particular Corporate Image jigsaw puzzle.

We've already covered some of what is necessary for the 'Sellers' piece of the Corporate Image jigsaw puzzle, in the previous chapter – 'If you want to beat the competition you've got to be **better** – in the eyes of the customers.'

But there are many more ways of coming over better – upmarket – than those covered in Chapter 7. Let's start by looking in the hall mirror, first thing in the morning, just about to leave home for a hard day in the field. There you are, newly pressed suit, clean silk handkerchief in top pocket, subdued tie, polished shoes, smart briefcase, hair brushed and recently trimmed, teeth brushed, no blood clots from shaving, faint smell of Eau Sauvage in the air.

Not a bad sight for so early in the morning. But wait! Put yourself in the customer's shoes.

Would *you* buy anything *better* from a guy like *you*?

Look in that mirror and think about it. That briefcase is a family heirloom and hasn't seen a tin of polish in twenty years. That bright red tie isn't really what you'd call subdued, is it? And those three pens clipped in your top pocket – they give you an identity more like a clerk than an executive. The mud on your shoes and trouser turn-ups doesn't show much, but what about when you sit down next to the customer in half an hour's time. Knees a bit baggy, but the suit'll do for another week before it's due for the dry cleaners. Been meaning to get to the hairdressers for about three months now, but there's always been too many people waiting. Maybe next week.

Do I need to say any more? If you cannot get this bit right – **every single selling day** – then there's not much hope for either you or your Corporate Image.

If you yourself **look** more expensive, you'll get less hassle and price objections from your customers and a hell of a lot more respect from everyone – receptionist up to managing director. But don't overdo it. Just look the part.

Talking about respect, there's another kind of respect important in the Corporate Image jigsaw puzzle. The respect you give your company and your products.

Sellers at the top of the Quality league table never ever moan about their company, or any of its personnel, or its products. They never run anything down. They never pass the buck. If a mistake is made, **they** carry the can and take the blame, even if it was someone else's mistake. They praise their company, its personnel, its products, at every opportunity. They show pride in everything they do. And the customer gets the message.

Sellers at the top of the Quality league table never abuse or denigrate their products by their actions. They never kick or slap or toss them around. They treat their products with the utmost respect and, as a result, their products come over as superior in the eyes of their customers.

If you're selling the best pocket calculator on the market, it's no good tossing it to a customer and saying: 'What do you think of that?' Hand it to him reverently and say: 'I'd like your opinion of our new calculator. We think it's the very best that's been produced so far.'

There's a true story about two company directors who set out one day to look for a quantity of five drawer filing cabinets. They wanted to see the cabinets for themselves before ordering.

They called at one large office equipment supplier. 'Yes', said the salesman, 'we've got some very good five drawer filing cabinets. Here is one, over here.'

The salesman proceeded to show off the filing cabinet to the two directors. 'Very strong, these are,' he extolled, slapping the side of the cabinet – doiiinnggg! Empty cabinets make a lot of tinny noise! 'Drawers have very smooth action, rollers all the way, good strong stops to prevent the drawers falling out.' The salesman flicked open a drawer so that it shot out to its full reach and jarred against its stops. Then he flicked it back in again and the drawer bounced out from its shut position. With a nudge of his elbow, the salesman pushed the drawer properly shut. Prices and delivery were discussed and the two directors departed with the promise that they would give the purchase serious consideration. The filing cabinet they'd seen would certainly do the job they wanted done.

They found another large office equipment supplier. 'Yes,' said the salesman, a more refined type and some fifteen years older, 'we do indeed have some very good quality five drawer filing cabinets. Would you care to follow me?'

The salesman introduced the two directors to his filing cabinet. He didn't slap it, he flicked a speck of dust off its top. When he opened and closed the drawer, he kept his hand on the drawer handle all the time, so that the drawer slid open and shut without a sound other than the smooth rumble of the rollers in their tracks. The cabinet was a different colour from the first one they'd seen, but perfectly acceptable.

Price and delivery were discussed. The cabinets were £5 each more expensive than the first ones they'd examined. The two directors departed to continue their search, but by the end of the day they hadn't found any more suppliers with five drawer filing cabinets. They discussed the pros and cons of the two cabinets they'd seen and agreed that the second cabinet was of much better quality than the first. They ordered the better quality cabinets, notwithstanding the £5 extra price.

The point of this story is that *both* cabinets were manufactured on the same production line at the same time. Only the colour and labelling was different, to the specification of each office equipment supplier. But no one would have convinced those two directors that this was so.

That's the intangible part of Selling Quality.

You won't believe the incredible blunders companies make on colours; blunders made in all innocence, because the powers-that-be know nothing about the Corporate Image jigsaw puzzle. If I may quote the Bible: 'God forgive them for they know not what they do.'

There was a classic example at the 1980 International Machine Tool Exhibition. One exhibitor was introducing two new machines into its existing range of machines. The whole range, including the two new models, ran in a line across the front of the exhibition stand. The two new machines were better, faster, more reliable, produced better quality components and, of course, were more expensive.

But very few visitors to the exhibition showed interest in buying the new models. All the interest was on the existing range. The powers-that-be couldn't understand it, yet the reason stuck out like a sore thumb.

The colour scheme for the existing range of machines was a nice, darker shade of British Racing Green with the guards over the moving parts finished in a subdued yellow. The combination was very pleasing to the eye. The two new models, however, were painted in a different colour. The powers-that-be had decided, before the exhibition, that the new models should be painted a different colour for the show so that they stood out on the stand. An instruction was passed to the paint shop. 'Paint new models in different colour'. No thought was given to *what* colour, or why. The paint shop used what paints they had in stock and mixed a special. They knew nothing about the Corporate Image jigsaw puzzle either.

The resulting colour scheme for the new models was a particularly bilious shade of what I call 'Puke Green' with the guards in bright orange. To the eye of the beholder, the beauty had been turned into 'Cheap and Cheerful'.

For the exhibitor to convince its customers that the two new models were better than the existing range was henceforth next to impossible. They didn't look better, they looked inferior.

It's that easy to get it wrong. Why has Lansing Bagnall, one of the UK's largest fork lift truck manufacturers, always finished its trucks in a rich dark red, while all the other manufacturers have finished theirs in yellow? Because the rich dark red bestows an aura of quality on the LB trucks that none of the yellow trucks can match.

The Alfred Herbert group, long before its demise, was reputed to have spent a lot of money having a new Corporate Identity prepared for it. The main theme of the new CI was a colour – a special magenta. But it was a down-market colour and *reduced* the perceived value of the company in the eyes of its customers. It was also hellish difficult to re-produce, which probably added 20% to Herbert's print bills. This major blunder must have cost the company millions in lost business and speeded up a death which otherwise might have been avoided.

The natural colours project quality best. The buffs, the beiges, the creams, the mushrooms, the creamy browns, the leaf and olive greens. Yellows, oranges and bright greens are cheap and cheerful. Red can be cheap, if post-office red, or expensive if Mercedes red. Blues can be good or bad with subtle differences in shade taking a product ten points up or down the league table.

Combinations can do more for quality than single colours. A two-tone cabinet in light grey and dark grey comes over very well. Black and green gives a good result. Black and satin aluminium, or black and gold, is superb – think about the effect John Player Special and Benson & Hedges get from their cigarette packets. Yellow and red is a dangerous combination. Yet Kodak has made it work wonderfully well. It depends on the product.

The colour of a Seller's suit, tie, shirt, socks, briefcase and company car all contribute to the Corporate Image picture which the customer sees. All should be carefully and consciously assessed and efforts made to increase their quality factors.

In 1980, UK publishers Mitchell Beazley Ltd brought out a book on the subject, entitled *Colour*, which for the first time presented the many complexities of using colour in business in an easy-to-understand and very comprehensive form. Here is a short quote from this extremely valuable book:

The language of colour is a vital living thing, our most potent means of perception and communication. It impinges on our every waking moment and even invades our sleep. Consciously or subconsciously, it influences every decision we make.

Today's supermarkets present an avalanche of coloured tins, packets, jars and bottles, all carefully calculated to catch our attention and convince us to buy. Some succeed – J-Cloths, for example, are reputed to have boosted sales some 23% by an apparently simple change in coloured packaging – others fail and vanish for ever . . . why?

And why is it that the safest, most sensible colours for cars – the ones which show up best in poor light – are the ones we are least likely to choose?

Even the clothes we wear pose some intriguing questions about our reactions to colour - why blue jeans, for example, and not brown or red or green?

Colours are the basic elements of the modern alchemist's art – 'the magic touch that can turn dross into gold'. Red is warm. Blue is cool. Yellow is cheeful. Black depresses . . . sometimes. But the human eye can distinguish some ten million variations in colour, so we mix them together and seek to 'cast a spell'.

Colour can dictate our moods and condition our reflexes. It has been used successfully in factories to increase production, cut absenteeism and prevent accidents – and in boardrooms to reduce aggression and enhance decision-making.

Today, in our modern, sophisticated and often artificial world, our skilful use of colour becomes ever more important – we must even colour much of the food we eat to make it acceptable.

Yet, not surprisingly, few of us can claim any real fluency in this most potent of all languages.

Consider the two advertisements on the next page. They are both mono (black and white). They are both half a page vertical in an A4 size trade magazine. How does the Corporate Image of the company advertising come over to you?

Which is the quality company? Which is the cheap and cheerful company? It's obvious, isn't it? But only the choice of words, pictures and type style are different.

On type styles, serif faces tend to project better quality than sans faces (serif has the twiddly bits, like Times Roman; sans is just plain, like Univers. Get a book of typefaces free from your printers to see what options are available to you.)

Advertisements don't have to be full colour and big to project quality. Small classified adverts can do it just as well, providing the type style is right and there's plenty of white space. Obviously, a full page in full colour gives more scope, but many a business has let its advertising agency mess it all up by allowing the agency to pursue a gimmick idea in bold lurid colours. Sometimes it bashes a dirty great hole in the Corporate Image which takes months to patch up.

Again, the natural colours are best in advertisements that aim to upgrade quality. And use photographs with real people in them – people who look as good as your Sellers should look. Above all, don't ever use heavily touched up 'still-life' pictures of the products.

Same thing applies to your other kinds of sales promotion. Mail shots, press releases, exhibition stands and business gifts.

Let's dwell for a couple of minutes on business gifts. These are not just restricted to Christmas time, although calendars and diaries, of course, always will be. Don't get business gifts that are part of sales promotion mixed up with gifts which are 'Thank You's' for past business, such as bottles of whisky and a dinner for four at a sumptuous restaurant or club.

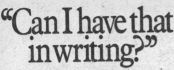

A business gift promotes business. It should be designed for use or display by your customers and prospective customers in or at their place of business. Okay, if you do business in their homes, that's the place.

Business gifts should have the longest possible life and should **always** carry your business name, address and telephone number – in the right place! (I've seen cubic memo pads with the supplier's number printed on all four sides, **at the top**! So after the first fifty or so sheets of the pads have been used by the customers, the gift becomes useless – the telephone number has gone!)

Business gifts should **always** reflect your Corporate Image. If you're seeking to go up-market in the Quality league table, it's no good spreading around a cheap and cheerful business gift. Likewise, if you're at the bottom of the league table and happy to stay there, you'd be wasting your money on **quality** business gifts.

The very best business gifts are tailor-made for specific, very good customers. They give the customer much pleasure, they demoralize your competitors' Sellers and they really stimulate **your** salesforce. Here's one of my favourites:

Let's assume you have a budget for this particular very good customer that would buy you a case of good whisky. But the last thing you want to do is spend the money on whisky. Once drunk, soon forgotten, **and** usually taken home. You know a lot about this customer. You know his hobbies and his habits, his likes and his dislikes. You know he's a sailing fanatic – every weekend, out on the reservoir. Small dinghy, but dreams about something much better and much bigger.

You're sitting in his office. You've concluded business. You have your eye on a particular section of his office wall, above his book case. You dangle the carrot.

'I've been wondering about that piece of wall above your bookcase, Mr Arnold.' He looks somewhat puzzled. You go on. 'My company has been putting together some rather different sales promotion gifts for this year; a bit out of the ordinary you might say. Just for our very best customers. One of the ideas we've come up with is to produce some original oil paintings, each one on a particular subject.

'One of the artists we've commissioned is pretty near as good as

Montague Dawson. His seascapes are fantastic. I was thinking how nice a painting of that 46 footer you told me about last time I was here, would look over your bookcase, with Cowes or something similar in the background.'

You watch his eyes light up. His posture changes from casually relaxed to keenly interested. 'What sort of frame do you think would be most suitable?' you ask.

Ten minutes later, you have the full specification for the picture and the frame, plus a brochure containing a colour picture of the 46 footer he's always wanted but will never be able to afford.

Your sales promotion people make contact with a few young artists. (If you're in London on a Sunday, just walk down Piccadilly and see how many you can find who will do you a **good** original oil for under £50. In Worcester there are 40 young artists who have joined together as a syndicate to produce and sell paintings. Good artists are falling off trees!)

Two months later, you deliver the finished, framed, oil painting. Inset into the lower horizontal frame is an engraved brass plate which reads:

**Presented to Walter Arnold
by Acme Distributions Limited
November 1984**

You've come armed with picture hooks, hammer, measuring tape, and pliers (just in case!). You and he spend a happy half hour hanging the picture over the bookcase. Then you both sit back for a few minutes, drinking coffee and admiring the picture before you get down to the business reason for this particular visit.

Your picture is there for life – or for the life of Walter Arnold as an executive of that company. He can't take the picture home without offending you and your company greatly. It serves as a constant reminder of what a professional, top quality supplier is really like. And every time one of your competitors sits in that office, he's grinding his teeth, dying to say to Mr Arnold, 'Why do you keep that dreadful picture hanging there? We could give you something *much* better than that.'

But the competitors know they can never say that.
That's demoralization for you!

## The Pirelli Calendar Classic

Throughout the sixties, one particular business gift became a legend in its own lifetime – the Pirelli Calendar.

By 1970, if you wanted one, it was a question of how many tyres you ordered, rather than how much you'd pay for the calendar. By 1980, you could get £100 for an *old* Pirelli Calendar.

As I write this, after an absence of ten years, the Pirelli Calendar is back. But you're not likely to see one. They're all safely tucked away in customer's attics, waiting for their value to escalate again. This time round, the Pirelli Calendar has backfired.

As perhaps you'd expect, one of my companies produces rather different business gifts. I've been working on one in particular which I reckon could be as good as the Pirelli Calendar. It lends itself to a large organization which has divisions in each region of the UK. Let's assume there are seven divisions.

My business gift is a set of seven limited edition prints, all nicely framed. The subject matter for the prints is classified (sorry) but of universal appeal and a certain laughter generator. Each of the seven divisions uses **only one** of the set of prints in any one year, but each division uses a **different** one of the set. Thus, the business gift has a full seven years' life and 'collectors' of the limited edition set have to stay doing business with a division for that long to be sure of securing the complete set. The organization's name, address and telephone number, and the name of the customer who receives the print, is included in a particularly ingenious way.

Of course, you **can** secure the complete set in the first year, but, like Pirelli, that depends on how much of the product you buy!

Calendars – the normal kind, girlie or whatever – are not very good business gifts, because, like diaries, they depend upon the personal choice of the customer. The customer probably receives a dozen calendars and a dozen diaries from his suppliers every Christmas. What is going to make him select and display only yours?

If you buy 1,000 similar calendars or diaries, you'll be lucky if 100 are ever used by the people to whom you give them. Consider your own diary. How long have you used that particular format? Will you want to continue using that same format next year, because you're used to it? Chances are you will. So if you are given a diary of a different format, you'll probably pass it on to someone else. You'll even go out and **buy** the diary you really like using; if you have to. Customers are no different.

Calendars also have a very short life. One year maximum. Your business gifts should last longer than that. The **best** calendar I've ever developed so that it is nearly always selected by the customers for display in their offices and has an unlimited life, is, in fact, useless as a calendar. This is the now famous Rush Jobs Calendar. Here is the version used by my own organization, where every day is a potential Mirday. Every day in *your* business could be, too!'

# Rush Job Calendar

| Mir | Fri | Fri | Fri | Thu | Wed | Tue |
|-----|-----|-----|-----|-----|-----|-----|
| 8 | 7 | 6 | 5 | 4 | 3 | 2 |
| 15 | 14 | | 12 | 11 | 10 | 9 |
| 22 | 21 | 20 | 19 | 18 | 17 | 16 |
| 29 | 28 | 27 | 26 | 25 | 24 | 23 |
| 36 | 35 | 34 | 33 | 32 | 31 | 30 |

This is a special calendar which has been developed to handle "rush jobs." As all rush jobs are wanted yesterday, dates run backwards so that work ordered on the 7th can be delivered on the 3rd. The 13th is omitted to please the superstitious. There are three Fridays in every week because everbody wants his job done by Friday. Five new days at the end of the month cater for "end-of-month" jobs, late completion of which is discouraged by having no 1st of the month. Mondays have been abolished because nobody likes them. There are no Saturdays or Sundays so that overtime payments can be kept to a minimum. Every week includes a special day–MIRDAY –for the performance of miracles.

On Structured Training's Calendar, every day is a potential MIRDAY

**Structured Training Limited**
Concorde House, 24 Warwick New Road,
Royal Leamington Spa, Warwickshire CV32 5JH
Tel: 0926 37621/4   Telex: 311746

If you want to rise to near the top of your market's Quality league table, then the letters you write and the letterheads you write them on have to be top notch.

Electronic typewriters with proportional spacing. Or word-processors. (You'll need these before you reach the end of Chapter 9, anyway!) Layout of the letters carefully thought out. Wide margins. Plenty of space. Short, easy-to-read paragraphs. Meaningful, quality-oriented words.

I spend a fair bit of my time copy-writing. Often I'm asked to advise on why a certain standard sales letter or circular isn't achieving the required results. Here are two examples, together with my suggested improved letters. Hopefully, these will guide you into writing your own better letters which bring this piece in the jigsaw puzzle up to its desired position.

### Letter One

The company in question is already in the top three in its market's Quality league table.

### Re: Pre-qualification – Commercial Catering Equipment

*We would confirm our interest in pre-qualifying for the supply and installation of Commercial Catering Equipment for your various projects.*

*As part of . . . we have first-hand experience in all types of catering operations while our corporate buying power renders us truly competitive. Whatever your requirement, we can offer a partial or total service covering all aspects from free planning and design, to supply, installation, commissioning and, if required, even maintenance. Where needed we can also offer an integrated package including building works and services installation, restaurant furnishing and equipment.*

*As requested, we enclose herewith a copy of our brochure which outlines our organization and its capabilities and would welcome the opportunity of providing any additional information you may require.*

*Yours faithfully*

Full of Victoriana, stilted phrases, strange terminology (pre-qualifying means 'can we go on your list of suppliers?') and rather cheaply duplicated so that it was impossible to match in the recipient's address without shouting to him that it is a circular, not a personal, letter.

Writing better letters isn't **just** for the Corporate Image jigsaw piece. Any selling letter must live and breathe; be full of carrots and benefits; tell the prospective customer what's in it for **him**, not just what you, the writer, have done; although the letter must *finish* with what you are *after* – what you want the prospective customer to **do** or what *you* intend to do.

There is a clear-cut formula for selling letters – AIDA. In strict order, start to finish: Attention, Interest, Desire, Action. Follow this formula, make your letter live, use words which bestow status, rather than give a cheap and cheerful impression, use the best quality paper and typewriter, and you won't go far wrong. Above all, write English as she is spoke!

Here's my submission for bettering the 'Pre-Qualification – Commercial Catering Equipment' letter:

*Dear Sirs*

*What do you or your clients look for from a new catering installation – be it a kitchen, a complete restaurant or whatever?*

*We would suggest – the very best equipment*

*– the most efficient equipment*

*– at the most equitable cost.*

*And after the installation – the longest maintenance free life*

*– the minimum possible running costs.*

*Can we give you all this? It is quite likely. Being part of the . . . group we have probably acquired more know-how (UK and internationally) than most quality suppliers. Our corporate purchasing power enables us to match anyone on price while maintaining top quality, and, when it matters, to acquire equipment faster.*

*We are also innovators – often the first to introduce new ideas, new applications and new equipment, but always thoroughly testing the innovation within our group's many hotels and restaurants before adding it to our portfolio.*

*Can we come and talk to you? Show you some of the projects we have worked on and some of the operating figures and publicity that our installations have subsequently achieved?*

*We will telephone in about one week's time to arrange a firm appointment. Meanwhile, if anything is currently 'cooking' do not hesitate to ring us.*

*Yours faithfully*

*Letter Two*

The company is the UK division of an American group operating at the cheap and cheerful end of the market and needing to move up the Quality league table as far as it can at minimum cost.

**For the attention of the General Manager**

*Dear Sir*

*—, America's leading on-site Rustproofing system, is now expanding its already established activities into dealerships throughout the UK.*

*— is making available to dealerships, without any capital outlay for equipment, the unique – on-site Rustproofing System, which has been developed by our Associate Company, —, one of the world's foremost and progressive chemical companies, specializing in anti-corrosion treatments to major International Automobile Manufacturers and Industrial business concerns.*

*Many UK motor dealerships, large and small, are fully operative with the — on-site system, and are happy to confirm substantially increased profitability compared with sending vehicles out to Treatment Centres and thereby reducing potential profit opportunities. The continuing adverse economic climate forces many Motor Dealerships to look closely at retaining as much In-House profit as possible. What better way – The — way?*

*This is reckoned by many dealerships to be the cleanest Rustproofing System available, while retaining the traditional appearance, and is simplicity itself regarding application. It comes in kit form for easy inventory/stock control – one kit per car. There's no spillage, no waste, and no need for special buildings or isolated workshop areas. All that is needed is an airline and a workshop ramp. We train your Staff:* **free.**

*The system is fully supported by a 5-year Warranty, covered by an insurance policy underwritten by one of the world's leading Insurance groups, for the entire period of the Warranty from Day One – unlike some major rustproofing companies, who renew insurance cover on an annual basis, or through their own internal reserve funds. — gives one of the finest Insurance Protection Schemes available in the world.*

*Retain your In-House profit opportunities with the — On-Site System by allowing us the opportunity to discuss how competitive we are with any current Rustproofing System you might already have. For further details please complete the freepost reply card or contact our UK office at —.*

*Yours sincerely*

Now you've got to admit that's pretty dreadful. Far too long. Far too much detail. Far too difficult to read. Far too much of a PR blast for the Rustproofing company. Starts 'Dear Sir' and finishes 'Yours sincerely'. Random use of capitals. No chance of more than a handful of replies.

Putting yourself in the shoes of a motor dealership general manager, what would *you* want to know? Here's my re-write:

*Dear General Manager*

*Like most other motor dealers, one of your biggest headaches has to be the need to give discounts away in order to sell enough vehicles to keep the manufacturers happy and stay profitable.*

*We have a package that could probably **halve** the discounts you are giving away. Over a year the effect on your bottom line would be dramatic.*

*Our package, if it is sold correctly by **your** staff to your customers, could also radically reduce that edge the urban big dealers tend to have over dealers like you in more rural areas.*

*The package involves rustproofing, paint protection and fabric protection – but with a big difference. For example, part of the package is a five year guarantee, point of sale tools which will positively help your staff to **sell** more cars, and you get absolutely no mess in your service bay.*

*We estimate that, used to maximum effect, our package could boost your profits 7 to 10% per year.*

*Can we come and talk to you about it, and give you a demonstration? We'll telephone in a week's time, hopefully to fix a firm appointment.*

*Yours sincerely*

*If you're Managing Sales . . .*

Go through all your standard selling letters. Re-write anything that doesn't fit your chosen Corporate Image. (You should re-write all your standard letters every three months, anyway!) Brief your typists, secretaries and executives on the changes in objective, format, and on AIDA. Do it today or tomorrow. Any delay is costing you business. Your competitors may be reading this, too.

Remember the old TV series *Never Mind the Quality, Feel the Width*? When it comes to quality sales literature, it is pretty near the truth. Apart from colour and type styles and decent pictures (preferably but not essentially colour) the key two factors which make sales literature top quality are:

1 the thickness, smoothness, colour, texture and *feel* of the paper or board used;
2 the words, the prose, the 'poetry' put into the explanations, descriptions, 'picture-painting'.

Never penny pinch on the paper quality. If you do, you'll lose. Go **up** in thickness every time, if in doubt. Collect samples, always have dummies prepared by your printers so that you can get the true 'feel', and *always* thoroughly proof read your copy, with all the pictures, graphs and columns of figures where they should be. For an example of word poetry, the topmost quality verbage I've ever read, I've chosen the text from the brochure on the Shadow I Rolls-Royce, circa 1966. Even Rolls-Royce has never surpassed this particular prose for simply oozing quality.

Read it carefully. There are many lessons to be learnt from it. Like how to get across that 80,000 components means 'excellence' not potential trouble. Like how to explain why the leather on the seats is the very best, and the walnut used in the facias cannot be bettered. Have a long, relaxed drool. As the text says – 'It's not so much *what* it did as the *way* in which it was done.'

**The Shadow . . .**
The day's triumphs and tragedies have been replayed stroke by stroke, hole by hole. Then the conversation can become general.

But this is the second half of the twentieth century. Eventually, inevitably, the talk turns to motor cars. And then, almost equally inevitably, to one motor car in particular.

'You can't buy one, you know, unless you're in *Who's Who*!' 'They almost never break down, of course. But when one does it's taken away in a plain van.' 'That mascot on the front's made of solid silver. There's a hallmark to prove it.'

And so yet another dimension is added to the vast complex of myth and legend centered on 'The Best Car in the World'.

Just why so many millions of people should develop so much respect and affection for a vehicle few of them are likely to ride in, let alone own, is one of the more amazing social phenomena of our time. Perhaps the names given to successive Rolls-Royce motor cars have something to do with it. Names like Phantom and the famous Silver series . . . Ghost . . .

Wraith . . . Dawn . . . Cloud . . . Shadow. They are invocations rather than names, with a hint of something magical, more than mortal.

Yet the hard, commercial fact is these names are carefully chosen to convey something of the smoothness, silence, speed and safety on which the reputation of Rolls-Royce motor cars has been built for over seventy years. There's no place for whimsy in the substance of the Shadow!

## . . . and the Substance

First and foremost the Silver Shadow is a machine. If mechanical excellence can be defined as efficiency in carrying out the tasks for which it is designed, then the Silver Shadow is probably the most perfect machine of its time. And you can reasonably say the same of every Rolls-Royce motor car that has ever been made. At this point it is worth recalling that the original Rolls (the Hon. C.S.) was a racing motorist and Sir Henry Royce an engineer. The first cars produced by this partnership made their name by performing feats which up to then had been thought impossible and by winning races and trials in spectacular fashion. In the 1907 Isle of Man T.T. race, for example, the Rolls-Royce beat the second car home by nearly twenty-seven minutes.

But this alone was not enough. The history of motoring is filled with stars that blazed brightly for a time and are now remembered by just the occasional enthusiast.

Rolls-Royce added an entirely new combination of qualities: comfort, reliability, silence, smoothness. It was in 1907 that the famous trick of balancing a coin on edge on the radiator of a Silver Ghost with the motor running was first demonstrated. Over 65 years and 800,000 km (500,000 *miles*) later, the same demonstration can be made on the same car!

Then, as now, the fundamental difference between a Roll-Royce and other cars was not so much *what* it did as the *way* in which it was done. And this has remained true ever since.

In the pages that follow, we hope to show you a little – necessarily a very little – of what makes 'The Best Car in the World' *the* best car in the world.

## The Whole is Greater than the Sum of the Parts

The Silver Shadow is not the biggest car in the world. Nor is it the fastest: though it can show a clean pair of heels to most 'sports' cars. It is not the trendiest: innovation for the sake of innovation is not encouraged by Rolls-Royce Motors. It is not even the most expensive car in the world.

And although the jigsaw that builds up into a Silver Shadow does have many unique features, on the surface a lot of the pieces are similar to those of other quite ordinary cars. A rugged steel monocoque body, a V-8 engine, automatic transmission, independent suspension, disc brakes, and so on. What makes the difference is the detail of the design of the 80,000 individual parts (the average car makes do with about 12,000), the materials they are made of, the fine tolerances they are made to, their finish, their precise relationship one to another.

The first time you set eyes on a Silver Shadow, you begin to see what the Rolls-Royce Motors approach to motor engineering is all about. The car looks right. Its line is clean and timeless. It is relaxed and elegant yet full of power and purpose. In a word, the Silver Shadow has *breeding* – and it shows.

Endless thought, care and testing have been lavished on each detail, right down to the individual nuts and bolts – and this shows, too. Nothing has been skimped. Nothing has been done the easy, quick way when longer, more painstaking methods will produce better results. No expense has been spared. Equally, there is no waste: you will not find meaningless embellishments on the Silver Shadow.

For example, many cars have headlamp rims; but the Silver Shadow's are individually hand beaten and polished to perfection. All cars are painted; before the colour coats are applied, the Silver Shadow is rinsed with de-mineralized water to prevent streaks that would mar its beauty. Down in the engine, cylinder-head studs are waisted – a feature found elsewhere on aero-engines. In the brake system, hydraulic lock is prevented by slightly 'barrelling' valves – by 0.005 mm (*2/10,000th inch*)! These are details you might not notice. But you certainly would note, with pleasure, that every time you close an ashtray after use, it automatically empties itself into a bin below.

But refinement is still possible and goes on all the time. Since the Silver Shadow was launched, over 2,000 alterations have been made to its specification, with each significant change tested over 80,000 km (*50,000 miles*) in France where roads are less crowded than in Britain – and where some very rough ones can still be found.

Someone once remarked: 'There is nothing in the world that cannot be made just a little cheaper – and just a little worse'. In an age dominated by this shabby philosophy, the Silver Shadow continues serenely on its way rewarding both its owner and its maker. Here, if you seek it, is living proof that Gresham's law is wrong. The bad does *not* necessarily drive out the good.

**Built by the Book**
There are still areas in industry where the most precise machine tool is the human eye; the sternest quality control the human conscience. In the

building of the Silver Shadow, there are enough examples to fill a book.

This, in fact, is exactly what does happen. Every Silver Shadow has its own history book, a plump volume of some seventy pages. This book accompanies the car right through the construction process. It logs details, not only of all materials used, but of all processes carried out and tests undergone, together with the signatures of those responsible. Then, after the car leaves the factory, the book becomes the basis of the service file.

The book begins with the monocoque body shell. This arrives from the body-builder protected by a thin coat of wax.

You would probably pronounce it perfect. The Rolls-Royce Motors inspector's critical eye sees it in a different light.

He slides a swift rule across a curved surface and detects imperceptible deviations from the norm. Panels swabbed with a special highlighting fluid reveal hidden hills and valleys.

Marked on the body shell itself and duplicated on an accompanying check chart these observations guide the four-day programme that beats, blasts, fills, grinds and polishes the body contours of the Silver Shadow to a smoothness which delights the eye.

Equally rigorous visual inspections monitor each of the filler, primer and top coats (at least 10 in all) that underwrite a finish for which superlative is entirely inadequate. Even its final accolade, the coachline, is added entirely by eye and an artist's fitch.

The tree that dominates this chapter is Italian walnut: it will eventually furnish fascia and window trim for a whole year's production of Silver Shadows – about 2,500 cars. Following the precepts of Sheraton and other makers of fine furniture, fascias and door trims are veneered into two halfs, each a mirror image of the other.

The woodwork is lacquered and buffed by hand to a finish that looks like glass and is almost as hard. You could (though you wouldn't) stub a cigarette on it without leaving a trace. It is also termite-proof.

Rolls-Royce Motors think walnut sufficiently important to send an annual two-man expedition to Milan to choose the tree of the year. Owners agree: the very far-sighted among them have been known to ask for three sets of their favourite veneer to be put aside for incorporation into future cars.

Each car requires eight hides – about 24 sq. m (260 sq. ft) of leather – and upwards of 500 are inspected for every one chosen. Rejects are likely to end up as expensive handbags.

Those that win through invariably come from clean-living animals grazed in fields protected by electric fences. Lacerations produced by barbed wire and lesions caused by ticks and parasites are equally unacceptable. The chosen hides are made up into matching sets and the individual car's chassis number stamped on each one.

Seats are designed on ergonomic principles and padded where necessary with impact-absorbent material, each piece of which has been individually tested. Springing is matched to the car's suspension and is adjusted accordingly should the owner be larger than average. There are limits, however. The operating limits of the electric seat adjusting mechanism are set at 190 kg (30 stone).

Possibly the most instantly distinctive feature of the Silver Shadow is the radiator. Dimensionally, this hardly differs from that of the 1906 Silver Ghost.

Only ten men in the whole world can make a Rolls-Royce radiator. The slender stainless steel panels are about 2.5 mm (1/10th inch) thick. To produce the clean, sharp line, edges are mitred and rebates worked behind bends. The pieces are hand-soldered with large, old-fashioned soldering-irons heated by gas. Modern electric ones have been tried and found wanting. Incidentally, you now have chapter and verse to throw at the next wiseacre who assures you that it is impossible to solder stainless steel.

The guardsman-straight columns look straight only because they are slightly curved. The Greeks called this effect **entasis** and built it into the Parthenon. At Rolls-Royce Motors craftsmen build it into the radiator by hand and eye alone.

The original 'Spirit of Ecstasy' figure that tops the radiator was created in 1911 by Charles Sykes, A.R.B.S. It is cast in stainless steel by the lost wax process. This originated in China about 4,000 years ago. Another contemporary use of this antique process is in the casting of turbine blades for jet engines.

## Command Post

The first thing that strikes you about the driver's seat of the Silver Shadow is the convenience as well as the elegance of your command post. Every control is at your fingertips. For instance, you can raise or lower any window, lock all the doors and the luggage compartment, without so much as turning in your seat. And you are very definitely in command: *you* can over-ride the individual door switches and handles. Even the door mirror is adjusted from inside the car by remote control.

Switches function smoothly and cleanly, with a carefully balanced 'feel'. Great care is taken to achieve this. Where heavy current is involved, relays are used. The correct tension in the seat 'joy-stick' is produced by tiny springs about half an inch long overall. And Rolls-Royce Motors engineers have seen to it that the system unobtrusively puts right any little slip you may make. For example, should you forget to turn off the heated rear window and later turn the air-conditioning to 'cool', the heated window will automatically be switched off.

The instrument panel provides all the information you need without submerging you in a torrent of unnecessary data. The Silver Shadow does not ask for unnecessary mental effort any more than it does physical effort. But what other car gives you an audible warning if the engine starts to overheat? Enables you to check that all warning lights are working? Or to check the coolant level in the radiator and the oil level in the sump without leaving your seat?

Finally, a few words on a very remarkable feature even of this remarkable motor car – automatic speed control. All you do is to accelerate to the speed at which you wish to travel and touch the speed control button. Then you can take your foot off the accelerator, and the car maintains speed automatically. If you need to go faster, put your foot down by all means: when you lift it again, the car resumes the chosen speed. If you brake, the system is automatically disengaged – unless you press the 'resume' button, when once again the car accelerates to your chosen speed. Choose the right speed, and the automatic speed control becomes an invaluable aid to economy.

As well as being beautiful, durable, safe, silent and comfortable, the Silver Shadow is an unusually *practical* motor car!

This text from the brochure 'The Substance of a Shadow' is reproduced by kind permission of Rolls-Royce Motors Ltd, Crewe.

If your company cars, delivery vans, lorries, service estate cars and whatever else you use aren't kept clean, aren't properly sign written under the same rules I've already mentioned for advertising, and aren't the most appropriate colours for your chosen position in the Quality league table – you'll down-grade yourself yet again.

Most companies allow their salesforce to choose the colour of their cars. Other companies don't care what colour their cars are, as long as they've got four wheels and an engine. Both wrong.

If you have a quality house colour, try to match it up on everything. If that isn't possible for cars because it's a special, pick a colour that is complementary to your house colour so that you have a quality colour combination. It doesn't cost any more to get this right. Think what the cigarette firms do with *their* company cars.

Never use those vacuum formed plastic stick-on signs for the sides of your delivery vans and lorries. If you want to portray the Corporate Image of a **temporary** supplier that won't be in business next week, this is as good a way as any. And when the sign writing on your vans starts getting worn and thin, so that it's difficult to read completely – have it done again, **fast**. You must have followed many vans and lorries that look like this. Remember what you thought about it at the time?

If you want the **worst** combination for a quality corporate image, try worn sign writing, un-washed vehicle and **rust**!

I'm not going to say much about this particular piece of the Quality jigsaw puzzle, because the next chapter of this book goes into Proposals in considerable depth.

Suffice it to say that the way you present your proposals, your quotations, your offer, is critically important in many ways, not the least of which is your enhanced position in the Quality league table.

Are your proposals packaged in a professional looking quality binder or folder? Is the paper they are typed and printed on as good as the paper you use for your quality sales literature and selling letters? Are the colours right?

Do you take the important ones in and present them properly, rather than simply stick them in the post?

Is there anything you include in your proposals that sticks out like a sore thumb? The odd piece of cheaply duplicated specification or servicing instructions amongst the quality paperwork. If there is, dig it out and do it properly on decent paper.

The best example I've ever seen of a really quality proposal was back in 1970. Coventry-based fighting vehicle manufacturers Alvis Ltd were going for a £15 million order for Saracen troop carriers from the Saudi Arabian Government. Okay, when you've the potential profit from £15 million to play with, you can push the boat out a bit with your proposals, but this one was still exceptional, notwithstanding this advantage, and what Alvis achieved can be emulated at very low cost by most businesses.

There were twelve people on the Government's buying team, headed by the Commander of the National Guard, who was also a member of the Saudi Royal Family. Thus, Alvis prepared twelve copies of its proposals, plus a few more, just in case. **All** the copies were **top** copies. No carbon paper or duplicating or photocopying. Each copy of the proposals was bound into a white, grained plastic, padded front ring binder. (If you want to do business with the Middle East, be *very* careful with colours. White is by far the best.)

On the front face of each white binder, the name of the recipient, the individual member of the Government's team, was printed in **gold leaf**. The one for the team's leader, a copy of which is one of my treasured possessions, reads:

### ALVIS LTD
## PROPOSAL
## RELATED TO WHEELED ARMOURED VEHICLES

for

### H.R.H. ABDULLAH BIN ABDUL AZIZ
## COMMANDER
## NATIONAL GUARD
## APRIL 1970

### ALVIS LTD, COVENTRY, ENGLAND

Inside the binder, as well as all the technical and commercial information, was a full colour picture of a squadron of Saracen troop carriers travelling fast across the desert. A well-known artist had been commissioned to paint, in oils, the original picture, which had then been given to Alvis's printers, to be used as artwork for a run of just fifty full colour prints on top quality art paper. The Saudi Government team was very impressed with this artist's impression of what their new troop carriers would look like travelling across the Saudi Arabian desert.

The team leader was even more impressed when, at an appropriate time during Alvis's presentation of its proposals, he was personally presented with the original oil painting, in a most gorgeous intricately gilded frame, by Alvis's managing director.

Who could lose when this much trouble was taken? Alvis certainly didn't.

Original oil paintings may be stretching things a bit for *your* proposals – but individual gold blocking and top quality binders aren't. The gold blocking would cost you around £5 to £10 a binder. The binder itself less than £5.

'HOW MUCH?' the prospective customer's eyebrows rise as much as his voice.

There you are, well on the way to selling him this top quality merchandise, his objectives clearly defined, his doubt about its performance, life, market reputation and your company's ditto all professionally handled, you thought, to his complete satisfaction. Quantities established. Starting dates provisionally considered. And now this. The usual thorny problem. Time and again, just when everything is going well, the customer goes and ruins it all with those two terrible words.

Your inner self starts sweating again. It sees an attack of 'Price Fright' coming on. It hasn't yet realized fully that because you are now a **positive** and have bags of confidence that has come from all the extra knowledge you've been acquiring since you picked up this book, things are changing.

Now you're beginning to feel **proud** of your prices – because you know in detail how and why they are justified. But maybe your inner self isn't so sure that the customers realize this. After all, if they did, if you were **really** putting the benefits and the justification over properly, they wouldn't keep shouting '**How much?**' at you so often, would they?

**Yes they would.** It makes no difference how good you are at presenting your case – the customer has **his** job to do, and part of that job is to get the best possible products and services for the lowest possible price.

He's going to **test** you on price, whatever and however you do. He's going to see how firm you're going to be. He's going to watch your reaction to his '**How much?**' and gauge, in his own mind, the kind of reduction or discount you're likely to give him.

Play poker with him. With complete sincerity. Without flinching. Without batting an eyelid.

'Don't you think the quality, the performance, the longer life, the lower servicing cost, the extra demand we've been discussing, is **worth** that much, Mr Dobson?'

If he splutters, hedges, laughs or plays poker back at you with something like, 'That's not the point,' you can continue: 'Just like any business that puts quality first, as, I suspect, yours does, if we didn't maintain our margins, we wouldn't be able to maintain our quality for very long, either. It's a fair price for the value you'll be getting, don't you think?'

If it's an average test, he's likely to give up about there. If he's a man of principle, he might persist a while longer.

'No, it's too expensive.'

'When you say it's too expensive, do you mean you can't afford to pay our price? Is there something I've missed?' or 'Do you mean you don't feel this is going to be an economical proposition for your company?'

Depending on the reply you get to this, you might continue: 'How much too expensive do you feel we are?' or 'How much more is this than you wanted to spend?'

**You are seeking to establish the difference between your price and what he sees as reasonable.**

You **must** define the difference. This is absolutely critical. Then, when you know how much or how little he is worrying about, you go back to your bag of justification benefits and you reduce the difference to the lowest common denominator.

Say you are selling something that has a working life of five years and the difference he's worrying about is £130. That's 50p a week for 260 weeks. Or 7p a day.

'Isn't getting the *best* worth an extra 50p a week, Mr Dobson?'

Another way of dealing with 'It's too expensive' is to ask back: 'In relation to what?' and see which way he goes. You'll get a specific objection with which you can easily deal.

Then you can back it up with: 'Let's face it Mr Dobson, you're not interested in *raw cost* – you're interested in *value for money*, aren't you? I think I've shown that you will get the best possible value for money if you buy from us. You get this, and this, and this, and you get **me**. Being the best goes right across our company.'

Normally, if you are progressing **up** the Quality league table, your price will also progressively rise. That Perceived Value factor will look after your profit margins. Of course, if you are happy with your profit margins and you can rise up the Quality league table at very little extra cost, you can afford to hold your prices down and take a significantly larger share of the market. But don't hold your prices down too much, otherwise cognitive dissonance will set in and the customers won't believe you can be that good with prices that low. Keep the balance right.

Up against competition, your customer, considering the four or five quotations he's received, might say to you, 'You are the most expensive!' You'll get the utmost satisfaction from saying, 'Yes, we are' and then saying **nothing** for four or five seconds. It's amazing how many customers will then say to you – 'I suppose that's because you're the best.' To which you reply – 'Yes – absolutely right.'

If you find yourself up against just one competitor and that competitor is down at the bottom of the Quality league table, the customer might say – 'You're a lot more expensive than ——!'

There is an awful temptation to knock the competition here. Don't do it. You can get the point over by inference without anyone laying a knock at your door. Sell the difference.

'Yes, we are a lot more expensive. But let me ask you a question. Isn't it true that in every kind of business, there are companies that provide a service that does as much as possible for their customers and there are companies that provide a service which does just enough for them to get by with?'

'Yes, I suppose that's true,' says the customer.

'Well, what would you like us to do for you – as much as possible or just enough to get by with?'

If you can devise a simple sales aid – a visual aid – to help you overcome the 'How much' merchants, this always makes justifying your higher price much easier.

Here's one for a capital equipment Seller at the top end of the market.

The customer has said, 'You're a lot more expensive than your competitors.' The Seller brings out his **profit/cost** chart and says, 'Yes, we are. But this isn't going to be very relevant to you. You see, if I've done my sums correctly, you're not going to spend a

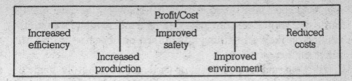

penny in real terms.' He points to his chart. 'Because of how our equipment is going to increase your efficiency, your production, improve your safety, your working conditions and reduce your production and stocking costs – and we can quantify every one of these – you're going to show a profit almost from day one.

'With us you'll be buying the **best**. So your profit will be greater than if you bought from our competitors, and you'll be getting that profit for a longer period of time.'

The most effective way of all to deal with problems on Price is to scotch them all – right at the **beginning** of your presentation. Here is a technique I put together for a double glazing company in 1983. The Sellers dealt with husbands and wives in the home.

Ten minutes into the first discussion, during the initial tour of the house or browse through the range of products, it doesn't matter which, the Seller says to his prospective customers –

'Before we go any further, rather than waste your time, can I ask you a question? When you buy things for your home, especially things that have to last a long time, do you shop around for the cheapest thing you can buy, or do you look for best value for money?'

The only answer anyone is going to get to that question is – 'Oh, we look for best value for money, of course.' Even if it isn't true, no one is going to admit to being a cheap jack. Their egos would never let them.

'Good,' continues the Seller, 'because that's precisely what my company stands for – Best value for Money. We aren't the cheapest, and we aren't the most expensive either, but we are the best.'

Then, a switch to phase two of this technique.

'Hey, I was talking to someone in this area only the other day who has exactly the same view of the importance of going for best value for money as you do. You might know him. What was his name? (*Think, then search in pockets.*) Hang on, he gave me his card. I've got it here somewhere. I remember, it had something printed on the back I thought summed our business up beautifully. Ah, here it is.'

The Seller pulls out a business card and reads out the name of the person printed on the front. 'George Thomson. Do you know him?' (*They won't.*) Then he turns the card over. 'How about this . . .' and reads the quotation printed on the card.

When he's read the quotation completely to his prospective customers, the Seller says 'Nothing's new, is it? 1819 to 1900. A hundred years ago and people were just the same as they are now.' Then he hands the card to the husband and says – 'Here, you have it. One of your friends might know him.'

Both husband and wife will read the quotation again, during which time the Seller keeps quiet. After that, no problems with price, as long as the customers can *afford* the double glazing, of course.

---

## Value ...

It's unwise to pay too much, but it's unwise to pay too little. When you pay too much you lose a little money, that is all.
When you pay too little, you sometimes lose everything, because the thing you bought was incapable of doing the thing you bought it to do.
The common law of business balance prohibits paying a little and getting a lot. It can't be done. If you deal with the lowest bidder, it's well to add something for the risk you run.
And if you do that, you will have enough to pay for something better.

John Ruskin (1819-1900)

---

You can simplify this technique by printing the John Ruskin quotation on the back of your *own* business card, and also having it in your literature, but that's not as effective as having it on **someone else's** card.

The oldest and still very effective method of justifying a higher price uses the four arithmetic symbols

+   &minus;   &divide;   ✕

**Add** . . . all the benefits of the higher-priced product.
**Take away** . . . what the customer will lose by *not* buying the higher-priced product.
**Divide** . . . the cost by time or by other parameters.
**Multiply** . . . the savings or gains over the life of the higher-priced product.

That's Selling Quality!

*Do* you reckon your prices are too high? If so, *why* do you think they are too high? In relation to what? So how do your 'extras' compare with your competitors?

Here's another interesting factor. Quite a few customers who say to you, 'It's too expensive' or 'It costs too much' are lying to you. They're saying that because they don't want to tell you their *real* problem.

The customer who's got into financial difficulties because of his own bad management isn't going to admit this to you and say, 'I can't afford to buy your goods just now'. He's going to say, 'They cost too much'.

The customer who bought too much last month and is stuck with a warehouse full of slow-moving products isn't going to say to you, 'First I have to make some space in my warehouse'. He's going to say, 'They are too expensive'.

The cut-price customer who has a reputation for only selling the cheapest products isn't going to say, 'My own style has made it impossible for me to handle your quality goods'. He's going to say, 'My word, they're too expensive'.

The customer whose company has a turnover much smaller than its PR department has been making out recently, isn't going to say to you, 'We haven't got enough work for this machine for it to earn its keep'. He's going to say (all together now) **It's too expensive!**'

**So question it – every time.**

'What do you really mean when you say it's too expensive?'

Don't **ever** accept it. Not the first time, not the second time, not even the third time. You're not selling prices, you're selling **quality, value, lower costs, longer life, satisfaction, safety,**

**peace of mind**, and a hundred other things for which it's worth paying a **higher price**.

Now a thought or two for those salespeople who sell to retailers.

A retailer should not be over-concerned about price, unless it is his concern to make sure he is selling the **highest-priced** goods he can safely move.

A retailer should be concerned with:

1 **Volume** – the number of units he can sell in a given time; and
2 **Profit** – the money he makes every time he sells one unit.

If the retailer sells the highest-priced units, he will logically make the most profit on each unit. He should know this (but some retailers don't seem to!), but his fears are focused on **moving his stock**. If he stocks too much high-priced merchandise, will he get stuck with it if his customers choose to go for the cheaper brands?

The salesperson therefore has to dispel the retailer's fears by talking about how effective his company's forthcoming advertising campaigns will be in stimulating consumer demand in this area. And how his company is going to back-up the retailer with point-of-sale displays so as to *make sure* the retailer's stocks move fast.

And at the same time the salesperson tickles the retailer's greed taste-buds with projections for a year based on a higher profit per unit multiplied by the number of units he expects the retailer to sell in a year

If it's a high-priced piece of equipment that needs servicing and the retailer is responsible for the servicing because of the prevailing trend for manufacturers to pass this buck down the line as far as they can go, then the salesperson has an additional arrow to fire.

The cost of the servicing comes out of the retailer's profit. The more units he sells, the more servicing costs and servicing 'aggro' he gets. Logically, the higher the price of the unit, the more reliable it is, and the less the retailer's servicing costs per unit anyway.

So let's make up a set of calculations for our retail salesperson to use:

The retailer is currently buying XYZ equipment at £200 per unit. His servicing cost per year averages £20 per unit. His gross profit per unit is £70. He currently sells 150 units per year. Thus his net profit per year is £50×150=£7,500.

The sales proposal is that the retailer switches to the more expensive ABC equipment at £300 per unit. Servicing costs per year will average £10 per unit. The gross profit per unit will be £110. The salesperson estimates the retailer will sell 100 units per year. Thus his projected net profit will be £100×100=£10,000, with fewer selling problems.

Of course, it will rarely be a clear-cut case of switching from one product to another. No retailer will risk an all-or-nothing situation. Unit ABC will be introduced alongside unit XYZ and, if the saleperson's estimates are proven in the ensuing year, the XYZ units will be steadily phased out or down to a minimum level consistent with consumer demand.

Whichever way the salesperson plays it, faced with these profit projections, most retailers are going to remain doubtful. But this final doubt is just what the salesperson needs for a cast-iron, certain 'try it for size' close:

'Look, I can see you're still not sure. Why don't we go for *half* this quantity for the first quarter? Then, if my projections are right, you can double-up from the second quarter onwards. That way you've *got* to be safe.'

# SOLD

Finally, let's look at a different kind of 'How much?' reaction from a prospective customer. The kind who doesn't react violently to your high price – he sits there calmly and says, 'Can I have a discount?'

It's another way the customer tries to do his job – best value for money; lowest price!

Look worried. Frown for a few seconds. Slowly shake your head and say:

'Oh dear. That does give us a problem. You see, we don't give our old-established, very large customers a discount. What do you think they'd think of us if they found out we'd given you one?'

If he smiles and says, 'Don't worry, I won't tell them!' you keep going with:

'That's not the point really, is it? It's simply not our policy to give discounts. We aim to offer best value for money, best service, best quality, best reliability, longest life. To be able to do that, we must protect our margins.'

Stick to your guns. He's getting a bargain, really. **You** know that. All you've got to do is convince **him**.

Often, top quality suppliers take longer to deliver than cheap and cheerful suppliers. If your delivery is shorter than your lesser quality competitors, great. Turn to the next piece of the puzzle. If your delivery is longer than you feel it should be to compete, read on.

Why is your delivery longer? 'Because so many forward-looking customers want to buy from us.'

If this were a fast food restaurant, you'd be in and out in ten minutes. But it's not; it's a top quality restaurant. There's something printed on the bottom of the menu – 'Good food takes time to prepare – please be patient'.

'Quality is worth waiting for.' That's what you've got to get over to the customer who wants delivery **now**! In his mind, time is the essence. A sense of urgency is in the air. You need to change the most important factor in his mind from **time** to **quality**.

'I can appreciate that delivery seems vital to you at this stage, but surely, in the long run, the fact that you are ordering the **best** equipment **must** be the deciding factor?'

If you're in trouble because of a **past** delivery problem, try this one.

The customer's saying to you: 'That widget crusher we bought from you a year ago. It was seven weeks late. It cost us thousands. We decided then – never again.'

'I can understand that, but let me ask you – if you were running a business where products were going out seven weeks late, what would you do about it?'

You might not get the answer you want, but, then again, you might. If you do, you then say:

'That's precisely (or more or less) what we did,' and you tell the customer in detail. After that, your troubles are either little ones or over.

If you find out you're going to be late on delivery, before it actually happens, telephone the customer fast and tell him. The Ostrich Complex is not for Quality league leaders, only for cheap and cheerfuls.

The packaging of your product is **not** just so much waste paper, board and polystyrene chunks. The packaging is the first glimpse of your product that many customers see. If the packaging is rubbish, cheap, badly put together, the best product in the world will come out of it with a much lower Perceived Value.

They'll maybe buy once, but what about the second time, and all the people they talk to?

Don't skimp on your packaging. Make it earn business for you. It's part of your sales promotion, just like the sides of your delivery vehicles. What's wrong with printing your guarantee on the outside of the packaging in big bold letters? What's wrong with printing some of your more choice Selling Quality head-lines, from your sales literature, on your packaging?

Like Hartmann Luggage

**'ENJOY IT . . .**
**YOU HAVE BOUGHT THE BEST'**

Like Rank Xerox for the 'Diplomat Copier'

### 'THE COPIER YOU WON'T
### WANT TO HIDE IN A CORNER'

Don't forget to get the colours right again. It's still important.

If your product is bought in retail stores and you want to persuade browsing prospective customers to pay a little more and buy something which will last a lot longer, maybe your packaging should have added to it a 'Share Certificate'.

# INVESTMENT
## 1,000 SHARES

**With Inflation still likely to run rampant and the Economy soft, an investment in a top quality product is a necessity in all your personal purchases.**

**A top quality product will last longer. It won't break down or wear out as fast, giving you an investment in enduring quality.**

**A top quality product never goes out of style.**

**By spending a little more now, you'll avoid repeating your purchase soon because it wore out or went out of style. This means real savings in the long run.**

**Make that investment now and get as a dividend the only full warranty 18 months guarantee in the industry, backed by the oldest and most reliable company in the industry.**

### INVEST IN A
### HARTMANN

Your back-up starts with the switchboard operator and receptionist and goes right through the organization and up to the managing director. **No one** is excluded. Rank Audio Visual produced a superb training film in the early seventies which has never been bettered for getting across to every employee the importance of the customer and the importance of providing the right kind of back-up. The film is called 'Who Killed the Sale?' Show it to **all** your people, including the managing director, once every three months. Video Arts also has a superb training film for resolving back-up problems, featuring John Cleese and Ronnie Barker, called 'It's All Right, It's Only a Customer!' Both titles portray the complete message!

Remember 'Think a Smile' for incoming calls to the sales office? Well, 'Think a Smile' begins with the company's switchboard operator. Where **do** they find these girls? It's as if they were selected for the most depressing voices and for how long they can hold their breath before answering a call!

If you want to be top on Quality, you've got to get these kind of things right and **keep** them right. One bad day and you lose. And you'll never know what you lost; that's the problem. Out of sight, out of mind, so you don't worry enough about this perpetual problem area.

To illustrate what kind of back-up you need for Selling Quality, turn to Chapter 10, where I take you through what *should* happen when a prospective customer visits your company for what I call a **conducted tour of the works**.

Selling is the most important job in the world. That's where we began. Service – servicing the products that you've sold or performing the service you've sold – is the **second** most important job. Get the Service wrong, and you don't have any repeat business. Worse than that, your unhappy customers tell their friends and then you don't have as much **new** business, either.

The very first training film Video Arts ever made featured John Cleese and was titled, 'Who Sold You This Then?' John Cleese is Charlie Jenkins, current world record holder as a service engineer, for **un-selling** more customers than anyone else. He runs down the product, he runs down his company, he runs down the customer and he runs down the Seller who sold the product he is servicing. As a result, customers run shrieking into the night.

Everyone who sees that film laughs their socks off – except service engineers. They hardly ever laugh. You see, the film leaves them nowhere to go, because, the world over, service engineers **are** like Charlie Jenkins.

If you want to aspire to a higher level in the Quality league table, or if you simply want to win and keep more business away from your competitors, you've got to make your service people more professional than the vast majority.

In fmcg markets (fast moving consumer goods) the service people **are** already highly professional, however. For businesses that sell to retail stores, service is called Merchandising, and a Merchandiser is responsible for making sure that his company's products are properly and prominently displayed, that the point-of-sale material provided by his company is in good condition, dusted regularly and replaced where necessary. He has an on-going objective which is steadily to get a bit more shelf space for his company's products every time he visits the retailer.

To achieve all this, a Merchandiser is very thoroughly trained, and this training is all very near to the training any Seller should receive.

And here lies the key to why service engineers of the industrial and domestic variety are so bad. The training **they** receive is on how to service the product. Very rarely indeed do these kind of service engineers receive training in Selling, or customer liaison, or basic communication, or even 'why we are in business!'

So if you really want to sell Quality, that's what you do first. Train your service people as if they were Sellers.

**Because they are!**

They get opportunities to sell that the Sellers themselves rarely, if ever, get. Customers, if the service engineers are really good, look upon them as impartial experts. Yes, impartial! Customers listen when this kind of service engineer recommends that a certain piece of equipment should be replaced, or that a certain competitor's product should be phased out in favour of his own company's MK47B. If the service engineer can justify, as a Seller has to justify, his recommendation with figures and proof, the customers will do what he recommends. Or he may alternatively set up a meeting between the customers and his colleague in the salesforce, so that the Seller takes over to clinch the deal.

That's another thing about the really professional service engineer – he works very closely with his Seller. Almost the Jekyll and Hyde technique again. The service force and the salesforce have regular meetings together, for training and for planning campaigns. Responsibility for service and for sales is carried by *one* senior executive in the best run Selling Quality companies. Where service is the responsibility of Production, warring tribes usually exist and the company plays straight into a more professional competitor's hands.

Service engineers are exceedingly well placed to sell spare parts, replacement units, maintenance contracts, as well as to advise the customers and their company's sales department on opportunities to sell. A well-tuned service force can generate as many leads as a well-planned advertising campaign. Service engineers can quite easily, when trained, use end of call question techniques. 'By the way, before I go, do you know anyone else in this area who could use this kind of equipment?' or 'By the way, before I go, Mrs Brown, could any of your friends in this neighbourhood do with a new washing machine?'

Service engineers who regularly look after postal franking machines are trained to watch for increases in usage of their machines. When usage reaches a certain level, they begin talking to the customer on their servicing visits about the imminent need for a larger machine. Then they set up a visit for their salesforce, who come in and sell the larger machine.

Photocopier and typewriter maintenance engineers do likewise. Many local typewriter engineers carry new machines in their cars and can effect on-the-spot sales with no one else needing to get involved.

Now what can I say about motor dealer service receptions, where you take your car for its regular 5,000 miles service, or for a repair? We all know the trauma we go through in this particular industry. They are diabolically bad.

It's absurdly easy to change all that – *and* make service reception a profit centre in its own right. A few drivers and a good quality mail shot letter is all you need. You've already got the necessary cars.

*Dear Customer*

*As from 1 March you don't have to bring your car to our service reception in Main Road any more for your regular service or a repair.*

*No more waiting. No more wasting your time twice in the same day. From 1 March* **we will collect your car from your home or place of business and return it to either.**

*At a time agreed with you, one of our experienced drivers will establish in detail your requirements for the service/repair and will bring your car to our service department. At the end of the day, again at a time agreed with you, the same driver will return your car. If you have an account with us, that's all there is to it; we'll invoice you as usual. If you're a cash customer, our driver will have the invoice with him and will accept your cheque.*

*There will be a small charge for this collection and delivery service, but we are sure you will find that, compared with the loss of your time, the charge is more than acceptable.*

*When you are ready for your next service, please ring the number below. From our records this should be around —*

*If you would rather continue to bring your car to us and collect it from us, as you have done in the past, then of course you can do this. Simply ignore this letter and we look forward to seeing you next time you are at Main Road. (By the way, we've now installed a coffee machine for our customers in our service reception.)*

Only penny pinching customers will be reluctant to take advantage of this new collection service. Only they will henceforth witness the trauma and hassle in service reception on a busy morning or evening. All the *good* customers, and certainly all the *business* customers, will be oblivious of any problems and will be telling their friends and colleagues about this 'different' motor dealer.

One motor dealership I know has gone one better than even this. It offers its business customers a '**Night shift service**', collecting the car for service after 6 pm in the evening and delivering it back to the customer's front door by 7.30 am the next morning.

If you actually **sell** a service, rather than a product, then your service people are the people who **perform** the service you sell. All I have said applies equally to them.

And throughout the service function, your people need to look and behave as up-market as the Sellers do in their piece of the Quality jigsaw puzzle. The service engineer's paperwork is just as important as the Seller's – in the eyes of the customers. Make it as professional as you can.

And now a word on the bit that comes between delivery of the product and its first service – the **operating instructions**.

It's a fact of life that every set of operating instructions says in bold type '**Read these instructions carefully before you touch the product**'.

It's also a fact of life that very few customers ever **do** read the instructions. So you get more early failures or malfunctions than you should get and instant dissatisfied customers.

Cracking this problem can save you a lot of money, enhance your product's perceived value **and** bring you new customers. Here are a few suggestions:

1 Make your operating instructions a sales brochure. Put some good action pictures in it. A few happy customers using the product, with quotes.
2 Print your instructions in big type, not small, hard-to-read type, and on good quality paper. Never duplicate or photocopy. Have plenty of **good** diagrams. Use colour. In other words, make the operating instructions look and feel important, expensive and interesting.
3 Have a really big main heading on the front of your instructions which hits the customer right between the eyes. Something like:

'**Our competitors tell us their customers never read their operating instructions.**
'**Maybe that's why our customers get so much more pleasure out of their —.**'

Or, if you want to challenge the customer:

'If this product were a sports car, these operating instructions would enable you to do 0–60 in 5 seconds on your first run.
'Without them, you'd probably do 0–30 in 3 hours!'

Finally, for this Service jigsaw piece, how do you **tell** the prospective customers about your incredibly good service back-up? I'm sure you don't make the mistake one manufacturer made a few years back. In the sales literature it said:

'Our equipment is utterly reliable and never goes wrong, but when it does we'll have a service engineer at your door within 48 hours.'

One of the **best** examples I've seen of putting over Service on paper is this.

### Service You Can Rely on

1,600 engineers in a nationwide network ensure that Rank Xerox delivers . . . quality, reliability and service.

'Choose a Rank Xerox copier or duplicator for your office and you're not just getting an advanced product. You'll also be gaining access to the most comprehensive copier and duplicator service network in the country. Service you can depend on, whether you rent, lease or buy.

'Service has always been a Rank Xerox priority. Wherever you are, we're not too far away. And we get to you fast when you need us.'

## The Success of the 'Diplomat'

A few years ago, Rank Xerox put into practice most of what I've said in this chapter. They did it as a test case for one product only, a 'limited edition' of their proven and very successful plain paper copier, the 3100. They called their limited edition the *Diplomat*.

It was an aesthetically delightful combination of top quality colours – beige, dark brown and black; a modern single tubular chromed column stand with streamlined, slimmed down copier unit and, to set everything off, delicate brown and black coach lines on the beige paintwork and a Royal Warrant, the Queen's coat of arms and 'By appointment to Her Majesty the Queen'.

The sales brochure produced to launch the Diplomat was equally different and impressive. Not large, A5 in fact, half as big as Rank Xerox's normal sales literature, but on very good quality board and printed full colour, the background colours setting off the pictures of the Diplomat to perfection. Plenty of plant life, cork wall tiles, that kind of thing.

| | |
|---|---|
| *The headline read:* | The Xerox 3100 Diplomat. Makes every other plain paper copier . . . look plain. |
| *The internal copy:* | Why settle for an ordinary plain paper copier when you can have a Xerox 3100 Diplomat – the exciting new copier with proven efficiency and good looks. |

(I'm going to give you the entire text, because, like the Rolls-Royce Shadow I brochure, there is so much to learn from this example.)

The copier you won't want to hide in a corner.

You own design sense will instantly tell you that here, at last, is a copier that looks as impressive as its performance.

The Xerox 3100 Diplomat is an efficient, functional piece of office equipment that's also smart enough to be the office showpiece. Whether it sits in reception, the MD's office or the typing pool.

**Wherever you place it, it never looks out of place.**

Where the space is at a premium, the Xerox 3100 Diplomat can actually contribute to the go-ahead, modern look of the working environment. It not only embodies the kind of style that appeals to every interior decorator's eye: it incorporates the business efficiency functions, reliability and service back-up you insist upon.

**It's image-conscious – and ruthlessly cost-conscious, too.**

The Xerox 3100 Diplomat is compact, completely portable and your accountant will approve of it for all the right economic reasons. Its pedigree is the world-renowned Xerox 3100 series, one of the most relied-upon low volume copiers in the business.

The name Rank Xerox speaks volumes about the efficiency of the Diplomat. Its impeccable styling means that now you can have a copier that also reflects your company's image.

**Good-looking, hard-working, easy-to-operate.**

20 copies a minute. First copy time eight seconds. The ability to copy virtually any original on to practically any material. Two way light/dark copy switch to improve the quality of poor originals. One quick automatic cycle for copying and paperfeeding. At a glance paper renewal display. All features designed to speed up the efficiency process.

**Lease or buy . . .**

And at the same time enjoy one of the most efficient back-up services in the country.

There are over 1,600 Service Engineers operating through a network of Service Centres, dedicated to keeping your Xerox equipment at the peak of efficiency.

**Tear off and post the Reply Paid Card now for details.**

This is a 'special edition' copier – and if you want the chance to obtain one at an equally attractive price – please hurry. Fill in and post the card. Now – while the image of this not-so-plain paper copier is still fresh in your mind.

The Diplomat was outstandingly successful. It hadn't got the storage cupboard that the standard 3100 copier was supplied with, but the customers didn't mind that. It hadn't got the second paper tray that the standard 3100 had, but the customers didn't mind that either. They were buying **style**. They liked the look of the Diplomat and were prepared to pay more for it. £410 more to be precise. During its last few months on the market, the Diplomat was selling for £1,925, against the standard 3100 copier at £1,515.

*That's really selling quality.*

### Now Back to 'A Day's Worth of USP'

Well, that's a sample dozen jigsaw puzzle pieces plus one complete example of how to put it all together. All you need to do now is decide how many pieces *your* particular Corporate Image jigsaw puzzle has, and what each piece is labelled. Because every business is different. The twelve pieces I've selected are probably the most universally common pieces, but there are many more.

How do you establish which pieces you need?

You go right back to Chapter 2 'How to Develop the Killer Instinct' and to that Day's Worth of USP I mentioned for speeding up the knowledge input. That same exercise will also show you clearly what your **edge** is over your competitors, for each of your products and markets. If your edge on any particular factor is not very bright, or if your competitors are beating you on that factor, you have a potential piece for your jigsaw puzzle.

You will also be able to *quantify* each piece. How much improvement you need for just the right amount of edge. There's no point in having too much on some pieces and not enough on others.

This has, of necessity, been a very long chapter, because this is such an important subject when you're Selling against competition.

# 9
# How to Present your Proposals

**90% of all the business that is quoted for throughout industry and commerce is lost because the Quotation doesn't do the job it is supposed to do.**

**The traditional Quotation is the most stupid document in business – only suppliers who are the cheapest price and the shortest delivery can win with it. The rest must change – or eventually die.**

**We certainly aren't the cheapest – so our options are clear.**

### Definitions – Quotation and Proposal

Let's get the definitions right before we get started.

A **quotation,** the traditional document used by most of industry and commerce the world over to confirm in writing what is being offered for sale, is **a legal document**. It contains just about every reason why the prospective customer should not place the order with you.

**Specification** (meaningless: doesn't have any 'what's in it for the customer!')
**Price** (How much???)
**Delivery** (Too long!)
**Terms of Payment** (Too short!)
**E & O E** (That little term at the bottom of the page that means 'Errors and Omissions Excepted' – a rough translation could be 'Whatever we've said we don't really mean!')
**Victoriana** (Phrases like 'Thank you for your esteemed enquiry' and 'We

look forward to the favour of your valued order which will receive our most careful attention', which make modern customers think this particular supplier is still living in the days of the *first* Industrial Revolution.)

**Your Terms and Conditions** (All that pale grey or blue small print on the back. Why now? Why this early, before the customer's agreed to buy? Wouldn't on the back of your acknowledgement of the order be more appropriate?)

**Price Only Holds Good for 30 Days** (then the customer has to start all over again? Did anyone consider how long it takes for the average customer to get through *his* decision-making process?)

You know, businesses that aren't trading at lowest price and shortest delivery and that are using these kind of legal 'Quotation' documents really **are** still thinking like they were in the first industrial revolution. That was the first big time when Demand outstripped supply by several hundred miles. So suppliers could dictate terms.

Now it's the other way round. Customers dictate terms and suppliers jump or lose the customers. At least that's the way the customers see it – and they've a pretty good edge – it's their money that pays our wages!

This book is about us Sellers getting that edge back again. But **not** by changing the Supply and Demand cycle round again. As I said earlier, we're going to do it by positive, aggressive professional **Selling**.

Quotations are **out**. Proposals are **in**.

So let's define what I mean by the word **Proposal**.

A **Proposal** is a Selling tool. A Quotation is not.

A Proposal contains all the reasons why the prospective customer **should** place the order with you. It is an invaluable selling aid, especially if your price is higher than your competitors'. Used correctly, it greatly increases the odds in your favour.

**Format for the Best Proposal**

The best Proposals are designed with five sections. These sections **must** be used in the proper order. They are these:

## 1 The Customer's Objectives

The Proposal should begin by re-stating the objectives which the customer wishes to achieve. These should be listed in priority order – the most important first. Thus, when the prospective customer picks up the Proposal and begins to read it, the first thing he reads after his name, address and introductory paragraph is what he and his business wants to achieve. Whatever he may have been wrapped up in before he began reading, this 'Objectives' first section is guaranteed to make him switch his concentration to the project for which you are presenting the Proposal. So he's in the right frame of mind before he gets into the meat of the matter.

## 2 Your Recommendations

Having defined the customer's objectives, you then present a **condensed** picture of the goods or services you are recommending that will achieve these objectives, together with brief outlines of how each objective will be achieved, using the same priority order. For complicated equipment, specification sheets can be added to the Proposal (at the back) and referred to in this section.

## 3 Summary of Additional Benefits

The principal benefits which this particular customer will derive from what you are proposing to sell him will undoubtedly have been mentioned in section 2. If there are any additional benefits which this customer will enjoy, other than those already mentioned, and providing they are relevant to this particular customer, they should be listed.

When you list them, make sure they **are** benefits, not features.

## 4 Financial Justification

This is the most important section. Very few people buy anything unless they can see clearly that the goods or services they are considering will show them an adequate profit; or saving, which ultimately comes to the same thing. They also look for that adequate profit happening in as short a time as they can achieve – the 'pay back' period or amortization of the purchase price.

The majority of Sellers expect their customers to work all

this out for themselves. Some of them do. Many of them don't. One thing I know for sure – a salesperson who works it all out **for** the customer, and presents the financial justification in the Proposal, always has a very appreciative customer and is always top in confidence and knowledge when the time comes to close the sale. So these kinds of salespeople usually win hands down.

Financial justification can be written into a Proposal in many different ways, as you'll see from the examples later in this chapter. The rule on which way to use is very clear and simple. If the purchase can be financially justified in three different ways, you use **all three ways**, the best first, and you finish by adding the three lots of savings or gains together to produce a final amortization figure, or total profit/savings figure.

## 5 Your Guarantees and After-Sales Service

Don't leave the guarantee, warranty and after-sales service details to the pale grey small print on the back of the Quotation. It's much more important. In the mind of that prospective customer, it might be the most important factor of all. If anything goes wrong, **he** carries the can, not you. He could even get fired for making a stupid decision and buying what you're proposing. That's maybe not the reality, but it's how they think. So put their minds at rest. Tell the customers how good your guarantees and your service are. How fast your service engineers respond.

And back it all up with some third party references. Customers who you know will be happy to take a call from one of your prospective customers and will sing your praises loud and clear – because you've asked them if they will do this, well in advance. Every really professional competition beater has at least a dozen such third party references tucked away, ready to use, at all times.

Such a five section Proposal can be constructed in the form of a letter, or as a series of separate sheets, one for each section, wrapped up in a professional-looking binder.

Whichever format you use, the good old legal Quotation document can **still** be added – at the back, after the specification sheets – if your company's legal eagles insist that traditions must be maintained at all costs!

## Some Examples of Good Proposals

Over the years, as a consultant, I've helped many businesses change over from the Quotation deterrent to the Selling Proposal. Here are a few examples.

The first five are all for the same product – a drinks vending machine. I give you all five so that you can clearly see how the basic format for the Proposal can be tailored to a particular customer requirement, and also to give you the most comprehensive input I can on that most important section of all – the financial justification.

Customer names have been omitted in some of these examples at the request of my clients.

*Dear Mr Holt*
*Thank you for your help last Thursday and for the very useful figures you supplied; the opportunity to carry out a survey of your plant was also much appreciated. From our conversation I understand your requirements are:*

1 *A drinks service for 325 shift workers plus 110 day workers and 28 staff.*
2 *Availability of this service throughout the 24 hours three shift working with minimum attention, and accessibility for office staff during the day.*
3 *A charge of 4p to be maintained for tea, but other drinks to be set initially at 5p. Provision for vend price increases to be built in.*
4 *The additional facility of a chilled drink selection to alleviate the humid working conditions in the moulding shop.*
5 *A Pepsi Cola or Coca-Cola selection as specifically requested by the female packers through their committee member.*
6 *The total operation to be self-supporting.*

**Our Recommendations**
*I believe your requirements will be adequately and economically covered by the provision on rental of 3 × Model S32 SUPERMATIC Hot 'n Cold drinks vending machines. One of these to be sited as shown at A on the enclosed layout plan of your plant. This is convenient to the packing and finishing section and is in a suitable location for the office staff. The remaining two machines to be sited as shown at B and C in the main and semi-automatic moulding machine shops.*

*All these locations are convenient for power and water supplies and give the best optimum sitings having regard to the proximity of the majority of the workforce.*

**The SUPERMATIC Rental Package Has the Following Benefits**

1 *The machine provides 29 selections of hot tea, coffee, chocolate, and soup plus 3 selections of refrigerated chilled drinks. Two of the latter are carbonated which means that fizzy drinks including Pepsi or Coca-Cola can be enjoyed by your packing girls.*

2 *The tea and coffee selections can be set to give a total of 29 variants to suit a wide range of personal preferences.*

3 *The unique Sankey coin handling system accepts 1p, 2p and 5p coins, inserted in any order to totalize up to 29 pence. Therefore your price level requirements of 4p and 5p can be catered for. In fact three price levels can be utilized, and possible future increases, caused perhaps by commodity prices, are a matter of simple on-site adjustment.*

4 *The cup capacity of 550 drinks in each machine ensures that your entire labour force can be catered for over a 24 hour period with only one daily filling and cleaning operation.*

5 *The fixed monthly rental payments are inclusive of:*
*Free delivery to your prepared site.*
*Comprehensive insurance cover.*
*Commissioning and full instruction.*
*Full maintenance including parts and labour.*
*An initial supply of cups and ingredients representing about 3,500 drinks, and are guaranteed inflation proof for the entire period of the agreement.*

6 *These payments will be more than covered by the income generated by revenue from the machines.*

**Financial Considerations**

1 *The basis for operating figures are* **cup costings** *including appropriate recommended ingredients and the cup itself. Average take-off figures are based on the findings of the Tavistock Institute of Human Relations, and statistics supplied by the Automatic Vending Association. They have been marginally adjusted to suit the special conditions existing in your plant.*

| Drink | Cost per cup | Average take-off (%) | Vend price | Cup profit | Profit per 100 |
|---|---|---|---|---|---|
| Tea | 1.57 | 10 | 4 | 2.43 | 24.03 |
| Coffee | 2.67 | 35 | 5 | 2.33 | 81.55 |
| Chocolate | 2.66 | 15 | 5 | 2.34 | 35.10 |
| Soup | 1.72 | 15 | 5 | 3.28 | 49.20 |
| Cold drink | 1.62 | 25 | 5 | 3.38 | 84.50 |
| | | 100 | | | 274.65p |

*Therefore average cup profit = 2.75 pence.*

2 *The monthly rental premium for each machine based on your current
Regional Development Grant qualification is . . . £60.95 which is equiva-
lent to a daily cost of . . . £3.04. If we divide this figure by the average
profit of 2.75p we arrive at a daily requirement of 110 drinks per 24 hours
per machine to break-even. At this point rental charges and ingredients' costs
have been covered.*

*If only 80% of your total workforce took a very conservative 2 drinks per
day this would account for an average daily offtake of 246 drinks per
machine.*

*463×80%=370*

*370×2 drinks=740*

*740÷3 machines=246 per machine*

*In these circumstances your break-even situation would be comfortably reached
and you could look forward to a daily profit of £11.22.*

*246−110*            *=136*

*136×2.75*          *=374p*

*374×3 machines*     *=£11.22*

*If we allow the odd £1.22 for daily cleaning labour cost, the total profit over
the 5 year period would be £12,000 (£10×20 days×60 months).*

*To this must be added the present cost in labour and materials of your
existing tea service. Your personnel manager's figures were £1,250 in 1976, of
which £1,020 was wages. Allowing for the projected rate of inflation in labour
costs over the next five years, we arrive at a figure of £8,827 and this amount
represents the additional saving which will be made.*

*Over the five years therefore we have:*

| | |
|---|---|
| *vending profit* | *£12,000* |
| *cost savings* | *£ 8,817* |
| | |
| **TOTAL** | *£20,827* |

*I would like to confirm that any service requirements will be cheerfully and
promptly attended to by our locally based engineer, Charlie Newman, who is
fully trained and adequately equipped. As part of the rental package this
service would be without charge.*

*I have enclosed a cup costing chart for your interest and in support of the
financial calculation; also a technical data leaflet which includes installation
requirements.*

*Finally, I have included a rental agreement and would be grateful if this
could be completed as indicated and signed by yourself as the authorized
signatory.*

*Yours sincerely*

*Dear Mr Jones*

*Confirming our discussions, when I visited your office on Monday 2 May, as agreed I am writing to you with details of our New Supermatic 32 selection Hot & Cold carbonated beverage machines.*

## The Present Situation and Objectives

*You have three CTCS/E 8 selection Hot beverage machines on a rental contract No. 5959, this contract coming to an end 12 June next.*

*As I understand it, you have had satisfactory service from your present machines and are looking for:*

1  *In addition to hot drinks, to provide at least one fizzy cold drink and one non-fizzy cold drink.*

2  *Improve the general image and acceptability of vending to your staff.*

3  *Keep costs to the minimum.*

## Our Recommendations

*Having discussed with you, at length, your present service and future requirements, we are recommending our New Supermatic 32 selection Hot & Cold Carbonated beverage machines. These will:*

1  *Provide 3 selections of cold drinks from two flavours. 1 high fizz level drink (for Pepsi Cola if desired), 1 with a variable fizz level and 1 non fizz, thereby catering for the majority.*

2  *Have new digital selector buttons, creating a modern image, making choosing more simple with a wider variety of drinks.*

3  *Be fitted with the New Sankey coin mechanism which will accept 3 coins and price 1p to 29p, giving flexibility of pricing to help counter inflation and reduce costs.*

## Summary of Benefits

(a) *Everpure water filters are provided with each machine; these remove any impurities and odours from the water, thus improving the quality of drink.*

(b) *New water system, easier accessibility within the machine making the cleaning operation simpler.*

(c) *Spare mixing bowls and pipes, reducing cleaning time, improving hygiene and the overall standards of this operation.*

## Finance

*Once again our G.K.N. Group Finance Company can provide you with a five year inflation proof rental contract, as you have enjoyed for the past five years.*

*You are currently vending approximately 500 drinks per week from each machine. With the proposed increase in vend price for hot drinks from 5p to 6p per cup and the introduction of cold drinks at 8p per cup, the overall increase in revenue will be approximately 1.5p per drink. Taking the increase into account the new rental figures should read:*

*3×New Supermatic drink machine . . . £46.43 per week (inflation proof)*
*Less increased revenue on 1,500 drinks*
*per week @ 1.5p per drink*         22.50 *per week*

                                23.93
*Less rental payments on old machines*   20.36

*overall increase* **only**         £ 3.57 *per week*

In addition to the usual rental term of providing service, spare parts and fully comprehensive insurance, we now supply each machine on RENTAL with an initial case of ingredients and a $CO_2$ gas bottle without any additional cost or charge to yourselves. What this means in terms of return to you is:

Coffee      1,600 cups approx.
Tea         2,700 cups approx.
Chocolate    500 cups approx.
Soup        650 cups approx.
Cold drink   2,500 cups approx.

Total       8,010 cups approx.×3 machines=    **24,030 drinks (F.O.C.)**

The total value to you of this number of drinks at an average of 6p each is £1,442 – we provide them all **without cost to you**.
Attached is our official quotation together with a technical specification sheet. We hope we will have your continued business for the next five years.
Yours sincerely

---

Dear Mr Lee
Following our discussion last week, I list below details of our Supermatic Drink Machine.

**Your Objectives**
As I understand it, you are looking for drinks machines that will:
1 Replace your 3 Hot Drinks Machines with Hot and Cold Drinks Machines.
2 Provide an automatic drinks service for your 210 works staff.
3 Recover all costs including the rental premiums at a 5p vend price for all drinks.
4 Equipment to be provided on a comprehensive rental system.

**Our Recommendations**
Three Model S32 Supermatic 32 selection Hot and Cold Drink Machines.
   This machine will provide your staff with a choice of 32 drinks giving the

*following alternatives: 18 selections of coffee, 9 selections of tea, 1 selection of chocolate, 1 selection of soup or lemon tea, 3 selections of cold drink from 2 flavours (2 fizzy and 1 still).*

*The S32 gives the following benefits:*
1 *Digital selection allows a fast positive drink selection.*
2 *Sankey electronic coin mechanism with a Ferranti chip allowing 3 selling prices and giving a coin acceptance of 1p, 2p and 5p; so drinks can be priced from 1p to 29p.*
3 *Coin acceptance lights that illuminate to indicate that drinks may be purchased to the value shown.*
4 *Water break tank that ensures a reserve of water in the machine and protects against mains pressure variations.*
5 *Insulated 1½ gallon boiler with a 3 KW heater ensuring consistent drink temperature under heavy usage.*
6 *High quality carbonator ensuring cold fizzy or still drinks.*

*Using G.K.N. Sankey's own finance company means that we will provide you with an inflation-proof rental contract which is inclusive of service, spare parts and comprehensive insurance, so ensuring a fixed monthly rental for the 5 year contract duration.*

### Accessories
*The S32 comes complete with the following:*
*Spare set of pipes and bowls.*
*Everpure water filter.*
*Initial supply of cups and ingredients including a swing top tidy bin and $CO_2$ cylinder.*

### Installation
*Connection of plumbing to machine by your personnel. We will commission the machine and train your staff on cleaning procedures. The machine has adjustable feet allowing for any unevenness in your concrete floor.*

### Rental Rates and Financial Breakdown
*$3 \times S32 = £200.70$ per month on Comprehensive Rental.*
    *I list below a breakdown of revenue and expenditure for the 5 year period including the following points we agreed on:*

1 *Your staff would consume at least 3 drinks per person per day.*
2 *20 day working month.*
3 *1 hour per day to clean machines.*
4 *14% inflation factor to be built in.*
5 *It would cost 2.5p to produce the drink from ingredients including the cup.*

| Daily revenue | Daily expenditure | |
|---|---|---|
| | Rental (fixed) | |
| | Cost per day | =£10.03 |
| Drinks | Drinks | |
| 630 per day at 5p=£31.50 | Cost per cup | |
| | 2.5p×630 | =£15.75 |
| | Labour | |
| | 1 hour at £3 | =£3.00 |
| | Expenditure per day | =£28.78 |
| Revenue per month=£630.00 | Expenditure per month | =£575.60 |

*As the rental stays fixed the inflation factor will affect only the drinks and labour costs and the annual first year figures would be: Revenue=£7,560.00; Expenditure=£6,907.20 and the 5 year figures would be: Revenue=£49,972; Expenditure=£41,780.*

### Reliability

*Our reputation goes a long way towards guaranteeing your satisfaction. We have installed Supermatics at The Mote Swimming Baths, Maidstone, South Eastern Electricity Board, Maidstone and Hercules Powder Company at Erith. I know these companies would not mind if you asked them about our Supermatics.*

*The comprehensive rental agreement allows for a fast, reliable after-sales service if ever required from our local service depot at Chessington, and all our highly trained engineers are on radio control.*

*I enclose with this proposal, our official quotation, rental document and leaflet.*

*I look forward to our next meeting to discuss this proposal on Tuesday, 24 May at 11.00 am.*

*Yours sincerely*

---

*For the attention of Mr N. Garner*
*Group Personnel Manager.*

*Dear Mr Garner*
*In confirming my visit to your company on 23 April, may I take this opportunity of thanking you for your time and courtesy and for the privilege of allowing me to survey your premises.*

### Your Objectives

*As I understand it, you are looking to:*

1 *Provide a 24 hour drinks service to all hourly and piece-work paid employees, totalling 350 persons.*
2 *Reduce time spent in obtaining beverages from existing trolley service.*

3 *Remove existing subsidy created by supplying drinks from a trolley and ensure a viable cost free operation by the use of automatic vending equipment which will be supplied under the terms of a comprehensive rental agreement and include labour and materials to maintain the equipment in full and efficient working order.*

4 *Ensure that all catering personnel will receive 'on site' training in the correct and hygienic operation of such equipment.*

## Our Recommendations

*Having given careful consideration to your requirements, I would recommend that Three – GKN Sankey Hot 'n Cold Drinks Machines Model S32 are most suited to meet your requirements.*

1 *Each machine has the capacity to provide over 500 drinks per machine without need to refill. Three machines will be sufficient to meet your maximum needs.*

2 *With the machines operating continuously time will not be lost waiting for drinks.*

3 *Using a vend price of 4p for tea and 5p for all other drinks, sufficient revenue will be obtained to cover both the cost of all ingredients and cups and the monthly rental premiums. Turnover is based on drink sales from existing trolley service.*

4 *On site training will be given by both our service engineer and myself to your staff at the time of commissioning with additional training available at any time in the future should staff leave or a change of duties be introduced.*

## Summary of Benefits

*These machines offer 32 selections of drinks including 3 choices of cold drink: no other equipment can supply such a personalized choice.*

*A choice of either 7 oz or 9 oz cup can be used and the changeover does not require modifications or specialized labour.*

*Having a lagged boiler ensures minimal heat loss, therefore reduced electricity consumption and ensures a constant temperature of drink when operated at maximum output.*

## Financial Justification and Price

*The conventional trolley service is operated by 3 female persons for a total of 6 hours per person per day; this represents a weekly cost as follows:*

| | |
|---|---|
| 18 hours×5 days×£1 per hour | £90.00 |
| Annual cost (48 week year) . . . | £4,320.00 |
| 5 year cost assuming an increase in labour cost of 15% per annum . . . | £28,628.00 |

*To clean and fill the recommended equipment would take 1 person 2 hours per day; this represents a weekly cost as follows:*

| | |
|---|---|
| 2 hours×5 days ×£1 per hour | £10.00 |
| Annual cost (48 week year) . . . | £480.00 |
| 5 year cost assuming an increase | |
| in labour cost of 15% per annum . . . | £3,233.00 |

To rent the equipment over 5 years, at a weekly cost of £46.30 represents an

| | |
|---|---|
| Annual cost of . . . | £2,408.00 |
| 5 year cost, fixed rental rate . . . | £12,042.00 |

With a combined machines rental cost together with labour to clean and fill totalling . . . £15,275.00 this to be offset against the cost of the existing conventional service calculated to cost £28,628.00 over the next five years, it can be projected that a saving of £13,353.00 would result. There are no additional costs.

## Accessories

The Model S32 comes complete with a spare set of all drink preparation attachments and ingredients to produce:

1,600 cups of coffee  (approx.)
2,700 cups of tea      (approx.)
500 cups of chocolate (approx.)
650 cups of soup      (approx.)

plus appropriate amounts of sugar and whitener and 2,000 plastic cups.

Delivery and commissioning is completed by our personnel.

The machine stands on a level floor and is connected only to power and water by your Works maintenance personnel.

## Reliability/Guarantee/Service

The reputation of GKN Sankey goes towards guaranteeing your satisfaction.

Our Nationwide Radio-Controlled Service Department is further evidence of the back-up facilities we supply to ensure customer satisfaction.

Equipment to the specification of the S32 machine is installed at:

1 A.B.C. Co. Ltd (Site address)
2 X.Y.Z. Co. Ltd (Site address)
3 C.B.A. Co. Ltd (Site address)

I am confident these Companies would not mind if you asked them their opinion of the reliable S32 Drinks Machine.

Enclosed with this proposal is our Official Quotation, our Rental Agreement and a leaflet giving the Specification of the Model S32.

Yours sincerely

Dear Mr Bloggs

Following my recent visit to your offices, as promised, I have put together the relevant facts appertaining to your vending machine requirements, and my proposals.

**Your Objectives**
*As I understand it, you wish to:*
1 *Supply Hot 'n Cold drinks around the clock for the 70 staff employed at your Long Road factory, by using Automatic Vending Machines.*
2 *This system to run on a break-even basis, thereby minimizing capital cost to your company, but the selling price of commodities to be reasonable to your work force.*
3 *The equipment must be fully maintained to ensure continuity of service at all times to your workers.*
4 *The drinks vended must not only be economical but of a quality acceptable to suit all tastes and this quality must be flexible to take into account any alterations in strength which you may require in the future.*

**Our Recommendations**
1 *Having discussed this in detail with you I would recommend the Sankey Supermatic Model S32 (specification enclosed).*
*This machine will give you a selection of drinks to suit all tastes as follows:*

| | |
|---|---|
| 9 × Tea | With or without extra sugar or milk |
| 18 × Coffee | With or without extra sugar or milk |
| 1 × Chocolate | Whipped |
| 1 × Soup | Whipped |
| 3 × Cold drinks | Both fizzy and plain |

2 *The Supermatic 32 can be obtained on inflation proof rental, through our own company thereby fixing your costs for the next 5 years, enabling you to keep the selling price of drinks to a minimum.*

**Your Fixed Monthly Rental Will Include**
(a) *The full cost of the machine.*
(b) *All parts and labour for the full contract period.*
(c) *A wide insurance cover, which includes replacement machine if machine burgled by intruder.*
(d) *An initial pack of ingredients providing in excess of 2,000 drinks to contribute to your first month's rental.*
(e) *Apart from VAT the price remains the same throughout the full contract period.*

3 *The continued performance of your machine is assured by using one of 14 trained engineers who cover the North West.*
*Each of these engineers carries £1,500 of spares and is in 2 way radio contact with our area office to ensure the quickest possible service, and our reputation, which is second to none, is your guarantee.*
4 *As well as machine maintenance we also supply all ingredients required together with on site quality control.*

5  *Each machine as standard will be supplied with:*

(a) *A spare set of mixing bowls for ease of cleaning.*
(b) *A water filter to ensure quality of drinks.*
(c) *An electronic coin acceptor to sell at any price you choose between 0–29p. This would therefore take into account any price increases within the life of the machine and no further acceptors would have to be purchased.*

## Financial Breakdown

*Because the rental includes all costs for the machine, its maintenance and its insurance – I will use the rental figure in these costings and these consequently have a known fixed cost not just this year but for the next 5 years.*

*Other items to take into account are:*

(a) *ingredient costs;*
(b) *labour to fill and clean.*

## Ingredients

*By using our ingredients the cost per cup is only*
*1.46p for tea, milk and sugar,*
*1.57p for coffee, milk and sugar*
*2.72p for chocolate, milk and sugar,*
*1.66p for soup,*
*1.23p for cold drinks.*

*1.73p is therefore the average cost per cup.*

*These prices based on 1–4 case rate.*

*Should your workers require stronger drinks than average, I will round this up to 2p for the following calculations, therefore allowing for any increase.*

## Recovering Ingredient Outlay

*We have found that most workers average 2 drinks per day: if we take this into account we arrive at the following equation:*

| | |
|---|---|
| 70 staff×2 cups per day | =140 per day |
| 140×5 days per week | = 700 per week |
| cost per cup average | =2p |
| your selling price | =5p |
| therefore gross profit | =3p per cup |
| 700 cups per week at 3p profit | =2,100p or £21.00 |
| £21 per week×4 | =£84.00 per month gross profit |

## Labour

*Because the Sankey machine is supplied with spare mixing bowls and cleaning kit this reduces the time spent at each machine by 15 minutes per day or 1¼ hours per week:*

*At £1.00 per hour your labour saving would be £1.25 per week or £5.00 per month or £300 over the next 5 years.*

**Financial Summary**
*The whole system therefore has taken into account the cost of:*
1 *the machine*
2 *service for 5 years*
3 *replacement parts for 5 years*
4 *insurance for 5 years*
5 *ingredients*
6 *labour savings.*

| | |
|---|---|
| *With a gross profit of* | *£84.00 per month* |
| *and savings of* | *£ 5.00 per month* |
| *we arrive at* | *£89.00 gross contribution* |
| *Less rental of machine* | *£66.90 per month* |
| *Current surplus therefore* | *£22.10 per month* |

**Installation**
*The rental price includes delivery to site and, after connection to power and water by your maintenance department, our engineer will commission the machine and give full operating instructions to your staff.*

**Conclusion**
*By installing the machine on rental from GKN Sankey you will not only rest assured of continuity of performance backed by the finest after-sales force in the country, but will have a fixed cost for the next 5 years.*

*I hope you decide to join the Sankey rental scheme. I know it will give you years of trouble-free service.*

*Yours sincerely*

---

This next example is for a core-making machine for a foundry. The machine is made in the USA and imported by the UK distributors.

*Dear Mr Bradley*
*Our Mr J. J. Docherty has asked me to write to you with details of our Dependable Shell Core Machines.*

**Your objectives**
*As I understand it, you are looking for a machine which will:*
1 *replace/supplement your existing system for core making;*
2 *provide a completely automatic operation which will increase your core production by 50% while not increasing your labour costs significantly;*

3 give provision for making cores up to 250mm in diameter and 700mm in length.

## Our Recommendations

I have discussed these requirements in detail with Mr Docherty and we recommend our **Model 100S Dependable Shell Core Machine** with fully automatic controls.

This machine will give you the most economical capital outlay and running costs while providing everything you need to cover your expansion programme for the foreseeable future.

The **Model 100S** gives you the following benefits:

1 Operation is on a continuous cycle basis, giving maximum possible output.
2 There is full temperature control automatically at all times, so there will be no fluctuation of core texture.
3 There is an automatic sand system which replenishes itself after each completed cycle, so no labour other than the operator is required.
4 Cores are ejected by air jets and vibrators into a box which is placed directly in front of the machine so that the operator can at all times check production.
5 The opening between the core faceplates can be set up to 150mm, to facilitate easy ejection, clearance and access.
6 There is a comprehensive filter system which prevents the valves and mechanism from abrasion by sand.
7 The faceplates are fine machined in cast iron and fitted with multiple tee slots for the easiest possible fitting of a wide variety of core boxes.

The design of the **Dependable** machine is such that all working parts are readily accessible, allowing maintenance of the machine to be carried out as swiftly as possible.

## Accessories

The **Model 100S** comes complete with the following accessories:
Lighting torch
Blow-off gun
Baffles
Silicone spray gun
Surface thermometer
Pair of heat resistant gloves
Clamps and all air and gas hoses and gauges and fittings.

## Installation

Installation will be carried out by our personnel. We will also commission the machine and train your operators in the running and maintenance of the machine.

*No foundation work is necessary for installation. The machine stands on a level concrete floor.*

## Price and Financial Breakdown

*The price of the* **Dependable Model 100S** *depends on how it is shipped from the USA.*

*If by air freight, this would be £2,858, delivered, installed and commissioned.*

*If by sea, the price reduces to £2,648.*

*There are absolutely no extras.*

*The capital cost of the* **Model 100S** *can be broken down into a unit cost per core produced.*

*Your present plant is producing 400 cores per day.*

*The new plant will produce 600 cores per day.*

*This gives you an extra capacity of 44,000 cores per year.*

*I understand that you depreciate your plant over 10 years. On this basis, the yearly cost of purchasing the Model 100S is £286 per year.*

*Thus, taking only the extra capacity produced, of 44,000 cores per year, your costs per core produced will be 0.65p.*

*The additional sand and gas costs for the extra production we have to leave to you to calculate, as we do not have the relevant figures.*

## Reliability

*As Mr Docherty has told you, we at Balbardie specialize in quality equipment. Everything we provide is built to last and the* **Dependable Model 100S** *is no exception.*

*Our reputation goes a long way towards guaranteeing your satisfaction. Our extensive service organization completes this reputation. We have installed similar core machines at J. & E. Hall Limited, Dartford, Kent; at British Industrial Sands Limited, Redhill, Surrey; at Evans Foundry Limited, Halstead, Essex and at Price & Tarling Limited, Christchurch, Hants. I know these companies would not mind if you asked them what they thought of the* **Dependable Core Machine.**

*I enclose with this Proposal our official quotation and a technical leaflet which gives the Specification of the Model 100S machine.*

*I hope you decide to install the machine. I am sure it will give you many years of excellent and trouble-free service.*

*Yours sincerely*

*D. A. R. Tennent*
*Commercial Manager*

The next example is in the 'report' format, a separate page for each section, and in real life is bound into a quality, but inexpensive, cover. The product is a system, similar to a computer, with hardware and software. The largest proportion of the price is in the part of the system which the customer does not see – the software development which makes the system work.

Many businesses have this kind of problem – justifying the price of an intangible which is part of a quite inexpensive tangible, making the whole look to the customer too much money for what he is apparently getting.

Without a Proposal, selling a quality intangible is very difficult indeed. Everything depends upon the skill of the salesperson and getting face to face with the decision-maker for a comprehensive presentation and demonstration.

With a proper Proposal, the task is made very much easier – and the odds on success very much greater.

# A
# PROPOSAL

for substantially and consistently increasing
your Sales Turnover
while steadily reducing your selling costs.

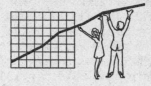

presented by

# SCRS

**Sales Control & Record Systems Ltd.**
Concorde House, 24 Warwick New Road, Royal Leamington Spa, Warwickshire CV32 5JH.
Tel: 0926 25103/6 or 37621/6  Telex: 311746 or 317488

**Assessing the Current Situation**

Let's begin with some irrefutable facts of business life.

Every salesforce, every selling operation, every individual sales person in the sales force, every manager, every director – each and every one has something in common. Never is performance, corporate or personal, anywhere near optimum. Life and human nature keep stopping 'optimum' from happening. Everything and everyone has 'slack' periods which occur quite regularly, and always will; when the pressure has to come off in order to preserve sanity. In some businesses, these slack periods manifest themselves as a kind of passive resistance to too much sustained hard work.

**SCRS HAS A SYSTEM FOR MINIMIZING THESE 'SLACK' PERIODS AND KEEPING BOTH PRESSURE AND SANITY AT PEAK.**

Everything and everyone has traditional ways of working, habits, pet likes and dislikes, and an inbuilt resistance to change. Every salesforce also contains a few people who fail to perform simply because they are downright lazy. Very often, therefore the best ways, the most effective ways, of doing the job are never used and results are thus never as good as they could be.

**SCRS HAS A SYSTEM FOR MAKING SURE THE MOST EFFECTIVE WAYS OF DOING THE JOBS ARE THE WAYS EMPLOYED, EVEN BY THOSE NATURALLY LAZY PEOPLE WHOSE CURRENT PERFORMANCE IS MAYBE NOT QUITE POOR ENOUGH TO CONSIDER 'SURGERY'.**

The pressures of everyday business bring yet another problem which limits performance and results. Management and sales-force alike are continually running out of TIME. For management, this reduces thinking time, leadership time and training time. For the salesforce, this invariably reduces the amount of essential planning and preparation that needs to be carried out before any really effective sales call can be made.

As a result, management loses real control and devotes most of the available time to 'fire fighting' while the salesforce spends most of its selling time making 'courtesy calls' on existing customers.

**THE SCRS SYSTEM HAS BEEN DEVELOPED TO GIVE MANAGEMENT MAXIMUM TIME FOR MANAGING AND THE SALESFORCE MAXIMUM TIME FOR EFFECTIVE SELLING.**

If you can identify with ALL these irrefutable facts, if you don't already hold more than a 30% market share and if your gestation period for converting an enquiry into an order is less than three months, the SCRS System can probably DOUBLE YOUR SALES TURNOVER WITHIN A YEAR and reduce your selling costs by a very conservative 10% in the same period.

Here's what one SCRS System user said in 1975 . . .

'We have increased our turnover five fold in the last four years with exactly the same number of sales personnel. The SCRS System has worked better than we ever envisaged.'

**What the SCRS System Will Achieve for You.**

This list is in what we feel is priority order for most businesses that want to substantially increase sales and reduce selling costs.

1. Maximize face-to-face **SELLING** time and make sure every call is an effective call. Minimize abortive calls and courtesy calls. Put customer records to work for your salesforce, so that everyone is chasing **BUSINESS**, not just customers. Increase the number of calls made **BY APPOINTMENT**.

2. Calculate accurately the number of new prospects each member of your salesforce needs to find to achieve his/her **NEW BUSINESS TARGET**, and **MAKE IT ALL HAPPEN**. Monitor by sales territory the effectiveness of sales promotion in generating leads for your salesforce to follow up, so as to maximize new opportunities to **SELL**.

3. Greatly improve the way in which each member of your salesforce plans the week and the month ahead, while at the same time reducing the time devoted to this essential planning. Keep track of next month's **'BEST BETS'**, improve the clarity and accuracy of Action Requests from your salesforce, and generally reduce the quantity of, and time spent on, paperwork to an absolute, practical minimum.

4. Delegate to your salesforce the task of producing accurate, detailed sales forecasts for every individual customer and known prospective customer, and so achieve a degree of **ADVANCE COMMITMENT** for both customer and salesperson which has never before been possible.

5. Measure the current performance of each member of your salesforce, both by **RESULTS** and by **ACTIVITY**. (Measuring just one of these is pretty useless. Both must be measured and used together.) Produce for each three months selling period individual performance ratios and company norms for your salesforce as a whole. Use these performance ratios and norms to set 'By the Inch it's a Cinch' targets for the following three months selling period for each member of your salesforce.

6. Use the performance ratios and norms to pin-point individual problems and training or retraining needs. Identify specific **STRENGTHS** which you can capitalize upon and specific **WEAKNESSES** which can be eliminated, both with all speed. Predict and thus avoid catastrophes.

7. Reduce to an absolute minimum the time spent by management on salesforce related paperwork, results and activity analysis, setting targets, salesforce counselling and 'firefighting', while at the same time knowing that everything is happening as it should be happening. Delegation (to the SCRS system) not Abdication!

8. Provide everything necessary for a new or relief field salesperson to be able to take over a sales territory with **IMMEDIATE FULL EFFECTIVENESS**, should a mem-

ber of your salesforce leave, go on holiday or fall sick.

9. Facilitate proper restructuring of sales territories without salesforce demotivation, to ensure the most effective and the most economical coverage.

10. Give accurate **EARLY WARNING** of products/services and markets which are on the way out or on the way in, and all necessary data for long range resource planning.


## An Example of How the SCRS System Can Double your Sales in Three Months

The activity and performance of each individual salesperson is monitored numerically throughout a thirteen week period. Performance is then summarized in a series of boxes. Individual performance is compared with the average performance for the salesforce as a whole for the same period (the Norm).

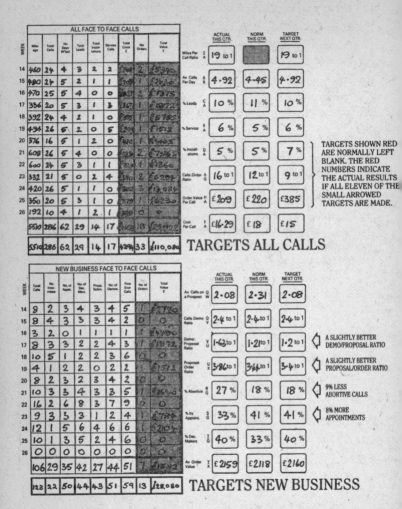

Up to 45 separate performance improvement targets can then be set for the individual for the NEXT thirteen week period – targets that are seen to be EASY to achieve and surpass. No fear complexes, no demotivation, and the flexibility to keep the high

### REPEAT BUSINESS FACE TO FACE CALLS

| WEEK | Total Calls | No Inter views | No of Appls | No of Dec Mkrs | Props Subm | No of Demos | No of Orders | Total Value £ |
|---|---|---|---|---|---|---|---|---|
| 14 | 16 | 1 | 7 | 8 | 2 | 4 | 1 | £2620 |
| 15 | 16 | 1 | 6 | 4 | 2 | 4 | 1 | £2130 |
| 16 | 22 | 0 | 6 | 1 | 1 | 12 | 1 | £2095 |
| 17 | 12 | 1 | 5 | 4 | 2 | 2 | 0 | 0 |
| 18 | 14 | 1 | 4 | 3 | 4 | 3 | 1 | £5755 |
| 19 | 22 | 0 | 6 | 1 | 1 | 4 | 0 | 0 |
| 20 | 8 | 1 | 2 | 2 | 0 | 4 | 1 | £405 |
| 21 | 16 | 2 | 4 | 3 | 2 | 3 | 1 | £5925 |
| 22 | 8 | 2 | 5 | 5 | 6 | 2 | 1 | £1360 |
| 23 | 12 | 2 | 3 | 2 | 2 | 3 | 1 | £2510 |
| 24 | 14 | 0 | 6 | 3 | 6 | 6 | 1 | £2050 |
| 25 | 10 | 0 | 2 | 2 | 2 | 2 | 1 | £4625 |
| 26 | 10 | 3 | 4 | 2 | 2 | 4 | 0 | 0 |
| | 180 | 14 | 60 | 40 | 32 | 53 | 11 | £44,310 |
| | 163 | 11 | 82 | 41 | 39 | 54 | 20 | £82,000 |

| | ACTUAL THIS QTR. | NORM THIS QTR. | TARGET NEXT QTR. | |
|---|---|---|---|---|
| Calls:Demo Ratio | 3·4 to 1 | 4·3 to 1 | 3·0 to 1 | A SLIGHTLY BETTER CALLS/DEMO RATIO |
| Demo:Proposal Ratio | 1·6 to 1 | 1·4 to 1 | 1·4 to 1 | A SLIGHTLY BETTER DEMO/PROPOSAL RATIO |
| Proposal:Order Ratio | 2·9 to 1 | 2·1 to 1 | 2·0 to 1 | WHICH BOTH HELP IMPROVE THE PROPOSAL/ORDER RATIO |
| % Abortive | 7·8% | 9% | 7% | 0.8% LESS ABORTIVE CALLS |
| % by Appoint. | 33% | 46% | 50% | 17% MORE APPOINTMENTS |
| % Dec. Makers | 22% | 15% | 25% | 3% MORE CALLS ON DECISION MAKERS |
| Av. Order Value | £4074 | £3107 | £4100 | A SLIGHTLY BETTER AVERAGE ORDER VALUE |

## TARGETS REPEAT BUSINESS

### PRODUCT GROUP ANALYSIS

| WEEK | 0 | 1 | 2 | 3 | 4 | 5 | 6 | 7 | 8 | 9 |
|---|---|---|---|---|---|---|---|---|---|---|
| 14 | 2 | 1 | 3 | 4 | 1 | - | 3 | 2 | 8 | 2 |
| 15 | 1 | 4 | 3 | 6 | - | - | 2 | 1 | 4 | 3 |
| 16 | 3 | 1 | 4 | 7 | 1 | 1 | 3 | 3 | 8 | 4 |
| 17 | 1 | 1 | 2 | 3 | - | - | 1 | 1 | 6 | 3 |
| 18 | 2 | 2 | 2 | 2 | 1 | - | 3 | 3 | 8 | 2 |
| 19 | 3 | 4 | 4 | 5 | 2 | 1 | 3 | 3 | 7 | 5 |
| 20 | 2 | 1 | 3 | 3 | 1 | 1 | 2 | 4 | 7 | 4 |
| 21 | 1 | - | 1 | 5 | 2 | - | 3 | 3 | 6 | 5 |
| 22 | 1 | 2 | 3 | 4 | 1 | - | 2 | 4 | 7 | 5 |
| 23 | - | - | 1 | 2 | - | - | 1 | 2 | 3 | 1 |
| 24 | 4 | 3 | 3 | 6 | 2 | 2 | 4 | 4 | 6 | 4 |
| 25 | 2 | 1 | 2 | 3 | 1 | 1 | 2 | 3 | 5 | 3 |
| 26 | 1 | 2 | 1 | 2 | - | - | 1 | 3 | 7 | 5 |
| TOTALS | 23 | 22 | 32 | 51 | 12 | 6 | 30 | 38 | 82 | 46 |
| NORM | 23 | 23 | 26 | 53 | 12 | 23 | 24 | 36 | 72 | 48 |
| TARGET | 23 | 23 | 30 | 48 | 15 | 25 | 25 | 35 | 70 | 46 |

### INDUSTRY CATEGORY ANALYSIS

| WEEK | A | B | C | D | E | F | G | H | J | K |
|---|---|---|---|---|---|---|---|---|---|---|
| 14 | 7 | 6 | 2 | 5 | - | - | 2 | - | 1 | 1 |
| 15 | 6 | 4 | 3 | 2 | 1 | 2 | 4 | - | 1 | 1 |
| 16 | 5 | 3 | 4 | 2 | 2 | 3 | 3 | 1 | 1 | 1 |
| 17 | 3 | 2 | 4 | 3 | 1 | 1 | 4 | - | 2 | - |
| 18 | 4 | 4 | 2 | 4 | 2 | 2 | 4 | - | 2 | - |
| 19 | 6 | 3 | 4 | 1 | 1 | 1 | 4 | 1 | 3 | 2 |
| 20 | - | 4 | 3 | - | - | 2 | 3 | 2 | - | 2 |
| 21 | 4 | 5 | 2 | 3 | 1 | 1 | 2 | 3 | 2 | 3 |
| 22 | 3 | 4 | 3 | 2 | 2 | - | 2 | 3 | 5 | - |
| 23 | 1 | 1 | 2 | - | 1 | - | 1 | - | 3 | 1 |
| 24 | 7 | 3 | 2 | 4 | 1 | 1 | 2 | 2 | 4 | - |
| 25 | 1 | 2 | 4 | 3 | - | - | 3 | 2 | 5 | - |
| 26 | 3 | - | 2 | 4 | 2 | 1 | 3 | 2 | 2 | 1 |
| TOTALS | 50 | 41 | 37 | 33 | 14 | 14 | 37 | 17 | 31 | 13 |
| NORM | 54 | 32 | 37 | 33 | 12 | 7 | 34 | 16 | 29 | 14 |
| TARGET | 50 | 30 | 35 | 35 | 20 | 20 | 35 | 15 | 30 | 15 |

> BY THE INCH IT'S A CINCH
>
> IF IT'S NUMBERS NOT WORDS
>
> AND YOU **DON'T** NEED A COMPUTER

### PRODUCTS – SECONDARY TARGETS – MARKETS

flyers stretching themselves further while properly guiding the new recruits until they've found their feet. In this example, eleven easy to achieve targets are shown arrowed. The RED figures show the catalytic effect on RESULTS of achieving these eleven easy targets – practically doubling sales in just three months.

After two such periods, performance improvement normally continues automatically, because everyone is doing the job the RIGHT way. Then it is only a matter of time before maximum market penetration is achieved – and at minimum cost.

## The SCRS System Overcomes that Inherent Dislike of Paperwork

Although it is a paper-based System, SCRS reduces salesforce paperwork to a practical minimum and quickly makes the members of your salesforce realize that the paper they HAVE to process is not only essential to their success – it also actually makes it EASIER for them to do their job well. Everyone knows that when it comes to work, salespeople tend to take the line of least resistance. SCRS harnesses this line.

The SCRS System is designed so that the sales manager can process the monitoring and measuring end of the system paperwork semi-automatically. For a salesforce of ten, about one hour per week is all that is necessary, plus no more than a day at the end of each thirteen week period. And all the data recorded is in permanent hard copy, easy to assimilate, form.

The SCRS System is very easy to use. It covers salesforce reporting, planning, forecasting and customer records as well as performance monitoring, target setting and performance improvements. It has proven itself a thousand times to be more acceptable as a change in operating procedure than any other type of system – both to the field salesforce and to management.

A key reason for SCRS's success lies in its pedigree. The System was devised in the late 1960's by John Fenton and has been developed over fifteen years from the combined experience and knowhow of many thousands of practising sales executives. There are currently more than 7000 users of the SCRS System in the UK alone.

The SCRS System is marketed in the UK by Sales Control & Record Systems Ltd. The Company is part of the Sales Augmentation International Group and works closely with sister company, Structured Training Limited and with the Institute of Sales & Marketing Management. Both these organizations have contributed to the development and perfecting of the SCRS System. The System is sold under licence in several other countries.

HARRISON & SONS (LONDON) LIMITED

A Member of the Harrison Group

Printing House Lane
Hayes Middlesex
UB3 1HQ England
Telephone 01 573 3628
Telex 23744

Directors
R T H Harrison MA Chairman
R A Boxall Managing Director
B L Hibbitt
K F H Leathers ACMA
D S Robinson

Registered Office
Harrison House Coates Lane
High Wycombe Buckinghamshire
HP13 5EZ England
Registered Number
882698 England

Mr. Peter Bosworth
Managing Director
Sales Control and Record Systems Limited
Concorde House
24 Warwick New Road
Royal Leamington Spa
West Midlands
CV32 5JH

14 March 1978

Dear Peter

Since our last meeting at Hayes I have carried out a new 20-day time log and analysis and, as agreed, I kept SCRS activities under a separate heading.

In the twenty working days following Monday, 6 February, SCRS for my six people occupied only 3hr. 05min (1.45%) of my time. Which is about half an hour per week for the whole group or five minutes per man per week.

It really is astonishing how little time is needed once the system is running smoothly and it is easy to find this amount of time and, more important, the return on the time spent is quite enormous.

I hope you find this information interesting and maybe useful to you.

Kind regards.

Yours sincerely

*Fred Pamphilion*

Fred Pamphilion
Graphic Design and Print Sales

## What You Buy When You Buy the SCRS System

SCRS is a System which has cost several hundred thousand pounds to develop and perfect – a System for salesforce performance improvement which no sales manager, setting out to design his own system from scratch, could hope to emulate, even if it were possible to devote a year to the task, to the exclusion of all other management duties. SCRS is the immediate solution to a major problem which, if it is not resolved, will continue to cost your business dearly.

When you buy the SCRS System, you are buying a share in this development. You are also buying the rights to use, for your business only, SCRS's copyrighted designs for the forms, files, cards and pads which are included in the System.

When you buy the SCRS System, you are buying everything you need to operate the System for one complete year; you are buying professional implementation training for your entire sales team and you are buying guidance notes, management check lists and back-up video and audio cassettes to help you use the System fully.

You are buying the peace of mind which comes from knowing you are using a System which has been proven highly effective for hundreds of other companies – proof you have seen with your own eyes. You are buying the long-term security which comes from knowing you are dealing direct with the Principal, not with a 'middle man', with a Principal that is British, financially stable and that employs top calibre people to make sure YOUR System continues to give you the best results.

When you buy the SCRS System, you are buying QUALITY. Everything about the System – customer record files, marine ply car storage cabinets, ring binders, survey pads, the paperwork and printing – is top quality. The SCRS System generates respect for itself by virtue of the quality it invests in its own packaging and presentation. Any salesforce prefers to use quality tools. From this respect comes proper use, not abuse.

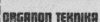

RJM/LAB

Organon Teknika Limited
Science Park
Milton Road
Cambridge CB4 4BH
Telephone Cambridge (0223) 313650
Telex 818866

3rd December, 1984

Mr. P. Bosworth,
Managing Director,
S.C.R.S. Limited,
Concorde House,
24 Warwick New Road,
Royal Leamington Spa,
Warwickshire.    CV32 5JH

Dear Peter,

It is now nearly two years since our company first introduced the S.C.R.S.
Recording System.

Over this period we have noticed 4 main improvements :-

1.  Increased 'face to face' time with customers.

2.  Better Journey and Call Plans, the end result being more cost effective.

3.  Increased sales for new business, particularly in the last year.

4.  A significant reduction in 'lost' orders.

In addition, new sales personnel joining the company have been able to adapt
to the system easily and quickly.

I believe we have already covered the cost of the system many times over.

Yours sincerely,

R. J. Melhuish,
Sales Manager

Directors A S Whitfield (Managing) B H M van Dommelen

Organon Teknika Limited
Registered Office Crown Lodge, Crown Road, Morden, Surrey SM4 5BY
Registered in England No 1231261

## The Cost of the SCRS System

The complete SCRS System, for both field salesforce and sales
manager, including customer record files and cards, storage cabi-

nets, sales manager's control files, company master file and manager's remedial action check lists – everything necessary for one full year's effective operation – costs £495 + VAT per salesperson.

A one-off extra charge is made for any special artwork required to tailor the System to a customer's unique requirements.

System forms and cards for a subsequent full year's operation cost approx. £75 + VAT per salesperson, including post and packing.

These prices apply to UK only.

The SCRS System can be RENTED on a three year all inclusive inflation proof rental agreement. Ask for full details if this is of interest.

### Implementation Training

One day's 'hands on' training for the customer's sales team at Concorde House, Royal Leamington Spa, at which the SCRS System is handed over to the customer's personnel; including back-up video and audio cassettes for management, coffees, luncheons and teas, costs £495 + VAT.

A subsequent day's training at Concorde House, to evaluate the first quarter's operation of the SCRS System, including coffees, luncheons and teas, costs £295 + VAT.

### But Does it REALLY Cost you a Penny?

Anyone seriously considering the acquisition of a System like SCRS is going to ask – 'How quickly will we get our investment back?'

There are probably a hundred ways you can get full pay back inside the first six months, so that in real terms, the SCRS System won't cost you a penny. Here are four specific examples:

## 30% More Sales and the Costs of SCRS Covered in Month One

A company in capital equipment, with a salesforce of 16, 3 regional managers and a general sales manager, decided to rent the SCRS System, rather than buy it outright.

Business was 20% below target. The main objective for the first six months from introducing SCRS was to get the company back on target and also to cover the monthly rentals for the SCRS System with savings made in selling costs.

The far greater objectivity introduced into the salesforce with SCRS sharpened up attitudes towards positive selling rather than technical consulting. After one month's monitoring, targets were set, with the help of one of SCRS's executives, for 'By the Inch it's a Cinch' performance improvements. All outstanding proposals were re-examined and every 'live' potential order was given top priority treatment. The target set was to improve the Proposals to Order ratio from 10 to 1 down to 8 to 1.

Being essentially a 'one-off' business, methods of prospecting were improved, in the light of the ratios generated by the SCRS System. Targets were set for increasing First Ever Calls, Appointments, calls on Decision Makers rather than on decision influencers, and for improving the ratio of Calls to Demonstrations.

Into month four, the company was back on target. By the end of month six, it was 10% over target and, as a result of the performance improvement achieved, the Gestation period – the average time needed to convert an enquiry into an order – had reduced from 5 months to 4 months.

The more detailed analysis of products being sold pin-pointed a greater potential for selling accessories and maintenance contracts. Targets were set for this 'Added Value' business and by month six the A.O.V. had increased by 4%.

One member of the salesforce was found, from the SCRS analysis, to be concentrating too heavily on one particular product (the one he'd lived with since his apprenticeship days). Straightening out this salesman improved his individual sales turnover by 45% in the first six months.

Only one member of the salesforce refused to adjust to the new ways of working that the SCRS System required and had to be replaced.

The cost of the SCRS System for the 16 salesforce, 3 regional managers and the general sales manager was £600 + VAT per month, this rental figure remaining fixed and inflation proof for the 3 years of the SCRS rental contract.

Over the six months subsequent to introducing SCRS, savings in selling costs, including petrol, abortive calls, a reduction in proposals submitted to non-serious prospects, use of referral techniques to find new prospects instead of direct mail shots, and the servicing of certain customers by telephone instead of by personal calls, was calculated to be around £14,500.

In SCRS terms (numbers not words) the Cost per Call reduced from £28 to £21 and the Sales Value per Call increased from £255 to £325.

## £7,400 Saved on Petrol

A salesforce of eight, using the SCRS System, pin-pointed that 35% of all calls being made were unnecessary calls (chasing customers, not chasing business). Four months into introducing SCRS, all these unnecessary calls had been eliminated and targets set for making a corresponding number of effective calls, but within the closest possible vicinity of the 65% of calls that were producing business.

As a result, orders increased dramatically and the mileage travelled by the salesforce reduced by 39%.

The salesforce averaged 34,000 miles per year per person. In a full year, this was reduced to 20,740. A total saving of 106,080 miles per year for the team. At an average of 26.5 miles per gallon and a price of £1.85 per gallon, the saving on petrol costs in this first full year was £7,400.

The cost of the SCRS System for the first year, salesforce and management attending a one-day implementation at SCRS's headquarters, was <u>£4,455 + VAT.</u>

### £1.5 Million Extra Sales by Increasing the A.O.V. and £75,000 Saved on Sales Promotion

The regional and national sales managers of a salesforce of 38, selling a range of regular repeating products into several markets, pin-pointed through using the SCRS System that the salesforce was under-selling four of the products and into two of the markets.

Some swift product training sessions on the four neglected products and a re-direction of some of the sales promotion to generate more enquiries from the two neglected markets, increased the average order value by 12%. Total sales volume increased in the month following the product training sessions and re-directed promotion by £128,000.

From this first month's success, the regional and national sales managers continued to use the SCRS System's analysis of products and markets to plan monthly product training sessions and sales promotion campaigns.

In the first full year of this programme, sales increased by £1.5 million as a direct result and the sales promotion spend reduced by £75,000.

The cost of the SCRS System for the 38 salesforce, 7 regional managers and 1 national sales manager, including 7 separate implementations by an SCRS executive for the regional sales teams, was <u>£19,820 + VAT.</u>

## A £24,400-per-month Boost in Sales

One of SCRS's customers had been monitoring its salesforce the SCRS way for a month. It had already established that the average order value for repeat business was £500 and the average order value for first orders from newly opened accounts was £400. 40% of its salesforce's calls had been repeat business calls, 60% had been new business calls. They'd been averaging 6 calls per day over a 20 working day month.

For repeat business, 6 calls resulted in 1 order, 20% of repeat business calls were abortive calls and 30% of calls were made by appointment.

For new business, for every 4 first ever calls made, 1 proposal was submitted, and for every 5 proposals submitted, 1 order was secured. 25% of new business calls were first ever calls.

Now that his ten salesmen had the SCRS System, the sales manager knew how to cut the 20% abortive calls down to easily 10% for the remaining two months of the first quarter and into the second quarter. He also knew how to get the salesforce to increase that 30% of calls made by appointment – he aimed for 50% for starters. As a result, the sales manager and the entire salesforce were confidently targeting to improve the repeat business calls to order ratio from 6 to 1 down to 4 to 1.

For new business, with the numbers and know-how he now had, the sales manager targeted his salesforce to aim for an improvement in the first ever calls to proposals and the proposals to order ratios. He targeted these at 3 to 1 and 4 to 1, reducing just by one digit in each case, and increased the 25% first ever calls to 33⅓%.

By the end of month three, the salesforce was well over half way there. By the end of the second quarter, they had achieved all these initial targets. The customer's resultant monthly sales turnover increased like this:

Total calls made = 10 salesmen x 6 calls/day x 20 days/month = 1200

40% repeat business = 480 calls. At 6 to 1 calls to order ratio = 80 orders.

At £500 average order value = £40,000.

Improving calls to order ratio to 4 to 1 . . . 480 calls will give 120 orders = £60,000.

60% new business = 720 calls. At 25% first ever calls = 180 f.e. calls.

At 4 to 1 f.e. calls to proposals ratio . . . 180 f.e. calls gives 45 proposals.

At 5 to 1 proposals to order ratio . . . 45 proposals give 9 orders.

At £400 average order value = £3,600

Improving % first ever calls to 33⅓% = 240 f.e. calls.

Improving f.e. calls to proposals ratio to 3 to 1 . . . 240 f.e. calls gives 80 proposals.

Improving proposals to orders ratio to 4 to 1 . . . 80 proposals give 20 orders.

At £400 average order value = £8,000.

Total improvement in sales turnover =
    £20,000 repeat business

plus £ 4,400 new business
    ——————
    £24,400 per month
    ——————

Cost of the SCRS System for the salesforce of 10, including implementation, was £5,445 + VAT.

Increase in selling costs to effect this extra sales turnover – Nil.

**EG&G SEALOL**

SEALOL LIMITED, SALISBURY ROAD, UXBRIDGE, UB8 2SN, ENGLAND
TELEPHONE UXBRIDGE 39411-4 (STD CODE 0895) TELEX 267849

YOUR REFERENCE                                OUR REFERENCE
                                              CJS/MY

                                              21st March, 1979

Sales Control & Record Systems Ltd.,
Concorde House,
24 Warwick New Road,
Royal Leamington Spa,
Warwickshire
CV32 5JH.

For the attention of Mr. P. Bosworth – Managing Director.

Dear Mr. Bosworth,

    We have now operated the S.C.R.S. system for eighteen months
and believe the time is now right to compliment S.C.R.S. Ltd. in
providing such a comprehensive aid to any field sales organisation.

    The system has been well received by all members of the sales
force and has assisted us in analysing our weak areas while
capitalising in areas of strength. The ease of access to such
information is one of the major advantages of this system.

    Wishing you every success in the future.

                          Yours sincerely,
                          SEALOL LIMITED

                          C.J. STRASZEWSKI
                          FIELD SALES MANAGER

**Hargreaves Fertiliser Industries Limited**

South Mills, Blunham, Bedford MK44 3PJ
Telephone: Biggleswade 40394 Telex: 82494 HARWIL

Directors
K T G Atkins Chairman and Managing Director
R D Dunn N.D.A          J N Hood B.Sc
D Goodwin               B Naylor F.C.M.A
G Hart                  J Steedman

4th August 1982

Our Ref: EBC/AM

S.C.R.S. Limited,
Concorde House,
24 Warwick New Road,
Royal Leamington Spa,
Warks.

For the attention of Mr. P. Bosworth

Dear Peter,

It is now just over 12 months since you helped us instal the SCRS into the
Company and I am writing to thank you for the help and support you have given us
during this time.

Besides reducing the amount of paperwork our salesforce and office handle we are
now in a position to give more objective help to our salesforce in terms of
training, counselling, appraisal and personal development.

Our managers have more confidence in planning since their judgements are
backed-up with important 'activity data' facts.

We are looking forward to our next stage in the system which involves full
computerisation and other activities which are helping in the success of our
sales operation.

Best Wishes.

Yours sincerely,

E.B. CHARNLEY  B.Sc. Dip. M.S.
General Sales Manager
Southern Sales Area.

A MEMBER OF HARGREAVES FERTILISERS LTD
Registered Office Skeldergate Bridge York YO1 1DR    Registered in England No 882661

**Some Words on Computerization**

Our final reference letter ends with a mention of computerization. Hargreaves Fertilizer Industries Ltd, employs 89 field salesmen who sell direct to farmers. They use a specially tailored SCRS System.

Hargreaves is a large company where the span of control – the number of salesmen controlled by one sales manager – made computerization of the SCRS numerical analysis data desirable. The company's existing mainframe computer was used and the SCRS data was merged into order and expenses data derived from other input sources.

SCRS does not recommend the computerization of its System on any kind of a 'stand alone' basis, because the System is much simpler and FASTER to use in its paper-based form. There are many thousands of micro salesmen who would argue this point and there is undoubtedly a temptation to 'keep up with the Joneses' by moving into the micro technology era, but never has 'stand alone' computerization of salesforce data proved cost effective.

SCRS is, however, deeply involved in the development of 'add-on' computerized hardware and software packages for specific functions.

One is the use of graphic tablets and light pens which recognize handwritten numbers and feed the data into a micro as it is being written by the sales manager on the System forms illustrated earlier. ZERO INPUT TIME and an even faster number crunching capability, for more detailed analysis, future projections and 'what if' forecasting, is the objective.

To SCRS, introducing a computer package is like introducing a new drug. All the experimentation, testing and proving-out has to be done very thoroughly indeed before the product reaches the market. The lack of thorough proving-out of new computer hardware and software, coupled with incompetent mis-matching, is one of the major problems faced by the micro industry today.

**The Rainbow Book**

The next example shows what can be done to systemize the production of a really good selling Proposal, with the salesforce collecting all the input they need from the prospective customer, at the Survey stage, in a specific format and order.

This input is then fed to the sales office and the resultant Proposal is developed on a word processor in minimum time, with minimum margin for errors, using standard printed sheets wherever possible.

The example I'm using, which came to be known as 'The Rainbow Book', is a kind of classic in the business. I developed the format for a company selling materials handling equipment, in 1974. It could be used, with only minor adjustments, for just about any kind of product which increases production or reduces costs.

The salesforce were equipped with A4 size ring binders, in which they carried eight different check lists, separated by black index cards. Each check list was in pad form, each pad containing about 25 sheets. Each different checklist pad was printed on a different coloured paper, for ease of identification. Thus, if you looked at the edge of the ring binder, you saw about an inch thick of multi-coloured rainbow striped paper. Hence the origin of 'The Rainbow Book'.

The first check list in the binder was the **objectives** checklist I referred to earlier in this book. Here it is again, so that you don't lose the thread of this example by turning back a hundred or so pages.

Following on from the first **objectives** check list were seven specific check lists, each one relating to one of the seven objectives on the first sheet.

Thus, if the sales engineer identified with his prospective customer that the objectives in this particular selling case were to reduce labour requirement, to increase production and to reduce handling time – in that priority order, he would turn to the three relevant check lists in his binder and use them, face-to-face with the prospective customer, to calculate the **financial justification**.

Doing this face-to-face really turned the customer on. He

# OBJECTIVES

Customer _____

Date _____

**What does the Customer want to do – and why does he want to do it?**

| Detailed objectives that this Customer wants to achieve (Strike out the sections which do not apply) | Order of Priority |
|---|---|
| INCREASE PRODUCTION/THROUGHPUT/VEHICLE TURNROUND | |
| REDUCE HANDLING TIME | |
| REDUCE LABOUR REQUIREMENT | |
| REDUCE MAINTENANCE COSTS | |
| BETTER UTILISATION OF EQUIPMENT | |
| BETTER UTILISATION OF SPACE | |
| IMPROVE LABOUR RELATIONS/SAFETY (Union attitude, accident rate, absenteeism, fatigue) | |
| OTHER FACTORS? | |

could see very clearly indeed how much he was going to make and save if he went ahead and bought the equipment which the sales engineer was proposing.

The sales engineer always told the prospective customer why he needed to define the objectives on his first check list in words which would be most meaningful to the customer – because those words would be featured in the resultant Proposal, precisely as agreed. He also told the customer that the Financial Justification check lists used for these objectives, would be included in the Proposal, in exactly the same format. So when the Proposal arrived, the customer knew precisely what to expect and was already half sold.

If the sales engineer was faced with a middle management contact who had to sell the idea to his own board of directors, he knew that he had put his contact through a kind of training course and given him the very best ammunition with which to sell the idea to the ultimate decision-makers.

Here are examples of three of the seven Financial Justification check lists:

**Reductions in Labour Requirement**

Customer _____

Date _____

|  | Present method | Proposed new method |
|---|---|---|
| Number of staff involved |  |  |
| Man hours per day |  |  |
| Man hours per week |  |  |
| Man hours per year |  |  |
| Cost per man hour (rate plus overheads) |  |  |
| Labour cost per year |  |  |

Target savings in labour costs in first year £_____ (figure A)

Customer's plant depreciation period _____ years

Assuming a _____ % per year increase in labour costs, the savings in labour costs for the entire plant depreciation period would be:

| First year (A) | _____ | £ |
| 2nd year (A + %) | _____ | £ |
| 3rd year (2nd + %) | _____ | £ |
| 4th year (3rd + %) | _____ | £ |
| 5th year (4th + %) | _____ | £ |
| 6th year (5th + %) | _____ | £ |
| 7th year (6th + %) | _____ | £ |
|  |  | £ _____ |

On labour savings alone, the cost of the new equipment is amortized over approximately _____ months/years

**Increases in Production**

Customer _____

Date _____

One Unit =

|  | Present method | Proposed new method |
|---|---|---|
| Units per hour | | |
| Units per day | | |
| Units per week | | |
| Units per year | | |
| Customer's plant depreciation period | | |
| Thus, Units produced over this period | | |

Target *increase* in Units produced – per year
                              – over depreciation period
Value of one Unit      £
Total money this value represents when
related to the increase in production
over the plant depreciation period _____ £

═══════════════════════════════════════════════

**Reductions in Handling Time**

Customer _____

Date _____

One Unit =

|  | Present method | Proposed new method |
|---|---|---|
| Units handled/hour | | |
| Units handled/day | | |
| Units handled/week | | |
| Units handled/year | | |

Improvement in number of Units handled/year

Number of staff
involved in handling

| | Present method | Proposed new method |
|---|---|---|
| time/day | man hours | man hours |
| time/week | man hours | man hours |
| time/year | man hours | man hours |

Thus, man hours available for re-deployment/ year _____

At £_____ per hour cost, this represents a
                         saving per year of _____

═══════════════════════════════════════════════

The Rainbow Book became a classic by accident. It was just a black ring binder until the accident happened.

One of the sales engineers ran out of space in his briefcase and walked into the office of a Yorkshire-based prospective customer with the ring binder under his arm. The customer took one look at the edge of the binder, guffawed and said, 'What've you got there, a bloody rainbow?'

The sales engineer didn't know where to put himself, crumbled and screwed up the call completely. A week later, he was relating the story at one of the monthly meetings I was running for the Company.

Another member of the salesforce commented that he'd had a similar occurrence. We put our thinking caps on and in half an hour had come up with a beautiful new technique.

Henceforth, every sales engineer, every call, went in with the Rainbow Book under his arm, in full view – inviting a ribald comment.

'What's that then, with all the different colours?'

'Ah. This is what I use to work out how much money we can make or save you,' the sales engineers were instructed to respond, patting the ring binder fondly.

And every time, the customer said just what we'd predicted he would say – 'Well, let's start with that, then!'

No preamble, no getting themselves comfortable, no outline of the product range. Open the Rainbow Book and get straight into the Objectives checklist, explaining for each objective how the Company's equipment could do it, and asking all the key questions, in the first five minutes. A veritable gold brick.

And the **fun** the salesforce got out of doing business this way!

When the Proposal was generated by the sales office, the first page looked like this, the gaps being filled in by the word processor typist from the sales engineer's very concise checklists.

Dear Mr—

Our Sales Engineer,—,has asked me to write to you following his recent visit to your factory, to confirm that we can certainly provide an economical answer to your (problem) and to outline our proposals on this project.

As I understand it, you want to achieve the following objectives:

1 _____

2 _____

3 _____

We believe these objectives can best be achieved by using the equipment I have detailed on the attached sheet.

The financial and other tangible benefits to you and your company of using this equipment are set out on the subsequent attached sheets, together with details of how quickly the cost of the equipment can be amortized, from the savings you will be making.

The final attached sheet details our guarantee and after-sales service scheme. It also lists some of the many companies who are currently using our equipment. I know these companies will not mind if you ask them what they think of the quality and reliability of the products we have supplied to them over the years.

Mr (Sales Engineer) tells me that you are hoping to have your equipment installed and in operation by—. To meet this deadline confidently, we will need your order or letter of intent by—, which will allow us the time necessary for us to manufacture, thoroughly test, deliver and instal this equipment.

I hope I have interpreted your requirements correctly and fully. If not, please will you let me know immediately.

Yours sincerely

---

## How to Win when Delivery is Critical and Yours is Longer

The last example of how to put together a good selling Proposal contains two paragraphs on delivery. You'll see that nowhere is delivery quoted as 10/12 weeks or 4/6 weeks or whatever is the current going rate.

The reason is, if you give a prospective customer a 10/12 weeks delivery date and your competitor gives him 4/6 weeks, you may lose the business on that point alone. And it's only a critical point if the customer needs the goods yesterday. If you're selling something which isn't going to be used for some time to come, the **last** thing you want to do is to quote the customer 10/12 weeks.

Agree with him a date for installation of the equipment, or a date most convenient for him to accept delivery – then work back from this date and **tell him** the date by which he needs to have placed the order with you.

Then there is no way the customer can compare your delivery time with your competitors. And you have a new found sense of urgency when you follow up that Proposal:

'Morning, Mr Jones. I'm getting a bit worried about your schedule. If we're going to meet your delivery date, we need your order by Friday. Any chance of you getting me the order number?'

Most times, the delay is only because the customer is dragging his feet, hoping for a better deal to come along or simply because he's not a very good decision-maker. So help him over the hump!

# How to use the Proposal when there's . . .

## Just You and the Decision-Maker

When you do business on a one-to-one basis, just you and your customer's key decision-maker, have you ever asked yourself **why** he asks you for a quotation or a Proposal in writing when you've just done the best selling job in your life?

Okay, if you're up against strong competition, he's going to compare your deal with someone else's. Maybe he's going to play dutch auctions. So you need a Proposal, not a quotation.

But what if you're **not** up against competition? Why does he want a quotation or Proposal from you then? Maybe because he's got just so much money to spend, and a number of different things he could spend it on. So he wants to be sure he's spending the money on the thing that'll do his business the most good. So you need a Proposal, not a quotation.

There are other reasons, however. The sneakier reasons. He just doesn't want to go ahead yet, and he's stalling for time. He isn't sure and wants time to think it over. He has decided 'NO', but lacks the guts to tell you No – so instead he says, 'Okay, looks promising. Send me a quotation and I'll consider it and let you know.'

Or maybe it's because he's always done business that way, or it's Company policy always to have a record of things bought, before they're bought, in case things go wrong and they need someone to blame. (Someone other than **him**!)

Or maybe **you** tender a quotation because it's **your** company policy, whether the customer asks for one or not.

Whatever the reason, you'll do more business, win more orders, if you submit a Proposal, not a quotation.

And when you have gone to the trouble of preparing a good Proposal and you're selling on a one-to-one basis, there is one absolutely critical golden rule: **If you want to win – take it in**.

Don't send the Proposal through the post. Okay, if you have to, you still have a better chance of winning if you're up against competition and the customer wants to compare two or more deals and decide which is best – it won't just be a question of price if you present him with a Proposal and your competitors send him quotations. But for all the other situations I've mentioned – if you want to win, take it in. Telephone and make a firm appointment.

'Morning, Mr Jones. We've completed our proposals and I'm ready to bring them in and go through them with you. I'd like to do this rather than post them to you, just to make absolutely sure we've got everything right. Would tomorrow morning suit you, or would you prefer the afternoon, say, about 4.30 pm?' The very best competitive Sellers stick to their guns even when the customer replies – 'I'm very busy just now. Put it in the post, will you?'

'With respect, Mr Jones, it's very important to us that we've got everything right, and I think it's very important to you. We're talking about being able to save you something like £27,000 a year. If this week's out, how about next week? I'd rather lose a week and make sure we've interpreted your requirements absolutely correctly. How does next Wednesday look, I'm within fifteen miles of you in the afternoon?'

So you take it in. Top copy for the customer, a copy for you, in case you need to make amendments, and the file copy. And you take the customer through the Proposal from start to finish, getting his agreement to everything you've said, step-by-step.

'When we conducted the survey, Mr Jones, you said these were the Objectives you wanted to achieve. (Go through the list of customer's objectives at beginning of Proposal.) Now, are these objectives still valid, or has anything happened since our survey to change them in any way?' (Pause: count silently to five, wait for his okay or information on changes. If changes, decide whether you can proceed or instead gather new information and re-submit the Proposal.)

It's incredible how quickly things change in any kind of business. How do you find out whether your listed Objectives are still valid if you **post** the Proposal?

Assuming the Objectives **are** still valid, you get his agreement to your list, then you move on to Your Recommendations. Once again, get his agreement that the way you are proposing the job is done meets with his approval – and that he fully understands **how** his objectives will be achieved.

Move on to the Summary of Benefits. Again, his agreement to your list. Then into the Financial Justification. Go through the calculations and projections, making sure he agrees with the figures and that you haven't exaggerated at all (a good basis is never to assume more than 80% of what you **know** you can do for him). At the end of this section, ask him, 'Are these kind of savings what you are looking for, or should we see if we can get more?' Your figures are likely to be a lot **more** than he was hoping for, so he'll probably say 'No, they look fine to me.' So you have agreement on the Justification.

One more step to go. Through the guarantee and after-sales service section. Through the third party references. Agreement on this last section.

Both of you lean back in your chairs. 'Fine, Mr Jones. Thank you very much for going through it all with me. You're happy with everything then?'

He can't say 'No'. He can't even say 'Maybe'. He's said 'Yes' to every section in the Proposal. He can only say '**yes**', now.

So you have the Proposal's wonderfully simple **built in, automatic close** . . .

'Can we go ahead, then?'

And he ain't got no place to go!

# How to use the Proposal when there's . . .

You          Your Contact and His Boss

This is why **most** people you sell to ask you for a quotation. They aren't the person who makes the decision. Often they never tell you this, because they feel they'd deflate their egos if they did. Some are simply full of their own self-importance, building their own empires, and have lost sight of the real reason they are there – which is to get the best deal they can for their company, make it as efficient as possible, save as much money as they can, whichever fits their job specification.

Where you should be selling to the boss, you find yourself selling to his lackey. And his lackey will **never** let you through to talk direct to the boss.

So you have to sell to your contact and he then has to persuade his boss that the deal is a good one. He's your classic unpaid, untrained, un-motivated amateur salesman.

Think about the problems. What do you want your contact to talk to his boss about? Which benefits do you want him to stress? What kind of things will turn his boss on – and turn his boss off?

What ammunition do you give your contact to help him sell the deal to his boss? (remember the Rainbow Book?) He has your sales brochures, your specification sheets, but will he be able to find them when he gets the opportunity to talk to his boss? Will he even bother to look?

You told him in detail about the benefits and you worked out for him how much better the deal should be in financial terms, didn't you? But will your contact remember much of this when he gets to talk to his boss? Not likely!

More often than not, it will be just your Proposal a contact uses when he's trying to sell a deal to his boss, plus what he can remember of what you told him when you were face-to-face, which won't be much.

Just imagine, therefore, what sort of job he does if all you've given him is the traditional legal Quotation document.

Here is a table of statistics on *recall* – the amount people remember of information conveyed to them after varying periods of time. There are three methods listed for the way the information is conveyed – the three methods we all use when we are Selling.

You can see clearly from this table how important it is to communicate properly – using all the senses, using your voice **and** appropriate visual aids. A sales presentation conducted with just the voice and no visual aids whatsoever is the worst of all when it comes to remembering afterwards what was said. Just pictures and no voice at all is better than just the voice.

Percentage recall of information

| Method of conveying information | 3 hours later (%) | 3 days later (%) | 3 weeks later (%) | 3 months later (%) |
|---|---|---|---|---|
| Telling and showing together | 85 | 65 | 28 | 16 |
| Showing (just pictures) | 72 | 20 | 12 | 7 |
| Telling (just voice) | 70 | 10 | 7 | 3 |

So couple these statistics to what I was saying about your contact and his efforts to sell on to his boss. He has no chance of success unless he desperately **wants** the deal you're proposing. He has no chance of success unless you arm him with a proper selling Proposal, complete with all relevant sales literature and specification sheets, in a format which will enable the boss to pick it up cold, read it, ask a few questions of your contact and say, 'Yes, we'll buy this.'

What chance of winning have you got if you **don't** – and your competitors **do**?

# How to use the Proposal when there's . . .

You        Your Contact and His Board

From your point of view, you're up against the same set of problems that you faced when your contact had to sell on to his boss. Except this time your contact has a bigger problem. Instead of just **one** boss, with pet things that turn him on and off, we now have several bosses, each with different backgrounds, expertise, attitudes, vested interests and phobias.

Some of them, if it's a highly technical Proposal, won't understand the first thing about the equipment you're proposing, but they'll still expect to make a contribution to the decision-making process – and they'll certainly understand your Financial Justification figures if you've done them correctly.

The very least you need to do when faced with this situation is to make sure that every member of the board has a copy of your Proposal, **in advance** of the board meeting, if a formal meeting has been scheduled during which your Proposal, and your competitors' proposals, are due to be considered. If your competitors haven't taken the trouble to do this, you're going to win hands down.

## How to use the Proposal when there's . . .

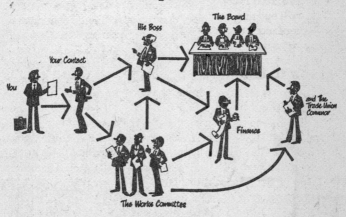

This is an extremely 'popular' situation, meaning it occurs all too frequently!

You sell to a single middle-management contact, who then has to sell to his boss. But your contact is also a member of the works committee, and your deal is discussed in committee.

The works committee can communicate directly with the boss – and does so daily. The boss can communicate directly with the works committee, but avoids this like the plague.

Then the boss has to sell the deal **again**, both to finance on budgetary grounds and to the board of directors on principle. It's called 'keeping your station!' Every medium to large business suffers from it. The multi-nationals and conglomerates are full of it.

Finance share the same feelings as the boss towards the works committee. Finance also has a direct line to the board of directors, of course.

Finally, the works committee discusses **everything** with the trade union convenor (or convenors; one per trade union) who is probably a member of the committee anyway. He has a secret passage to the board of directors but no one is sure to which member of the board.

Now you've really got problems. Conflicts of interest. 'Can't afford it' and 'Not in the departmental budget' objections from finance. Environmental considerations, safety considerations, protection of union members' jobs considerations, resistance to changes in procedures and methods of working, as well as cost/benefit considerations.

And if the deal you are proposing has the temerity to reduce labour requirements, you have no chance at all, even with a good selling Proposal. Why? Because **you're presenting it to the wrong person**.

Assuming you cannot get in front of the board of directors, you have two choices – if you have a Proposal and sound financial justification – the boss or finance. Anyone with close links to the works committee or the unions is death to the deal. The nearer the very top you can get the better.

# How to use the Proposal when there's . . .

Here you are selling direct to the buying committee. But the buying committee is made up of heads of departments and each department has its own self-interests and a deep set 'competitive spirit' against other departments. I've seen many a good deal deliberately sabotaged by one department 'tribe' because it saw its own interests or kudos in the company pecking order losing out to another department.

Your selling Proposal and its financial justification has to be pretty powerful to get through this lot. With a traditional legal quotation document you might as well give up before you start.

If you can make sure that your proposals cater equally for the interests of each of the departments involved in the buying committee, so that the *status quo* is maintained, you have the best chance of success. Copies of your Proposal to **everyone**, of course.

That's just a glimpse of the can of worms you're opening when you're selling in this modern, sophisticated world. And if you catch a touch of cynicism in those words, you're dead right. Don't kid yourself that I'm exaggerating. I've only given you five examples out of probably five hundred different selling situations you'll come up against. And there you were, not even thinking about how futile is your simple little quotation, looking more like an invoice, with all your terms and conditions on the back, posted to the prospective customers more often than not.

This book is about **How to Sell against Competition**, not about how to lose without really trying. A true 90% loss to turn into a gain, or at least a darned good chance of winning – that's what we're talking about in this chapter.

Proposals are **in**. Quotations are **out**.

### How Committees Behave – or Misbehave!

Of course, there are many buying committees that perform very effectively, just as there are many middle management contacts who communicate thoroughly and honestly to their bosses and to their boards. What I'm saying is – don't take chances on finding a good one. They're the minority, not the majority. I've been there, on both sides!

Let's look into the committee chamber and see what really happens. The bigger the committee, the worse it gets. Hospital or university boards are really something. They're comprised of a mixture of consultant surgeons and physicians, or professors, the administration chiefs and umpteen 'lay' persons, like the Lord High Sheriff, a couple of JPs and the chairman of the region's Women's Institute. Every committee has a Chairman who is usually elected to the post for his or her impartiality (and that's a laugh!). Every committee has a Secretary, whose job it is to formulate the agenda, take the minutes and organize the coffee and tea.

The agenda is always the same. Cutting out the formalities, minutes of the last meeting, apologies for absence, etc; the big projects and the big money are at the beginning and the small projects with small money are at the end.

Most big projects for these kind of committees are highly technical. Which means that only two or three members of the committee know anything about the project in detail. These two or three members monopolize the conversation. They also know that they are all-powerful on the big project. The rest of the committee very quickly get bored and begin doodling on their blotters. Five minutes and the 'experts' call for a vote on the big project. £5 million is okayed with only a casual examination and complete faith in the experts. No, it's not for that reason. The real reason is that all the 'lay' members of the committee who wanted to ask questions wouldn't ask them *for fear of looking stupid in the eyes of their fellow members*.

The meeting progresses. Projects are discussed in order of descending value and importance. For the first two hours, most of the 'lay' members haven't made a contribution. And they're getting pretty fed up about that. After all, they're on that committee because they **want** to contribute.

So when the agenda approaches its final items, and the Chairman announces – 'Main gates, re-painting of' or 'Mattresses for wards E to G, soft or hard' – these very minor items can consume several hours of heated discussion, because every single member of the committee understands fully the subject and most of the members have been waiting in frustration all day for the opportunity to make their contributions.

Five minutes to okay £5 million. Five hours to decide what colour to paint the main gate! That's committees!

How do you structure your proposals, therefore, if you are going to be up against this kind of thing? Cater for the 'lay' people as well as the 'experts' and make sure every member of the committee has a copy of your Proposal in advance of the meeting. A letter to the Secretary, enclosing the appropriate number of copies, which says: 'This project will, we understand, be discussed at your next full committee meeting on Wednesday, 21 November. Please will you make sure each member of your committee receives a copy of our proposals well in advance of this meeting.'

Full marks to the committee Secretary who turns her agenda upside down and deals with the minor items first. But how is she going to get such a change agreed by her committee?

## Tactics for Coping with the Internal Politics

This bit is not really about Proposals, but as we've now delved into a few selling situations and how committees behave, it seems a logical place to put it.

What I call 'Internal Politics' the academics are now calling 'Transactional Analysis'. You can't keep a good academic down and I bet a few people make a lot of money peddling TA around and running courses on it.

From time to time every Seller will suffer the effects of these internal customer politics. An idea is sold to a certain customer executive, but another executive who has a say in the matter dislikes the first executive and so vetoes the idea for no other reason. Every time this happens, your **ace** has to be that financial justification in your Proposal.

A particular customer executive tells you – 'You only need see me. I'll handle all the liaison with the technical department.' Then out of the blue, you are asked to call on the chief engineer, who tells you, 'Don't waste your time with him. I'm the man who makes the decisions on this kind of equipment.'

What's to be done? Well, you could call for a meeting with both the executive and the chief engineer, perhaps over a lunch on you if it's the only way to get them together. Then you outline the problem you're faced with. 'Gentlemen, I am trying to do the best job I can for your Company. I have no wish to offend either of you, but I am in an impossible position. You (the executive) tell me only to call and see you about this project, and you, (the chief engineer) tell me only to call and see you. Yet I need to keep talking to both of you about a number of other ways we can be of value to your Company. Please will you help me? How can I make both of you happy?'

Or you pass the problem up the line to your sales manager, who will personally call on someone else, senior to both the problems.

There are only two levels in any company hierarchy which are comparatively free from internal politics – the very top and the very bottom. So to find out who all the key-decision-makers and decision-influencers are, ask the managing director, or ask the workers on the factory or sales floor. The workers will normally be delighted to talk about the internal politics. They hate those kind of people. But be careful, they also talk to those kinds of people. Managing directors are much safer, as well as being the ultimate decision-makers. It's always good to have been sent down from God to talk to a lesser being, especially if you can keep that top door open and send a copy of your Proposal to the m.d.

If you are up against an empire-building middle-management executive who won't let you by-pass him, and you work for a managing director who backs you up all the way (sadly not a frequent phenomenon!) you might be able to say to your customer contact:

'My managing director has asked me to try to arrange a meeting for him with your managing director. I think he has a few cards up his sleeve which even I don't know about. Can we fix up a date and time, and include you in the meeting, of course?'

## 'No Terms and Conditions'

At the beginning of this chapter I criticized quotations for having all that pale grey small print on the back. Okay, if you're selling boilers, or lifting tackle, or building bridges, there are certain conditions that must be stated, but outside these kinds of businesses, why have terms and conditions at all? Except, of course, terms of payment.

I've thrown out terms and conditions for two of my consultancy clients over the past ten years. Just two. That's how hard they dig their toes in. Both clients are doing much more business as a result.

Consider the selling situation where you are going through your Proposal, and at a suitable point you say 'By the way, you'll see there are no terms and conditions for doing business on the back of any of these sheets. We don't have any. Only, I should say, the terms of payment. We're a customer-oriented company. If one of our customers gets a problem, before, during or after we've delivered the goods, we sort the problem out first, and fast, and we worry about whose fault it was much later. And if the customer doesn't come out and admit it was his fault, we stand the cost. There's no future for either of us if we start nitpicking on the small print, and we're looking for a long and lasting relationship. So no terms and conditions.'

It's incredible how much confidence this gives the customer in you, as a supplier, if you can say this – and mean it. And straight away you have a beautiful opportunity to get advance commitment on another very important point.

## How to Make Sure you Get Paid on Time

'While we're on the subject of terms and conditions, you'll see that our one and only term is Payment in 30 days promptly. Can I ask you a question on this? It's important to us because if we can't maintain our cash in-flow, it could jeopardize the service we give our customers, and we'd hate that to happen.

'Assuming we go ahead with the order, do you see any problems with your accounts department or computer that would make payment difficult within our normal 30 day terms?

'Do you need invoices in by a specific "no later than" day of the month for them to be processed that month?'

See how easy it is to talk money to the person to whom you're selling. If you don't, and you have to chase the customer later for payment, he won't care less about seeing that you get paid on time. But if you get an okay from him when you go through the Proposal, you've also got a **commitment** from him. And when you telephone **him** to chase payment, rather than his accounts department, he'll move heaven and earth to honour that commitment to you.

## *How to Use the Proposal to Deal with 'We Can't Afford it Yet'*

This selling technique applies to products that can be leased or sold on hire purchase, as well as for cash. If you sell such products, it **always** behoves you to have set up a deal with one particular finance company so that you can **sell** the finance rather than have to wait for the finance company's representative to close the sale for you. My ego wouldn't like that and I doubt if yours would either!

So let's assume you're armed to sell any of four ways – cash, lease, lease purchase or hire purchase. You go through the Proposal, your customer agrees step by step, but when you get to the automatic close, 'Can we go ahead, then?' he says – 'Not just yet. We can't afford to buy it yet.'

And because of all that financial justification you've put together and just gone through with him, you look him in the eye, surprised, and with full confidence and sincerity you say – 'You can't afford *not* to have it. Look at all these costings we've gone through. It will save you at least £450 a week on your loading and unloading work.'

'Yes, I know, but we still can't afford to buy it **yet**.'

'Why don't you buy it over two or three years? That way, you'll only need to find 10% of the price now, and you'll be saving far more each month than you'll have to pay out. We can only offer this for widget handlers over £2,000, and our group deal with the Industrial Bank of Scotland means our interest rates are the best. Here's what your monthly repayments would be (bring out repayments table). Look, you're going to be in profit even in month one.

'Is there anyone in finance we can get to now, or can you okay a lease or finance deal without checking with them?'

But try this technique **without** the Proposal's financial justification and see what happens.

### *How to Use the Proposal to Deal with 'It's Too Expensive' and 'Your Price is Too High'*

Sometimes your price **is** going to be too high! Too high for the customer's budget. Here is another technique which can be adopted to fit hundreds of products.

The first thing to do when the customer says 'It's too expensive' or 'Your price is too high' is to look concerned and say – 'Oh dear. How much too expensive?' or 'How much too high?'

As I said in Chapter 8, you need to establish the **difference** between your price and what the customer is prepared to pay. It could just be a try-on, don't forget – another way of asking for a discount.

You may get a precise answer – 'It's £24,000 over our budget for the project'. Or you may get a vaguer reply – 'Well, it just looks a hell of a lot of money and I don't think the board will go that high'.

Now you turn up the page in your Proposal that actually gives the price. The secret of how to handle this kind of problem is that you **never** just wrap the deal up in a single, total price. You break it down into as many items as you can.

Here is an example which itemizes the specification which the customer asked for when you conducted your detailed survey of his requirements.

'Let's see what we can reduce if we adjust the specification a bit. How important is the Satin Chroming? That would save you £8,120 if you could accept our standard finish. Satin Chroming **is** a bit of a luxury. We've got customers still using the standard

| | Standard control unit | £100,260 | |
|---|---|---|---|
| **Standard extras** | Rubber wheels | 530 | |
| | Voltage regulator | 4,650 | |
| | Transfer table | 1,040 | |
| | Optical unit | 32,250 | |
| | Variable converter | 9,250 | |
| | | | 147,980 |
| **Accessories** | Collector unit | 550 | |
| | Electronic calculator | 2,070 | |
| | Automatic aligner | 14,450 | |
| | | | 17,070 |
| **Customer variations** | 'Square' configuration | 10,350 | |
| | Satin chroming | 8,120 | |
| | Design changes | 7,500 | |
| | | | 25,970 |
| | Assembly on site | | 20,930 |
| | | | £211,950 |

**The cost of components from the other divisions amounts to £45,500 which is included in the cost of the Standard Control Unit.**

finish equipment happily after 15 years, in conditions much worse than yours.'

If the customer bites and agrees that would solve the problem; great. Sacrifice the Satin Chroming and ask for the order again.

If you get a vague reply to your first question, 'How much too high?' and the customer bites on your suggestion but then goes on to say he **needs** the Satin Chroming, **you know what kind of figure he has in mind for a discount.**

'How much could your people help us on Assembly on site? If you could supply some labour, we might be able to get £8,000 off this £20,930. Our labour is bound to cost more than yours, when you include travelling and subsistence.'

Give and take. Don't give anything away unless you get something in return. Those are the rules when you work with a good financially justified, selling proposal. Discounts are **out**.

*The Ultimate Gambit –*
*UWC's Instructions to the Prospective Suppliers*

Imagine you are sitting in your sales office and a fairly large enquiry comes in out of the blue. You need to prepare a quotation (this is happening before you bought this book) but – wow! – attached to the enquiry is a set of instructions telling you **how to quote**. It isn't a local government or an architectural tendering job, where they always tell you the way they want it done: this one is for ordinary commercial/industrial 50,000 grade B widgets, or something like that.

The instructions read as shown (UWC is, of course, the Universal Widget Corporation).

# To all Suppliers

## Procedure for submitting quotations to UWC and its subsidiaries

All quotations should give the following information in the sequence as listed.
Quotations which do not follow this procedure will not be considered.

1. Begin all quotations with a brief statement of the objectives we wish to achieve by having your equipment/products/services.

2. Follow this statement of objectives with a brief outline of your recommendations, and explain – briefly – how your recommendations fulfil our objectives.

3. Elaborate on 2, with a list of any additional benefits we will receive from your recommendations.

4. Explain with the full use of figures, finance, times, labour rates, maintenance costs, depreciation periods, production outputs, verifiable comparisons, whichever are relevant, how we can justify the purchase of the equipment/products/services or how we can justify changing from our present suppliers to you.

   All prices must be inclusive, i.e. include delivery, installation, commissioning or whatever necessary.

   If the quotation is for supplies of products over a contract period, detail the options you can offer for regular call-offs so that we can achieve one of our objectives of minimizing our stock levels without adversely affecting our production flow.

5. State the guarantees you provide. Give details of your after-sales service facilities and how they operate.

6. Give at least three names, addresses and telephone numbers of firms we can contact and with which you do business on the equipment/products/services concerned in your quotation. Preferably, firms situated near us.

Now if this enquiry has arrived out of the blue with no previous contact having been made by anyone in the salesforce, it wouldn't be very fair, would it? There is no way you could respond as instructed without first talking to the prospective customer and asking a lot of questions.

But, however you quote, if an enquiry comes out of the blue, you must get back to the enquirer fast to ask the questions anyway. Only an idiot sends off a quotation straight away in response. Flying blind is nowhere compared to **this** risk!

So let us suppose you have established all the answers to the questions you need to ask this prospective customer to be able to follow his instructions. Even then – **would you be allowed to draft a quotation that way?**

Would the sales office manager allow it? Would you need a board meeting to get the approval to do it? Would anyone get on their high horse and cry – 'Who do they think they are, telling us how to quote? Send 'em our standard quotation – they can take it or leave it.'

And they **will**! Leave it, I mean. Let's face it, you only have two choices – do it as the prospective customer instructs, or don't bother doing it at all.

There is a reason for this little story, as you'll see. What I really want to suggest is that you don't wait for a prospective customer to tell you what to do – you **do it yourself**, for every single one of your quotations. You follow those UWC instructions to the letter. This will **double** your resulting orders.

It'll take a while to get it right. On jobs in the pipeline you won't have all the information you need. But there is nothing in the rule book that says you can't submit a second, better quotation, if you have enough data to improve on the first one.

It really impresses a prospective customer to have a salesperson telephone and say – 'We've been giving your problem a lot of thought since we submitted our quotation and we've come up with some extra data which makes the deal we're offering even more attractive. I've prepared a second Proposal which contains all this extra data. Can I come in and go through it with you? How about Tuesday at 9.50, or would early afternoon be better for you?'

And now you are in a position to use the ultimate gambit – a technique that really gets you some fun out of the job, at the expense of your competitors.

During the weeks you are perfecting this UWC format for your Proposals (about the time you stop calling them quotations), you take some copies of the UWC instruction sheet over to your own purchasing department and you encourage your company's buyers to use the set of instructions on all their suppliers and prospective suppliers. It will halve their enquiry/quotation processing time and make sure they select the best value for money deal for your company, every time.

You arm yourself with another dozen copies of the set of instructions, this time with your company's name on the top, not UWC.

Now you can apply the ultimate gambit. You take in your Proposal to go through it with a prospective customer. You go through it in the way we've already described. At the end, you close with 'Are you happy with everything? Can we go ahead then?' If he says 'Yes, don't see why not' you don't need to play your ace.

But if he says – 'Not yet; I'd better wait until the other quotations come in, so that I can compare them with yours,' it's time for your ace.

'You've no doubt noticed, Mr Jones, our Proposal is quite a lot different from most quotations you see (pause: get an affirmative). It follows the format we use in our own purchasing department when we go out to suppliers for quotations. Our buyers send out a set of instructions to all our suppliers and prospective suppliers, telling them precisely how to quote.

'By doing this, they have three or four identical format quotations to consider; they can therefore compare like with like and they can guarantee to select the best all-round offer every time, and much faster.

'How do the other quotations you've received so far measure up to ours?' (It's nice if you're first and he hasn't received any of the others yet, but no matter . . .)

'Can I make a suggestion?' (and here you bring out half a dozen of your purchasing department's instruction sheets). 'Why don't you try this for yourself? Send one of these – with **your** name on top, of course – to each of the other suppliers that are quoting on this job, and see how much easier it will be for you to compare the quotations and come to a decision. Have you got time in your schedule to do this?'

If he's got the time, he'll do it. It's irresistible. If he hasn't got the time, you've still made a friend, given him something to try out on his next job, and enhanced your chances of getting this particular order. (Your idea is worth 10% on price as a consultancy fee!)

So now you see the reason for the introductory story. Your **competitors** are now the ones crying – 'Who the hell do these people think they are – telling us how to quote!'

Most of them will lose by default. Some will completely ignore the instructions. All will have to do the survey again because they didn't ask the right questions first time round.

If only you could be a fly on the wall in **their** sales office when those instructions arrive out of the blue.

But don't forget who else might be reading this!

## *How to Use the Proposal to Set Up a Demonstration*

When you go through that Proposal with your prospective customer, he will not agree with everything you've said every time. Sometimes he'll be doubtful on some major or minor point. Sometimes it will be a doubt based on an inability to understand fully – and you won't get very far by telling him, or even inferring, that he's thick!

Sometimes, the doubt will be based on a misunderstanding.

Whatever, you clear up the doubt if you can, and keep going. If you can't clear it up, set it to one side, and secure complete agreements on everything else.

Then try a different close. 'You're happy with everything except this one doubt on the crushing capabilities, then, Mr Jones?' Get his agreeement to this. Then move on. 'So if we can clear up this doubt to your complete satisfaction, may I assume you'll go ahead?'

It'll be very difficult for him to say 'No'. Worst you're likely to get is – 'All other things considered, I wouldn't be surprised.'

So you propose a demonstration – at your works or at one of your customer's premises, or whatever is most appropriate. A demonstration with one clear-cut objective in mind – to clear up that doubt. The best kind of demonstration, as you'll see in the next chapter.

And if there are a number of decision-makers and influencers involved in the project, your last question should be – 'Can we get Mr Brown and Miss Smith and Mr Humphries to attend the demonstration? We could lay on a tour of our works at the same time.'

## Would YOU Buy it, if you Were the Customer?

This is the acid test for a Proposal. And the measure of a really professional Seller. That he or she can put himself or herself into the customer's shoes; really into the customer's personality and working situation; empathize with the customer; read through the Proposal before it's taken in and answer honestly and truthfully – 'Would I buy this, if I were this customer?'

Would you really? Why would you? Think about the reasons in detail. Think about **all** the reasons why you would buy it.

Then go in and **sell** it to him – with more confidence and sincerity than you'd ever dreamed you could muster. You'll do it, you'll convince him, because now – **you believe**.

Go in and **sell** it to him, because you've thought out exactly what best to do – and why.

And if you find yourself answering, 'No, I don't think I would buy it if I were him' – tear the Proposal apart and do it again until you can answer truthfully, 'Yes, I'll buy it now.'

You're a **winner**, remember!

# 10
# How to Demonstrate your Superiority

**Every Demonstration has an objective, usually to prove
to a customer that what the Seller says will happen *does*
happen.**

**But Demonstrations can come in all shapes and sizes.
Some are very different from others – and much more
successful because of it.**

**Our Demonstrations must help us to win – so they're
going to be very different from those of our competitors.**

Why is it so many demonstrations go wrong? Here we are in the
heydays of the fastest expanding industry we've seen for decades
– Information Technology. Micro-computer Sellers are coming
out of the woodwork everywhere. And more times than not, the
demonstration you get of the latest, or past latest, micro leaves
you wondering why you ever wanted to discard that lever arch
filing system.

Before that it was photocopiers. How many people in business
**have not** been subjected to a photocopier demonstration that
went wrong?

Whenever an industry booms, so that salesforces expand so
rapidly the training of those salesforces can't keep up with the
recruitment rate, your demonstrations are the first things to
suffer.

The people conducting the demonstrations haven't been
taught enough about the product in general, or about the art of
conducting a good demonstration in particular. Yet we all know,
with absolute certainty, that if a product demonstration goes
wrong, the sale is **lost**. Irretrievably lost. For ever. **And** that
prospective customer talks about it to his friends.

Commercial suicide is being committed every day by businesses everywhere that really know better, and should be doing better.

Then there's the other kind of 'demonstration'. The Seller picks up the customer from his premises at around 11.45 am. They drive straight to the Seller's favourite top class restaurant.

An hour in the bar and then they roll into the dining room. Two bottles of vino over the lunch, two double brandies over the coffee and by 3 pm they're ready for the demonstration. Short drive to the works, ten minutes talking about the product and the prospective customer looks at his watch and says, 'I've got to get back to sign the post!'

I know salesmen who have lost their driving licence, and the order, trying to get the prospective customer back to base in a hurry after this kind of 'demonstration'. And why bother? Let's face it, if the objective of the exercise is to get the customer well and truly tipsy at your expense, you can do it much more effectively if you didn't have a demonstration to get in the way of progress!

If you want to win against serious competition, your demonstrations have got to go right, not wrong. Every time. And that needs systematic planning, preparation and technique. It also needs the active co-operation of quite a few other people.

Here are the rules.

**The Objectives**

Once you have committed yourself and your prospective customer to a demonstration, sit down alone with your A4 survey pad and list the objectives on paper. Why are you conducting this demonstration? What specific doubts do you need to dispel from the prospective customer's mind? How can you best dispel these doubts? What other things could you demonstrate which would enhance the customer's appreciation of your product and your company's prowess, without detracting from the key objectives which you **must** achieve?

Now that you have this information on paper, you can begin planning and preparing for the demonstration.

**The Administration**

Still with your survey pad, make a second list. What will be required to achieve the objectives? Where would be the best place to hold the demonstration? When? Who will be attending from the customer company? Who will be required from your company, other than you? What literature and samples will be needed? Will any food and drink be required during the time the customer is in your hands?

Now you can get to work and tie all the pieces together. Memos to any of the company's staff from whom you need assistance. Requisitions for the appropriate equipment. Firm booking of your demonstration unit if the demonstration is to be conducted on your premises or on the prospective customer's premises. Telephone your old established customer and make sure the date is convenient, if the demonstration is to be held at another customer's premises. Which brings me to the third critical point.

**Check up Beforehand**

This is absolutely essential if you plan to conduct a demonstration at one of your customer's premises, using his product, the one you sold him a year ago and with which as far as you know, he's very happy.

**Don't**, under any circumstances, rely on just the telephone call when you agreed the date and time. Visit that customer personally beforehand to make sure everything is okay, that your product will be being used on the day in question, that it will be used by a competent person. Brief that person on why you are bringing this prospective customer to see this particular equipment, and what you need to have demonstrated to that customer, and why. Come over to that person in a way which makes that demonstration and the responsibility you've given him the most important thing in his life as well as yours. Fuss over him. Ask him if he needs anything from you to make his charge perform like it's never performed before.

I know one very successful machine tool sales engineer who carries a few spare control wheels and levers in the boot of his car, ready for just such situations. He knows from experience that the operators of his machine tools don't use the machine's wheels and levers as they should be used, they take a copper hammer and hit them every few seconds to clamp components tight or to reset tooling. It's faster for the operators, easier on the muscles, and does the machine no harm. But after a few months, it makes the wheels and levers look a mess. Scars and dents in the satin chrome finish. Spoils the overall aesthetics of his product.

So the day before a demonstration, the sales engineer visits the customer, checks out everything, briefs the machine operator, and *changes the wheels and levers for new ones*, making the operator promise that he won't use his copper hammer until after the old wheels and levers have been replaced, the day after the demonstration.

This so impresses the operator, the sales engineer claims, that he sometimes goes to the trouble of turning up to work for the day of the demonstration in freshly cleaned and pressed overalls, hair cut, shaved properly that morning, all the junk has been cleared away from around the machine and the machine itself performs 20% faster than it does in normal production.

He's the only one in his salesforce who takes that kind of trouble to get things right, and he's top of the sales league table consistently. Another Flo Wright!

I was privy to a demonstration a few years ago where the salesman **didn't** check up beforehand. I was one of the three prospective customers looking at a particular piece of office machinery. We arrived at the customer's premises, were introduced to the commercial manager, who escorted us to the piece of machinery we'd come to see. I wondered at the time why the commercial manager seemed a touch distant and tight lipped.

When we reached the salesman's equipment, he exclaimed in surprise, 'It's not working!' The commercial manager just looked at him and said quietly – 'No. It hasn't worked for a week. And can we get one of your service engineers out here – can we hell!' And he walked away and left us standing by the machinery.

The salesman couldn't understand why I couldn't stop laughing. The customer got his service engineer within the hour, but it didn't do the salesman much good. He still lost three potential orders and the goodwill of that existing customer, whom he certainly couldn't use for a demonstration ever again.

Do check up beforehand – personally.

## The Demonstration Itself

During the demonstration itself, there is a specific format you should try to follow – it's called **Tell – Show – Tell**.

You should break the whole demonstration down into a series of separate operations, using the Tell – Show – Tell technique several times in several ways. Start to finish, it might go like this.

You sit down with your prospective customer and you **tell** him what you propose to show him. You tell him at the start **all** the things you propose to show him.

Then you proceed with the demonstration, taking each separate operation and using Tell – Show – Tell again, this time reminding the customer of what you told him you would show him, then **showing** him, with **no talking**, then telling him again what he's just seen and asking if he's happy with that or would he like to see it again. (You'll need to read this paragraph slowly at least three times, just as if you were attending a demonstration!)

When you've completed all the Tell – Show – Tell separate

operations, you recap on everything the customer has seen, **telling** him everything once again, then you ask if he's any questions or if he'd like to go through the entire demonstration again, from the start to finish, or any specific part of the demonstration.

If you are demonstrating something which **must** go from start to finish non-stop, so that it's not possible to break it down into separate operations, then demonstrate the entire process at least twice, preferably three times, using the Tell – Show –Tell technique each time.

I know this all sounds far too much trouble, even patronizing for the customer. I just know it's the best way, the most thorough way, to conduct a demonstration, that's all. It's the winner's way.

### Closing Time!

All doubts resolved: all Tell – Show – Tells completed; you can now provide him with whatever literature is relevant to what you've just done and you can close in exactly the same way you would have if you'd been going through a Proposal with him.

'You're happy with everything? Can we go ahead then?'

Now let's look at some specific techniques and attitudes which can help and hinder **during** a demonstration.

### Getting the Customer Involved

It's always good to get the customer involved – to let him try it for himself. But *only* if you are confident that the customer will be able to do it right first time. If you have any kind of situation where there is a knack required, or training and experience required to master a procedure or function, *don't let the customer anywhere near it*.

Whatever you say, if he muffs it he'll go away thinking it's going to be too complicated or too difficult for his staff to handle. His ego will lose you the order.

I'll never forget a visit many years ago to an old-fashioned toffee factory. During the tour of the factory, our party passed through a quaint little room, completely bare except for several wooden stakes sticking a foot out of the walls, about head high. This ancient chap in a brown smock was kneading a hefty chunk of semi-molten toffee. He'd manipulate the toffee with incredibly smooth, flowing motions, turning it from a round ball into a sausage shape and then, with a kind of flick of his wrists, he'd throw the sausage up over the wooden stake, catch the two ends as they slowly flowed downwards and knead the two halves into a ball again. Guess you should have been there!

Our guide asked if any of the party would like to have a go. It was an obvious set up, but we all tried. And every time, all we got were two lumps of molten toffee on the floor. None of us could master the wooden stake bit. Half of our party couldn't even throw the toffee high enough to reach the stake. Everyone had a good laugh. Our guide explained that old George, the guy in the brown smock, had been doing this for forty years, and was the only employee who could knead toffee properly. 'Don't know what we're going to do when he retires. He's 68 now. He learned his trade from his father, but his daughter doesn't want to know. Quality's bound to suffer when we have to knead with these new fangled machines!'

You're not likely to suffer from any 'knack traps' like this one, but the message is clear.

## Respect your Product

Don't bang it, slap it, kick it, toss it, lean on it or abuse it in any way whatsoever. Caress it, drool over it, revere it. It's the best product in the whole world and that's what the customer has to go away thinking.

Your superiority depends entirely on the respect you show your product. Remember the two directors who went shopping for filing cabinets?

## Don't Be an Exhibitionist

Things *will* go wrong from time to time. Murphy's law strikes anywhere, in spite of the best-laid plans and preparations. When they do, play it down. Often the customer won't even be aware that something's gone wrong unless you tell him.

A classic example of this occurred several years ago in Birmingham. A regional manager and one of his salesmen were demonstrating a small offset printing machine to two prospective customers. Half-way through the demonstration, a panel in the side of the machine came undone. The manager saw the panel beginning to fall away and, with the flat of his hand, pushed it back into place. The customers were on the other side of the machine, watching it perform, and saw nothing of the problem. But the manager caught the palm of his hand on the edge of the panel, and gashed his hand pretty dreadfully – about a two inch cut.

Now most Sellers in that predicament would instantly become martyrs, holding their blood dripping hand high and screaming, 'Oh my God!' The customers would thereupon be convinced that they'd been looking at a highly dangerous piece of equipment, and wouldn't buy it at any price.

This particular manager was a professional. His bleeding hand went instantly into his trouser pocket and he kept going with the demonstration as if nothing had happened. Five minutes later he could feel blood trickling into his shoe, so he passed the demonstration to his salesman and excused himself, pleading that nature called.

A few minutes later, his secretary goes up to the salesman to apologize, on behalf of the manager that he's been called home urgently as one of his children had fallen and broken a leg, and his wife needed help. Sympathetic understanding from the customers. The demonstration was concluded. The order was won.

## Privacy and Thanks

Two golden rules for demonstrations which are conducted at other customers' premises.

Allow the prospective customer and your existing customer to talk privately together out of your earshot. If you hover, and are seen to be hovering, the prospective customer will get the idea you **don't** want him to talk privately to your customer, and he'll wonder why. Much better if you say to both of them – 'I'm sure you two would like to discuss things without me being around, so that you can get a really impartial picture of what our products can do. I'll just pop over to the toilets and be back in ten minutes, okay?'

Second golden rule – make a point of thanking everyone concerned. It's so easy, in the heat and pressure of the moment, to forget to do this, and it's critical if you want to use this customer again for a future demonstration. Be appreciative and they'll appreciate you and be happy to help. Be appreciative in front of your prospective customer. He'll see for himself the pleasure your thanks gives those people. He'll see for himself how they want to help you. Your esteem as a professional goes up a few points in everyone's eyes.

## F.A.B.

When you're going through the Tell – Show – Tell routine, don't forget to use F.A.B.

Feature – Advantage – Benefit.

It's incredibly easy during a demonstration to talk about, point out, show, **features** of the product, and forget to explain the advantages and benefits which the customer gets from those features.

'You'll see that this machine has very large main bearings (*feature*) which means that you can take much deeper cuts than normal (*advantage*) and so your total machining time is drastically reduced (*benefit*).'

'The casting we use is minimum half-inch thick spheroidal graphite cast iron (*feature*) which means that even when the machine is not grouted into your factory floor there is absolutely no vibration (*advantage*), and that means you can expect a quality of surface finish which will cut out a lot of your grinding operations (*benefit*).'

## Across the Desk Demonstrations

Many products can be effectively demonstrated to a prospective customer across his desk. Even products too large for this can be miniaturized for use in the hands of the competent professional Seller.

Earlier in this book, I mentioned how samples can be used as focusers; exposed to the customer's view when the Seller walks into his office for the first time.

Now let's look at samples in a demonstrating role.

The range and the scope is enormous. The ordinary central heating water valve to the high pressure corrosive chemicals process plant butterfly valve, all can be part cut-away to show the actual workings of the valve, so that a Seller can demonstrate everything that needs to be demonstrated, across a desk.

Six different sizes of specially cut-away, nicely finished samples in the boot of the car, and the Seller can tailor the demonstration precisely to the size of valves this particular customer or that particular customer uses.

One British valve manufacturer produces what is called a Security valve – a gate valve or ball valve fitted with a special rod which slides through holes in the hand wheel and into a hole in the valve body. Once the valve is set to the required position for use, the rod is padlocked into place so that only the key holder can adjust the flow through the pipes that the valve controls.

The Seller might walk into a prospective customer's office with the security valve in his hand and ask: 'Do you get any problems in your process pipelines with vandals, or kids, or your own people changing the valve positions?'

Ten to one he does. Jam factories, breweries, oil depots, even the central heating system in a large office complex. As winter approaches, people don't put on sweaters, they turn the heating up. It costs thousands.

'What have you done about stopping these problems occurring?'

'Have you considered using valves like these?' The Seller hands over his security valve sample and proceeds to give an across-the-desk demonstration.

I haven't got an obsession about valves, it's just they're so easy for everyone to identify with. One sales engineer I know sells a particularly fine valve for corrosive chemicals which will seal absolutely 100% at pressures of 2000 pounds per square inch. He uses a cut-away sample to demonstrate the internal construction of his valve, its neoprene rubber seating and its superbly moulded ptfe butterfly. But he can't demonstrate to prove that it won't leak at 2000 psi.

So he compromises, and adds a bit of fun. 'I can't prove to you that this valve seals absolutely 100% at 2000 psi, Mr Jones, but I can prove to you that it does at room pressure. If you promise to be very careful – this is one of my best suits – pour some of your scalding hot coffee into this valve and I'll sit here for as long as you think is reasonable with it directly over myself just to show you it won't drip.'

'Nine out of ten customers laugh and say, "I believe you!" ', the sales engineer claims. 'But every now and again you get one awkward so-and-so with a shaky hand . . .!'

Like the regional manager with the cut hand, I bet he puts the cleaning bills on his expenses as 'fair wear and tear in the line of duty'.

## Demonstrating at Exhibitions

Whatever the exhibition, whatever the product, if a demonstration is being conducted on a trade exhibition stand, there's always a crowd of people around that stand. Nothing attracts casual prospects as effectively as the demonstration. That combination of noise and movement – and curiosity.

Demonstrations at exhibitions involve continuous preparation, demonstrating, clearing up, preparation, demonstration, clearing up, preparation – and so on. All day, all week. Exhausting work, but highly productive work.

I've seen stands selling rotary concrete floor levellers, a bit like rotary lawn mowers but with flat paddles like old Indian ceiling fans, where a gang of labourers were mixing and shovelling concrete all day so the demonstration could run. They filled a skip with the debris every day of the exhibition.

I've seen a true entrepreneurial salesman crack a big problem for his company's product with a way-out, but highly effective demonstration at an agricultural show. You won't believe the name of the product – it's called Bloat Guard!

The story goes like this. When cows eat fresh, dewy, green grass, they tend to make pigs of themselves. The fresh green grass effervesces in the cow's stomach and the cow gets very bloated. This affects the quality and quantity of the milk. One teaspoonful of Bloat Guard in the cow's drinking water twice a day and this problem is completely resolved.

Bloat Guard comes in bottles, so the agricultural show stand looked a lot like an old American West's medicine man's stall. And the farmers weren't having any! Farmers are by nature a very cynical lot.

This one salesman created queues, clamouring to buy Bloat Guard, with a very simple demonstration. He acquired a large clear pvc bag and a crate of Guinness. His assistant stood ready with a bottle of Bloat Guard and a spoon.

Barker fashion, he gathered a group of farmers around him.

'Imagine this plastic bag is your cow's stomach,' he told his audience. 'When the cow eats too much fresh dewy green grass, the inside of the stomach looks like this . . .' And he took an opened bottle of Guinness, put his thumb over the open top, shook the bottle violently for ten seconds and emptied its entire contents into the plastic bag, holding the bag in his fist, like a balloon about to be blown up. The Guinness, escaping into the larger area of the bag after being violently roused, frothed madly, filling the bag with brown foaming bubbles.

'And this is what Bloat Guard does' – the salesman's assistant adds one teaspoonful of Bloat Guard to the foaming mass of Guinness and, immediately, all the froth is gone and a flat calm is seen on the lake of Guinness in the bag. Incredibly effective. The speed of the transformation takes everyone completely by surprise.

What we don't know is whether those farmers who queued for a bottle intended to apply it to their cows, or to a bottle of Guinness down at the pub on Sunday! But does it matter? The word is spreading about Bloat Guard.

## A Braver Man than I

In 1977, I returned home from the USA with 50% of the patent on a portable 'hang it on your belt, campers' water purifier'. Two aluminium containers, one for the dirty stream water, one for the purified, drinkable water, and a plastic gubbins which contained the secret ingredient X. It all went into a neat little zip-up plastic case.

A few months later I came upon this brave chap from the Middle East, who went into raptures when he saw my water purifier and started chanting, 'We'll sell a million, we'll sell a million!'

'To whom?' I asked.

'The armies out there in the desert. They keep poisoning the wells, you know. The soldiers are falling like flies. Will it filter out metallic poisons? If it will, or sufficiently to get the chap to hospital before his toes turn up, we'll sell a million of 'em – maybe two million.'

I took a couple of sample water purifiers to a chemical analyst and asked him to test the unit's effectiveness with metallic poisons. The analyst didn't work up any enthusiasm for the job. Guess a million purifiers to the Middle East and a Queen's Award for Export didn't feature in his world. No sense of humour, either.

Three weeks later, I had the analyst's report. Yes. No problems with metallic poisons. I cabled my man in the Middle East.

Two weeks later, I received a telephone call from this very excitable individual. 'Sell five million!' he kept saying.

'Find out if it'll cope with **what**?' I had a bit of a problem grasping the significance of his latest request for an analyst's report. 'The man's mad,' I thought.

But I went back to my chemical analyst, conveyed our latest

request and, impressing upon him the urgency of the matter, waited for the results of the tests. It took him two hours. When he reported back there wasn't a glimmer of a smile on his face, not a twitch, as he said – 'Perfectly safe – but it will taste rather salty.'

He didn't even smile when I nearly fell off his chair with laughing so much.

Another cable to my man in the Middle East and I sat back to await results. A month later he was in my office, gleefully relating what had happened at his demonstration.

'It took me weeks to get all six of the Sheiks together,' he told me. 'I wanted to do this once only! At last I had 'em all lined up for the demonstration. Three interpreters going nineteen to the dozen. Twenty or more bodyguards on all sides. I went through the construction of the unit, its potential uses for their armies, the expected life of the active ingredients. I told 'em about our analyst's report on the metallic poisons – gave 'em each a copy.

'Then I took a deep breath, unzipped my fly, peed into the thing, filtered it, and drank it all down in one go.

'And do you know what those Sheiks did? They got down on their knees and they kissed the ground in front of me like I was Allah himself!'

I poured him a stiff drink. I only wish I could have been out there on the day of the demonstration to pour him one then. A braver man than I am, that's for sure.

## Conducted Tours of the Works

No way can your supremacy be better demonstrated than with a conducted tour of your works. Or the opposite: meaning your incompetence!

In the middle of the tour of the works might well be the demonstration, but we've adequately covered that bit. This final piece in this chapter is concerned with those aspects of the customer's visit to your place of business *not* directly involved with the demonstration itself.

Let's picture the **perfect** tour of the works, with a few alternatives to perfection thrown in.

The chairman's chauffeur picks up the prospective customer in the chairman's Rolls. It usually stands outside the front offices most of the day, if the chairman's in, just taking up space. It's an asset that costs the company a lot of money. So use it as an asset. Requisition it to bring this very important prospective customer to your place of business.

Second best: **you** collect the customer in your car. But your car has been specially prepared for the task. All the junk has been removed. All the literature is safely stowed away in the boot, along with the kiddy seat that usually hangs on the back seat. Interior is freshly vacuumed. Exterior freshly washed and leathered. No smoking inside the car until you're sure the customer does. No pop music, or any kind of music on the cassette player. And drive carefully, allowing plenty of time.

**Welcome to UWC.**

Another second best; the customer drives to your place of business in his own car, and when he arrives, **he's expected.** When he stops at the main gate, the security man says –'Ah yes sir, Mr Jones sir. Welcome to UWC. If you drive over there to the main entrance, you'll find a parking place to the left of the main doors. Your name will be on it. It's our chairman's spot, but he's not in today.'

And sure enough, there's a little notice hanging on the chairman's name stake saying 'Reserved for Mr Jones, Apex Distributors Ltd'.

When Mr Jones walks into your main reception, the first thing he sees is your notice 'UWC welcomes Mr Jones of Apex Distributors Ltd'. And, even better, everything has been spelt correctly. Your receptionist has been warned by the security man that Mr Jones is on his way in, and has telephoned you and your chief. She gets up as Mr Jones enters, walks towards him smiling, hand extended, and says, 'Mr Jones. Good morning. Welcome to UWC. Mr Fenton and Mr Carstairs are on their way down. Would you like to visit the men's room before they get here? Let me look after your coat.'

**'Customer on the Premises' mode.**

More than that. As soon as the customer drives past the main gate, the security man presses the 'Customer on the Premises' button, bells ring in every department and **everyone** changes into 'being happy and bustle' mode. Everywhere is a happy, throbbing hive of positive activity whilst the customer is around. Any dismal Jimmies get fired for sabotage!

The conducted tour of the works gets under way. It's planned like a royal procession, with drawings and route markers. And everyone on the route knows it's coming their way, and what to do and not to do. UWC is the kind of company in which everyone understands that it's the customers that pay their wages every week or every month.

The departments covered by the tour fall into **musts, shoulds** and **coulds** categories.

**Musts** include the **purchasing department** – 'We think you should see how our purchasing people make sure our lines of supply are always kept secure, with at least two sources of supply active for every bought-in component and sub-assembly. This is important to you because it plays a key part in our policy never to let any customer down on delivery.' Don't forget to show him the UWC instructions to suppliers' procedure in action.

**Goods inwards inspection** – 'These are the people who make sure that the bought-out items ordered by our purchasing people come in undamaged and at the right quality. George Goodwin here and his two assistants have a system for checking and chasing that they claim is absolutely infallible. I'll let George tell you about that.'

**Goods outwards inspection and despatch** – 'This is our last line of inspection before the product reaches the customer. Every single unit is thoroughly inspected and then packed for despatch, by the same staff. Any doubts whatsoever, and the unit goes back to final production inspection with a red "TOP PRIORITY" notice on it, because any delay from then on could mean we risk breaking our delivery promise.'

**Finished goods stores** – 'You'll see from just looking at all this how many of our products we keep in stock for immediate delivery. We aim never to fall below 90% of the total range at any one time, with 100% for anything that falls into the 80/20 law. You know, 20% of our products are used by 80% of our customers. That 20% we've always got in stock.'

**Quality control** – 'This is the quality control and final inspection department for everything we manufacture ourselves. You'll see we use the most up-to-date technology throughout. Coupled with our range of numerical controlled machines in production itself, this makes us a clear number one in our industry for quality, reliability and longest working life. Our Research and Development people are also number one, which is why we are so far ahead of our competitors. We can't show you R & D, I'm afraid. There's a fair bit going on in there for the Ministry of Defence and it's a classified area.'

**Production and assembly** – 'Let's start at the beginning and follow the manufacturing and assembly process through. Then you'll see our widget crusher taking shape as we go and when we get to the end you'll be able to test one yourself as it comes off final assembly.'

**The sales department** – 'I'm sure you'd like to meet the people who will be looking after your orders. I know they'd like to meet you. Putting a face to a voice on the telephone is very important, don't you think? This is Harry Chandley. He looks after our sales estimating. This is Gloria Prufrock. She sees that any telephone requests for information are dealt with speedily. As you can see, she's in communication with stores and other departments by VDU as well as by phone and personal bleeper. If the person with the answer is sitting on the loo, we can still reach him inside ten seconds.'

**After sales service** – 'You'll see here how we can get a service engineer to you within four hours, if one of your people backs a forklift truck into a unit or something. All twenty-seven of our service engineers drive a fully equipped van and are in constant radio communication with base. They have personal radios too, like the police, so that if they're away from their van, on a job, we can still get in touch with them and they with us.'

**Customer training school** – 'This is where your own people come for their three day course on how to get the best out of their widget crushers. This is optional and all part of the service we give our customers. About 85% take us up on the training course. It means our products are earning money for our customers a good deal sooner, and a bit faster every day thereafter.'

**Beware the junk room.**

Every conducted tour I've been on – and that's a lot – has had a classic Achilles heel; the part of the works no one thinks about, so no one allows for. The junk room!

It may not be a junk room; it may be the department or bay of the factory that's being redecorated, redeployed, re-organized or made redundant. Doesn't matter. To the customer it looks like a junk room, and it kills the conducted tour of the works stone dead.

Every conducted tour I've been on has passed right through the middle of the junk room. No one's thought of the significance. No one's planned, therefore, to avoid it.

You **must** avoid it at all costs, even to the extent of postponing the tour until the junk is cleared up, or, if the junk room is permanent and in a critically strategic place, until it's been moved to a rented garage about 3 miles away from the factory.

Chances are, as you read this, you don't even know where your junk room is, or how many of them you've got. Get out there and find out. Act like a professional golfer – walk the course before the match.

**The boardroom lunch.**

The highlight of any conducted tour of the works is when the

visiting customer is given lunch in the boardroom, and all the directors present (and that means **all** the directors, properly briefed) ply the customer with questions about his business and how he sees business in general. He walks out of that boardroom after lunch, ten feet tall. He'll buy from you for life. No one's ever before made him feel so important.

Hopefully, if you're the Seller looking after that customer, you get invited to that boardroom lunch, too. Nothing is more degrading than to be left out of the lunch, on the grounds that your salary scale is 4 and only executives at 7 or above are allowed into the boardroom. Nothing is more certain to make the customer himself very aware that the person who looks after his account is of minor importance in his future supplier's hierarchy.

I've seen salesmen who have been taking a customer round the works excluded from lunch in the senior staff canteen, let alone the boardroom. Sheer stupidity. Internal politics getting in the way of business, again. If they have to, then *always* use an outside quality restaurant.

**The farewells.**

The final crucial point to get right on a successful conducted tour of the works is the goodbye. It's essential that the most senior executive who has been involved in the tour, or part of the tour, walks all the way to the customer's car with him, opens the car door, shakes him by the hand, and stands and waves him goodbye as he drives away.

The security man has been phoned. The barrier is up and he too waves goodbye as the customer drives past.

Bells ring the all clear. Customer's **off** the premises. Phew! Now we can all get back to work. 'Harry! What the bloody 'ell went wrong with that meeting this morning? Never seen such a militant lot of morons. Can't you keep your people working for even one hour a day? And George, the mess we had to clear up in bay 3 before that customer came through. You'll do it yourself next time!'

**You don't have to be big.**

You don't have to be a big company to organize a successful conducted tour of the works. At Structured Training Ltd and SCRS Ltd, which have around thirty staff, we do several every week.

You should get used to doing them as often as you can, because, apart from their value as business generators, there's nothing remotely comparable as a reason for keeping the entire operation neat and tidy, and all the people on their toes. And that means *more efficient*.

# 11
# How to Close More Sales

**If we don't ask for the order and get it, we're not just wasting our time, we're working for the competition!**

The only reason a Seller is employed is to get orders. The only logical reason for a meeting between a Buyer and a Seller is to give and receive an order – if not now, at some definable time in the near future.

The only reason a Seller makes calls on customers and prospective customers is so that he can put himself in the situation where he is most likely to get an order.

The only reasons a customer or prospective customer grants a Seller some of his valuable time are because that customer needs something; or because he wants to make sure he's keeping up to date with what's available in the market place; or because he's looking to improve on something he's buying now from somewhere else.

**So what's the problem?**

How come so many Sellers grind to a halt when they get to the most important bit – asking for the order?

How come the very thought of coming straight out and *asking* for an order puts the fear of God into so many otherwise reasonably competent Sellers?

Statistically, no one has ever been struck by lightning for asking for an order. And let me remind you yet again – the world doesn't beat a path to many people's doors any more! Translation? It means few Buyers volunteer orders. They expect Sellers to **ask** for them and if they don't ask, they let the Sellers go away empty handed and wait for more professional Sellers to come along and pick up the order with minimum effort – just that one extra question – 'Can I have your order?' Can we call it a deal?' 'Can we go ahead and deliver?'

Way back in the 1950s, Alfred Tack made a statement: 'If you don't close – you're working for the Competition.'

This says it all. Imagine finding a good prospect, researching his needs, establishing the carrot, dangling it successfully, getting face to face, asking all the right questions, surveying the situation, preparing and submitting a proposal, carrying out a demonstration, dealing with all the prospect's objections – and then leaving him for a few days to think it over.

Three days later, your competitor calls on the prospect, or his company, by chance, sees your name in the visitors' book in reception, gets face to face fast because he correctly guesses the situation, establishes how far you've gone, adds or adjusts a few things, does a swift proposal, and does what you didn't do – asks for the order. The prospect has already thought it over. You did most of the work, but this other Seller actually asked for the order – 'And he's here now, right in my office. Why bother with the first guy. Okay, its a deal.'

Two lessons to be learned here:

**Lesson One: Ask for an order on every call**. Make this one of your fundamental rules. You'll be amazed how much extra business it gets you. And note, I say 'ask for *an* order,' not 'ask for *the* order.' You might be some way off the big one, but there might be a few odds and ends you can pick up along the way. 'Anything you want to order while I'm here, George?', 'Are we anywhere near getting you to place the order yet, Charlie? Every day's costing you £500 in lost revenue!'

**Lesson Two: Watch that visitors' book in reception**. Don't fill it in with the whole truth. Make your signature indecipherable and leave out the name of your company. But read it carefully while you're making your entry. Look back a few pages for your competitors. See to whom *they're* talking.

If you don't close, you're working for the competition. But when it comes to closing the sale, there is **no** substitute for a good presentation, based on adequate knowledge and confidence.

If your presentation has been sound; if you've asked the right questions, dealt with all his doubts and queries, presented the evidence and the proof in a businesslike, professional way – the Close will be easy, will feel right to you, is the only logical way the meeting can end.

Remember the Sales Proposal in Chapter 9, and my 'If you want to win, take it in' rule. That's the culmination of a sound, professional presentation. Go through the Proposal, with the prospect, step by step, gathering agreement and commitment as you go. Get to the end and recap – 'Are you happy with everything, then? He has to say yes; he said yes every step of the way. 'Can we go ahead then?' Or even 'Great, then I'm delighted to have you as a customer.' As easy as that.

Remember the second ingredient that makes up the Killer Instinct? The first is Confidence which comes from knowledge. The second is Determination.

At Closing time, Determination is what makes a good Seller refuse to take **no** for an answer when he's asked for the order, when he **knows** the deal, product or service is right for this customer and when he *knows* he's done a good job.

A **no** in these circumstances must have a reason behind it – either a sound reason which the Seller has so far failed to uncover, or *politics*!

A **no** in these circumstances gets a sincere, surprised, 'Why Not?' from the Seller; possibly preceded by a touch of padding to help the sincerity shine through.

Always remember also that there are two kinds of no.

'No, not yet' and 'No, not ever.'

You *must* establish which **no** you've got before asking 'Why not?'

**Lesson Three:** before we get into Closing proper, is very simple and in fact applies whatever and wherever you are in selling: whenever you ask a customer or prospective customer a question, especially a closing question, when you've asked the question – **shut up!**

Don't say another word. Not one.

If, after six or seven seconds (and count them off to yourself) the silence is unbearable and you crack before he does, **ask the same question again.**

Just don't let him off the hook!

## Pre-Closing

The more commitment a Seller gets as he progresses through his sales presentation, the earlier the final Close will be. It's akin to building something, where brick upon brick the something grows into a finished edifice. In our case the finished edifice is an order.

Small elements of commitment can be secured from the very beginning onwards:

'Yes, you can come and see me next Tuesday at 4.50 pm.'
'Yes, we can go down and take a look at the assembly line.'
'Yes, I am interested in increasing my sales next quarter.'
'Yes, you can quote for the job.'
'Yes, delivery by 10 July will suit our schedule.'
'Yes, your standard colour is acceptable.'
'Yes, I'll have some!'

Lots of customers give Sellers opportunities to go for commitment. And lots of Sellers wouldn't recognize such an opportunity if it jumped up and hit them between the eyes. Some examples:

'Do you supply in 25 litre drums?'
'Can I get these in yellow?'
'Do you have a larger size?'
'Could you deliver by the end of this week?'
'Do you give a discount for cash?'

Most Sellers who get questions like these fired at them during a presentation answer 'Yes, of course,' and go on to talk about the 25 litre drums, or yellow widgets, or larger sizes, or even how much discount they can give this month (aaagghh!!!).

But, where's the commitment? The customer asked a question and in return he got more information. That's all.

What the really professional Seller does is field the customer's question, turn it round 180 degrees and fire it back at the customer – but gently.

'Do you supply in 25 litre drums?'
'I think we should be able to. Do you want your supplies in 25 litre drums?'
'Could you deliver by the end of this week?'

'Probably. Do you need delivery by the end of this week?'

Now the Seller will get a **yes** from the customer. That's commitment.

Customers often ask Sellers dumb questions. Consider a prospective customer who finds himself stuck for something to say and he knows it's fast approaching Closing Time. He's faced with a Seller who doesn't talk too much, who asks a lot of questions. He's reasonably happy, just wants to keep his end up. So he asks a random question:

'When can I get delivery?'

The Seller replies with another question: 'When do you want it?'

The customer doesn't really care. Delivery doesn't bother him at all. So he replies: 'Well, I suppose I can put it to work just about any time.'

And the Seller closes: 'All right. If I guarantee delivery by Wednesday of next week, can I have your order now?'

The customer has nowhere to go. He was dumb enough to ask the first random question, 'When can I get delivery?' Now he's going to look dumb in the eyes of the Seller if he says **no**. So he says **yes**.

Sellers themselves can ask commitment-getting questions during the early part of th₂ presentation.

My favourite is 'What do we need to do to get you to buy some of your supplies from us?'

The customer tells you what you need to do; you do it to his complete satisfaction and the business must be yours.

Other such questions might begin and end with certain key phrases like:

'You do—don't you?'
'You will—won't you?'
'This is—isn't it?'
'We are—aren't we?'
'This could—couldn't it?'
'If we can—will you . . .?'
'Suppose we—would you . . .?'

For example:

'You do want to keep an edge over your competitor down the street, don't you?'
'You will be re-ordering for the Christmas rush next month, won't you?'
'If we can prove to you that this unit will cut your office cleaning costs by 25%, will you let us put one in on a week's trial?'
'Suppose we could increase the life of your tooling by 10%, would you give us a try then?'
'If we can link you into some of our local advertising, will you change over to us?'

Or the questions could be very straightforward:

'How many gallons a month do you need?'
'How long will your present stocks last?'
'Which gate do we deliver to?'
'Will six boxes be enough to get you started?'


## The Preferences

Really successful Sellers have definite preferred techniques when it comes to closing the sale. A survey of 100 successful Sellers who sell to industry or direct to users (Speciality Sellers) established that 74 out of the 100 preferred to use the Alternative Choice close.

'Do you want it in the primer or in our standard finish?'
'Single phase supply or three phase supply?'
'Do you prefer the white finish or the satin aluminium?'
'Will you be paying cash or do you want us to invoice your company?'
'Shall we deliver or will you collect?'
'Do you want to take delivery in 5 gallon drums or 50 litre?'
'Which would be best for you, deliveries on Tuesdays or Thursdays?'
'Would you like to pay cash or use our lease purchase scheme?'

These are still commitment-getting questions, but as the Seller approaches Closing Time, they also become Closing Questions, and the commitment is very nearly for the order itself. A couple of alternative choice closes and all the Seller has to do to wrap things up is say something like:

'Okay, I think we've covered everything. Can you let me have an order number so that we can get cracking straight away?' or

'Fine. That's all the details I need. If you'll just let me have your signature on this order form, I'll put the wheels in motion first thing tomorrow morning.'

Successful Sellers who sell to retailers (Staple Sellers) prefer to use the Order Form close. Out of the 100 surveyed, 64 preferred this method. Alternative choice came second with 16.

The Order Form close, in retail selling, is the nearest thing to an automatic close any Seller can achieve. The Seller has his order form out and at the ready when he enters the store. He also has a copy of the last month's order to which to refer. The order form has printed on it a list of the Seller's entire stock lines.

He first checks the store's stockroom, then the shelves where his company's goods are displayed, so that he knows how much stock has been sold since his last visit and how much is left to sell. (Overselling a retailer is suicide for a Seller.)

Then he talks to the store manager. He tries to get the manager to walk round the store with him and most times the manager is only too happy to do this. During the walk-about, referring to his order forms and to the displayed goods, the Seller asks questions:

'How's the new line moving? As good as I said it would? Great. Same again this month or should we increase it to six cases?'

'Is this one still slow? It's going to pick up, don't worry. We've got an advertising campaign next week. I should fill the shelf if I were you. Two cases enough to do that?'

'We've got a special offer this month on this one. Should make a big splash over the next few weeks. Bound to be plenty of demand. What do you think, four cases?'

When the seller has covered every relevant line on his order form, plus any new lines which the manager and he have not previously discussed, he makes a final check on the form, turns it round to the manager and says:

'Fine. I think we've covered everything. Would you just okay this for me as usual, here at the bottom?'

## It's Never too Early

Opportunities to close the sale can come to Sellers at any time during a presentation. Asking for the order doesn't **have** to be at the end. The Seller doesn't **have** to move elaborately, step by step, through a formal planned presentation.

For example, a Seller of advertising space for a magazine might hear a customer say early on in his visit: 'We got very good results from that whole page advertisement we took with you last month.'

So the Seller closes. 'Great. Can I put you down for a page next month, then?'

In and out in 10 minutes flat. **With** an order!

## Try it for Size

I used this technique very successfully back in the mid-sixties when I was selling small fork-lift trucks at about £500 a time. If I established a definite need and knew that the particular truck I was recommending would do the job – fit the pallets, negotiate all the gangways, suit the floor, all the basic specification bits – I'd suggest to the customer: "Try our truck for a week. No charge, no obligation. If it doesn't do the job, or if your people don't like it, we'll have it back. If you're happy with it after a week, we'll invoice.' They hardly ever said No!

I knew that the price difference between my truck and any of my competitors' trucks to do the same job could not be more than £50. A week later, barring accidents, who the hell wanted to go to the trouble of arranging to send it back or switch to another truck for a saving of a measly £50? The truck stayed and we invoiced.

The key point to watch out for if you use this technique is you must make sure the product that goes in on trial for a week is actually put to use. There is little risk with something like a fork lift truck, but a new kind of paint, or chemical cleaner, or office calculator, or fastener, or tool, or electronic component might just stay on the shelf for the week, no one getting around to trying it out.

After the week, when you call back, the customer is often too sheepish to admit he forgot to try it out, so he says instead: 'Our chaps don't like it' or 'The difference is so small it isn't worth us changing over.'

It's up to **you** to make sure that if the product goes in on trial, it is used as it should be. Monitor things very closely, by telephone will do, several times during the week. It will pay handsome dividends.

## A TV Classic

One guy in the mid-west of America took this 'Try it for Size' closing technique and really refined it to the ultimate. He refined it so much, in fact, that it finished up not being a close at all, but it was incredibly successful nevertheless – for just one year.

The year was, I think, 1957. The first year of colour television in America. That year this guy, by using his very refined 'Try it

for Size' technique, sold more colour television sets than any
other dealer in the entire U.S.A.

Of course, the powers-that-be sent out a posse to find out how
he did it.

They found he was doing a lot of simple and cheap local radio
and newspaper advertising aimed just at getting people to walk
into his place of business to have a first look at colour television.
He had a big bank of sets working for the people to stand and
look at. After a few minutes' looking, this guy or one of his
assistants would walk up to the people and say:

'Hi! Bet you're wondering whether you and your family could live with
one of these, aren't you? Seen the reports? Lots of families all over
America are going nuts – just can't live with colour television.

'Tell you what – we wouldn't even **sell** you one unless you'd first decided
you could live with it. All our sets go out on that basis. Two weeks
absolutely free, including aerial. No obligation. The research is just as
important to us as Selling television sets.

'You want to try one for two weeks?'

Did they want to try one for two weeks? You bet they did. So the
installation team descended on their home – van, engineers in

overalls marked 'Colour TV', ladders – the aerial goes up on the chimney stack. And all their neighbours watch.

Next day the kids have invited all the other kids in to have a look. By the end of the first week most of the adult neighbours have been in for coffee or cocktails. By the end of two weeks the family is building up its sales resistance ready for the call they are expecting. And, dead on time, the telephone rings.

'Here it comes,' says the husband to his wife, picking up the 'phone.
'TV store here,' says the voice on the 'phone. 'Just ringing to check on the trial set. Is it working okay or should we come out to adjust it?'
No close. No sales pitch. If the set's working okay, the store says, 'Fine. Goodbye!'

Three and a half weeks maximum – every time – the husband and wife were back in the store asking, 'How do we go about buying this damn thing?'

Could they **really** send it back – even if they wanted to? All the kids and folks in their neighbourhood had been round to see it. Some of their friends by then had trial sets of their own. Could they ever say to them: 'We sent it back!'?

The application of the Joneses principle *par excellence*. But it only worked in the first year, while colour television was a novelty.


## I'd Like to Think about it!

The only customers a good Seller will have problems with are the ones who have no intention of buying anyway – for political or corruptive reasons – and the ones who are still procrastinating and uncertain, mainly because they are not very good at making decisions.

Most people are very *bad* at making decisions. They worry about putting their necks on the block if anything goes wrong with something they buy on behalf of their company. They worry about jumping out of the frying pan into the fire. They worry about all those stories they've heard about con men in Selling.

Just because a person has the responsibility for buying a few million pounds worth of goods and services for his company every year, don't assume he's the cat's whiskers when it comes to making business-buying decisions. The opposite is often the case.

Customers like these need some extra help from the Seller when it comes to closing the sale. Without the extra help, 'I'd like to think about it' will take over and that's where the sale will end.

## The Summary Close

If you are quick mentally and you really know your products' USP, (refer to Chapter 2 for USP) and your presentation backwards, when the customer says, 'Right; okay so far, but I'd like to think it over for a while,' you could say:

'Fair enough, Mr Jones. I know you won't be wasting your time giving this a lot of thought. I know it's right for you. But, just in case I've missed something out, precisely what aspects of the proposals do you want to think over – is it the performance of the equipment?'

You **must** get the first 'is it . . .' question in without a pause. A pause for breath after 'do you want to think it over . . .' and you give him the opportunity to say 'The whole thing!' Then you're dead. What you're trying to do is to get him saying **no** to a whole list of things –

'Is it the performance of equipment?'
'No.'
'Is it a question of acceptability by your work force?'
'No.'
'Is it the running costs?'
'No.'
'Is it the maintenance and service aspects?'
'No.'

You should get one or two **yes** answers as you go down your mental list. These you can then concentrate on for another five minutes at least, having first established there are no other points to come, simply by asking: 'Are these the only things that are worrying you, Mr Jones?'

Quite often, something very pleasant happens, however. You complete your mental check list and the customer's said no to every 'is it' you've put forward. Then you raise your eyebrows, smile happily and say: 'Well, there isn't anything else, Mr Jones, unless you can think of anything I've missed (pause for three seconds to make sure). Can we call it a deal, then?'

If, in response to your 'Are these the only things that are worrying you, Mr Jones?' he says, 'No; there are a few more things,' you switch from oral to written, take out your A4 survey pad and say – 'Do you mind if I get *all* the things you're worried about down on my pad, while they're completely clear in your mind? What are they?' .

Now you have the full short list to get your teeth into. Think about 'I'd like to think about it!' The problem you're really up against when the customer first says those dreaded words is that you've got **nothing** to get your teeth into.

Deal with the short list to his complete satisfaction and you can close with a straightforward – 'Well, if you're now satisfied on all points, Mr Jones, can we go ahead?'

## The Advantage List

Consider the customer who can't make his mind up whether to buy **your** goods or to stick with one of your competitors. If the USP is tooled up ready in your mind for both you **and** the competitor, the A4 survey pad again wins the day.

'I'm going to need to think about this for a while before deciding to switch suppliers. After all, we've dealt with your competitors for some time now. And with relatively few problems.'

The Seller empathizes: 'I can appreciate the problem, Mr Giles. We've both got a lot to offer you. Can I suggest something that might help you decide? Why don't we take a sheet of paper, draw a line down the middle and on one side list all the benefits to you of buying from us and on the other side list all the benefits to you of staying with your present supplier. It might help clarify the situation and it certainly can't do any harm, can it?'

If the customer is truly uncertain, he will agree to the idea. So you draw a line vertically down your A4 note pad, write your company's name at the top of the *left*-hand column, write his present supplier's name at the top of the right-hand column and begin listing and discussing the benefits the customer will derive from changing over to you. (You **always**, but always, complete **your** list first. Never, never the competitor's list first. Apart from psychological reasons; what happens if he gets called away when you're half-way through? Do you want to leave him with just a list of your competitor's benefits – in *your* handwriting? Sellers have been shot for less!)

A good Seller, well versed on his USP and his competitors, has no trouble at all filling his side of the pad with a list of all the plus points his goods give the customer. He'll probably leave out the minus points unless the customer himself suggests they go in. Then the Seller puts them in happily.

On switching to the right-hand side of the pad – the competitor's list of benefits, the Seller still volunteers help. He doesn't clam up and let the customer do the second part on his own. But, what he *does* help on are the benefits which he knows – and which he figures the customer knows – are common to both suppliers. These can be crossed out from both sides of the pad, once they've been established as common.

Once this has been done, the left-hand list will always be longer than the right-hand list. If it isn't, the Seller needs to swap jobs with the customer or go back for a refresher course at the product training school.

With this advantage list – even a higher price can be outweighed with the list of additional benefits on the left-hand side of the pad, which often will more than justify the difference in money.

The final close? 'Well, that looks pretty conclusive, doesn't it, Mr Giles. How much of the business do you want to move to us for the first quarter? Can I suggest 40% or do you want to go for the extra 5% discount and make it 50%?'

## Quality Closing

If the Seller is blessed with the best products at the highest price, there is a refinement of the advantage list close which is probably the single most successful advantage closing technique in the Selling business. It can be used for just about any kind of product or service, big money or small, and it is particularly useful when the Seller is closing with a committee or a board of directors, rather than one person.

The technique is known to me by the mnemonic QUALITY, the letters of the word standing for each of the seven stages of the technique:

Qualify and Quantify
Uncover and Understand
Ask for Everything
Lock the Prospect in
Isolate and Answer
Test the Lock
Yes is the ONLY Finish.

Many sales trainers have tailored this QUALITY mnemonic to their own methods of teaching. One has re-named it NUMBERS, which stands for:

Number One to Ten
Uncover the Objections
Make sure you've got them all
Bring in the Close
Eliminate one by one
Re-state the Close
Sign him up.

Another British trainer has gone as far as registering as a Trade Mark his particular version of this technique, which he calls LACPAAC and which spells out:

List
Ask Back
Close-in
Pre-Close
Answer and Abandon
Ask Back Again
Close

Let's develop the QUALITY/NUMBERS technique as it might be used by a really proficient Seller, chasing a fair-sized bit of business and facing a board of directors. He's delivered an excellent presentation, he's done his best to answer all the questions the members of the board have thrown at him. He has a 'feel' for the situation which tells him that all his efforts are appreciated, but he knows there are a few dismal jimmies on that board who don't like any kind of change. He figures he'll get a 'We'd like to think about it for a couple of weeks' and he's ready for it. He knows he has a better deal for this customer than they're getting at present and he isn't about to quit.

He winds up his presentation: 'Well, that's our proposition. I think you can see that it is a very definite improvement over what you are doing at present. How do you feel about it?'

A spokesman for the board looks round at his colleagues, gets a couple of frowns as well as a couple of nods and says to the Seller: 'It looks fine the way you've presented it, but we'd like to mull it over ourselves for a while before going ahead.'

The Seller then moves into the first stage of QUALITY.

## Stage One: Qualify and Quantify

'I agree; you **should** think it over. But, in my experience, when someone says they want to think it over, it is usually because there are some specific points they are unsure about, would you agree?'

Enough of the board will agree.

'Fine; let's get the specific points down so that we can all see what we're talking about.'

Bearing in mind the Seller is presenting to a board of directors, he should be using a flip chart and easel. If he is, he turns his flip

chart over to a blank sheet and writes down on the left-hand side the numbers one to ten. As he writes, he says out loud the numbers he is writing: 'One, two, three, four, five, six, seven, eight, nine, ten.'

If he hasn't the benefit of a flip-chart, he does the same thing on his A4 size survey pad. (The A4 pad will be ideal when this same technique is used with a single customer.)

The reasons for writing down the numbers one to ten are very important. Into the minds of that board of directors go the thoughts: 'This guy knows his business, he can answer at least ten points or queries and *everyone* he sells to must have queries.'

But we all know that very rarely does any customer have more than two or three points to raise.

'What points are you unsure about?' The Seller asks when he has completed his numbers, his felt pen or pencil poised over the number one.

## Stage Two: Uncover and Understand

The Seller writes on his flip chart or pad the first point given him by the board – maybe it will be: 'It's a hell of a lot of money. Do we really have enough justification for spending it?' But he doesn't write down all that – he tries to condense the point to as near only one word as he can. Maybe in this case the word could be 'Price'; or 'Justification for spending that much money' might serve the Seller better.

Most important of all in this second stage, the Seller must **only** write down points, and words, he understands. He must clearly see what the customer is getting at **and** how he can set about answering the point when the time comes. If a member of that board of directors were to give him a point which seemed to him to be ambiguous, he would respond: 'What exactly do you mean by that?' and establish some words with which he *is* happy. Sometimes, in asking a customer 'what do you mean' the resulting reply seems so daft to the customer who is trying to explain what he means that he gives up and says: 'Oh, forget it, I can see now that's been covered.'

Maybe the second point will be: 'We're a bit uncertain how your delivery date will fit into our scheduling. Annual summer holiday shut down is our usual time for things like this.' The Seller may write down 'Delivery' against number two on his flip chart or pad.

Maybe the third point will be: 'Your service response seems a bit slow at forty-eight hours. That's a long time to be out of production.' So he may write down 'Service Response Time'.

If the Seller is lucky he may get a Credibility point: 'How do we know this will do everything you say it will do?' He may write down 'Credibility/Proof'.

He'll be very unlucky if he gets more than four points. The input from the members of the board ceases. He waits three or four seconds and then moves to stage three.

## Stage Three: Ask for Everything

'Are these *all* the points you have?'

The directors confer and then nod. 'Yes.'

And the Seller then draws a bold line horizontally across the flip chart or pad, immediately under the last of the listed points, so that the remaining un-used numbers down to ten are all below the line.

### Stage Four: Lock the Prospect In

The Seller now tries for what is sometimes called a Pre-Close. A firm commitment based on the list of points from which he can go on to secure the order.

'If I am able to answer each of these points to your complete satisfaction, then can I assume we are in business?'

The likelihood of a 'Yes' is greater than 80%.

### Stage Five: Isolate and Answer

The Seller now proceeds, one by one, to answer each of the listed points to the complete satisfaction of the board of directors. As he covers each point, and the board agrees that the point is no longer a problem, the Seller crosses the point out on his flip chart or pad. A line all the way through the point, not just a cross in the margin.

If one particular point is more difficult for the Seller to answer than the others, he is permitted to leave it until last, even though it may not be the last on the list. The customer will know that that point is the most difficult, and will agree if the Seller says: 'That's a very good point. Let me come back to that when I've dealt with the rest.'

Good tactics, because when the Seller has dealt with the rest of the points and crossed them out, he can go for an even firmer commitment, point to the last remaining point and say: 'So if we can answer this last point to your complete satisfaction, we're in business.'

### Stage Six: Test the Lock

All points have been crossed out. Decision time has arrived. One final question remains to be asked: 'Have I answered each of these points to your complete satisfaction?'

It's too late for any member of the board of directors to say **no**. All they can do is say **yes**. And that *is* stage seven.

## Stage Seven: Yes is the ONLY Finish

No more questions to close the sale. It's closed. A follow-up question 'Can I have the order, then?' is superfluous – and bad tactics. The Seller should instead make a final statement, which might be: 'Splendid. I'm delighted to have you as a customer. It's a decision you won't regret.'

There could be one final administrative question necessary if the Seller is selling to a board of directors or any other kind of group or committee, as he is in this example: 'Which one of you will be issuing the order?'

## The Objections Themselves

Suggestions for handling Price and Delivery objections you'll find in Chapter 8 – 'How to Sell Quality and Your Higher Price'. But a few paragraphs ago I wrote: If the Seller is lucky he may get a Credibility point! 'How do we know this will do everything you say it will do?'

A very effective way to answer this kind of objection is for the Seller to say: 'Suppose we had one or a number of directors here in this room with us today, of companies like yours but who have been using our products for some time. Would I be right in assuming that you'd be guided by those directors?'

'Of course we would,' the board will reply.

'Well, they're not here with us today, but this is what they've written about our products.'

And the Seller produces from his briefcase his collection of Third Party Reference letters from happy, satisfied customers. Objection resolved to customers' complete satisfaction.

It is incredible how many Sellers do not have such third party reference letters. Why? Because they've never thought of asking their customers to write them. When a customer says to them, 'Hey, we're delighted with that widget crusher you sold us a year ago; it's saving us a mint of money,' they just reply 'Oh, great,' rather than saying, 'That's absolutely splendid. Would you do me a great favour? Would you write me a letter to that effect. I'd love to show it to my sales director. And could I put a couple of my new customers in touch with you, so that they could ask you how you're finding our equipment? It would help me a lot.'

Every good Seller up against stiff competition needs at least twenty third party references that can be used when necessary. Two or three are better than none at all, but, nowhere near as credible as twenty. And they should be kept up to date – the oldest ones being replaced by new ones on a continuous basis.

A salesforce of, say, ten Sellers can do it the easy way, each Seller securing *two* third party reference letters and **all** the letters being used by **all** the Sellers.

Which brings us back to 'How to Close More Sales' and those 'I'd like to think about it' customers.


## Third Party Reference Closes

Very often, a third party reference can be elaborated upon, using the money savings or turnover gains the customer has achieved and building a story around this. Then this is what the situation becomes.

'I can understand you wanting to spend some time thinking this over, Mr Brown. In fact, I had a very similar situation some months ago over at Universal Widgets.

They had been using Snook's oils for years and it took their works manager a long time to decide to switch to us. But since they did, their oil stocks have reduced by a third because of our 24 hour delivery service, they've got much better tool life all round through using our special cutting oils, and they reckon that overall they're saving about £2,400 a week.

'Look, (produces third party reference letter) this is what UW's works manager said in a letter he wrote to us only last month.

'Would it help you decide if I had a word with UW and took you over to talk to your opposite number over there? Every week you think about it could be costing your company the same kind of money – £2,400 a week. That's £120,000 a year. Or can we get something started today?'

A good, true, relevant story, with figures, about another customer with whom your new prospect can identify. Followed up with an offer to set up a meeting. Followed up with reinforcement of the kind of money he's losing if he keeps thinking about it and doesn't act. Finishing with an alternative choice close – the meeting or give me an order now!

This is the winning combination for storytelling closing.

In the life insurance business, this technique is fondly known as the 'Back-the-hearse-up-to-the-door-and-let-them-smell-the-flowers' close. To use it well, the Seller must be sincere, must be senior in years and must have the bedside manner of a clergyman.

Picture a domestic sales situation. Husband, wife and little daughter. Not really interested in buying any life insurance. They aren't planning on dying for years yet. They're going to think about it – and not very much. The Seller tells a story:

'You know, sitting here talking to you and your wife and seeing your little girl – how old is she, six? – I keep remembering another family I talked to about three months ago. They had a little girl like yours.

'We were discussing the same kind of life policy we're discussing now but, I don't know, maybe they really couldn't afford the premiums just then. Anyway, I didn't succeed in persuading them that they should do it – they didn't have insurance at all, you see.

'And then, only a week later, I read in the local paper that both of them – the mother and father I mean – had been killed in a car crash. A lorry jackknifed or something. And ever since I keep thinking of that little girl and wishing I'd have been able to do something that night to get her parents to take out *some* cover.

'It happens so often, with no warning at all. You can't insure against it **not** happening, but – it's the helpless ones who are left who haunt me, with a whole life ahead of them and no way of fending for themselves.'

## Recap

Now none of this is new. It's all been around the business a long, long time. There isn't much about Selling that *is* new. But all these old techniques, if you practise them and apply them skilfully, still work superbly well. And see how much fun you get out of closing more sales if you put your mind to it.

If you *don't* close, remember, you're working for the competition – and you're in the wrong business.

# How to Win in the Exhibition Arena

**Our stand at a trade exhibition gives us an opportunity to get at all our competitors' customers.**

**But it also gives all our competitors an opportunity to get at *our* customers.**

**So this is a game we simply *must* be best at, or we shouldn't do it at all.**

There is still nothing to compare with a stand at a trade exhibition for launching a business and its products or services towards new customers, new contacts and new markets – providing the stand itself is properly designed, the products are properly displayed, the stand manning staff perform properly and the enquiries are logged properly.

90% of businesses that exhibit still get at least two of these four provisos wrong – and pour their exhibition budget money down the drain.

It's why quite a few past exhibitors have been heard to comment unfavourably about the 'sport'. A recent survey quoted exhibitors as saying things like 'Stand space costs £50 a square metre, more than five times the cost of a first class hotel, but without bed, bath, loo and colour TV. The stand itself costs about the same again!' and 'I'd rather increase coverage by other means without shows. Costs are becoming prohibitive' and 'In no other activity do managers leave themselves so exposed.'

But the exhibition business is booming – and likely to continue to boom. Most exhibition centres are booked for years ahead. So why are exhibitions good for some businesses and bad for others?

The answer is exhibitions should be good for every kind of

business. It's the approach to exhibiting and the way an exhibition cuts right across all departmental boundaries within the business, that gives senior executives a jaundiced opinion of this key element in sales promotion.

One big problem is that businesses tend to look at the cost of an exhibition stand in isolation. They rarely compare the costs with alternative ways to generate the same amount of orders, or enquiries.

Let me give you an example. If you were head of a machine tool manufacturing or distributing business and I walked into your office one day and told you I could supply you with a list of names and addresses of people who have already shown an interest in buying your machine tools, what would you say?

I'll bet your first question would be 'How much?'

'£25 per name and address,' I'd reply. And I'd stand a good chance of getting thrown out on my ear.

But consider the nature of the machine tool business. You have a salesforce out there, making most of their calls on prospective customers, rather than existing customers – because machine tools is essentially a 'one-off' business, and highly competitive. You'd be up against forty or more competitors on every sales territory.

Your salesforce makes a lot of Cold Canvass calls, without the benefit (so far) of the techniques we discussed in Chapter 4. On average, for every ten Cold Canvass calls, the salesforce gets face-to-face with one possible prospect – a 'warm one'. But a call, any kind of call, you know costs £25 to make. That's a simple piece of arithmetic – total cost of the salesforce divided by the number of calls made, for any given period of time.

So one 'warm one' costs £250 if you let your salesforce handle the job. And you threw me out on my ear when I offered you a list of warm ones for one-tenth of the cost.

That's how people often look at the cost of exhibiting.

I used this example because in 1976 I was involved, as a consultant, in the planning and manning of an exhibition stand at the International Machine Tool Exhibition.

The budget, not including the cost of the machines on display, was £30,000. Over the duration of the Exhibition, the stand manning staff **sold** all the machines on the stand **and** logged the names and addresses of more than 1,200 people they hitherto didn't know existed, who set foot on the stand and showed an interest in the machines.

If we assume that the sales of the actual machines on display covered the labour costs of all the staff involved on the stand, we're left with 1,200 'warm ones' and a cost of £30,000 for being there.

That's £25 per logged name and address!

Whatever your business, this is the way you should cost out the viability of the exhibitions in which you consider participating.

**Why are you Exhibiting?**

Are you aiming to increase your market share? Maintain your market share? Recover your past market share?

Does your market penetration need to spread, go deeper, or be re-directed?

Are you seeking to probe into a new market, explore the unknown, or infiltrate a competitor's market with malice aforethought?

Are you seeking to promote to your customers and potential customers new applications for your products, new features and benefits of your products, improved quality, longer life, new versatility, new design, colour, shape?

Are you aiming to show off products or services which are new to the Industry that the Exhibition caters for, or new to the markets for which you cater?

Are you aiming to introduce new trade marks or brand names or to pioneer 'ahead of its time' new technology?

Or are you just considering a stand because you have an uneasy feeling that because the competition is going to be there, you ought to be there?

Whatever the reason, you'd better be sure of it – and it had better be a good, valid reason – before you begin planning the event.

Here is another good reason for exhibiting. It is a table of statistics from Hugh Buckner's *How British Industry Buys* and concerns how the various executives in a customer company acquire information on products and services they need to buy.

| In industry, personnel with these functions (right) consider, in the percentages shown, the factors (below) to be amongst the two most important when obtaining information on products | Board (general management) | Operating management | Production engineering | Design and development engineering | Maintenance engineering | Research | Buying | Finance | Sales | Others |
|---|---|---|---|---|---|---|---|---|---|---|
| Catalogues | 39 | 36 | 45 | 64 | 34 | 64 | 52 | 32 | 44 | 76 |
| Direct mail | 12 | 9 | 14 | 6 | 31 | 21 | 23 | 14 | 5 | 27 |
| Salespersons' visits | 66 | 61 | 60 | 67 | 78 | 64 | 64 | 60 | 73 | 40 |
| Advertisements in trade press | 14 | 32 | 28 | 22 | 21 | 15 | 12 | 23 | 24 | 24 |
| Exhibitions | 15 | 17 | 11 | 11 | 47 | 15 | 9 | 19 | 14 | 12 |
| Demonstrations by manufacturers | 50 | 41 | 35 | 26 | 37 | 21 | 37 | 38 | 45 | 22 |
| Other | 6 | 4 | | 6 | | | 5 | 5 | 35 | |

## The Exhibition Budget

When it comes to putting together a budget for an exhibition stand, the 'ostrich complex' normally prevails. Items which should be included in the exhibition budget are hived off and buried elsewhere, to reduce the apparent expenditure. Few businesses tackle the budgeting task as it should be done – as if you were presenting a Proposal to a prospective customer: Cost/benefit ratios, objectives, recommendations for achieving the objectives, financial justification, even guarantees and third party references (past successful exhibitors and ABC past attendance figures).

Here's a list of most of the items which **should** be included in your exhibition budget (use the blank space for *your* figures).

### The Stand
1 Stand space
2 Stand design
3 Furniture and fittings
  functional
  protective
  for decoration
4 Exhibits
  main items
  auxiliary equipment
  sign writing
5 Publicity display equipment
6 Stand transport charges
  to exhibition
  from exhibition
  mechanical handling
  packing
7 Construction charges
  erection
  dismantling
  maintenance
  sundry labour
8 Other costs
  services
  communication
  insurance

entertainment
clerical aids
security
safety
cleaning
waste disposal
repairs
consumables

**The Staff**
1 Your own staff's salaries
2 Other staff's salaries
demonstrators
hostesses
interpreters
others
3 Expenses
travel (to, from, at)
hotel
living
equipment, clothing

**Promotion**
1 Advertising and PR
before
during
after
2 Sales and technical literature
3 Other publicity materials
4 Give-aways
5 Catalogue entry and advertising

## The 'Hilton' rule

Conrad Hilton, founder of the world famous hotel chain, claims there are only three factors which guarantee the success of a hotel:

### Position, position and position!

So it is with an exhibition stand. If you're stuck in some minor side gangway in the annex, you'll only attract a small fraction of the number of visitors who actually attend the exhibition. It's like advertising in the wrong publication. Not enough of your market notices your advertisement!

This means your planning has to begin early, so that you have the pick of the prime stand space (assuming, of course, you can afford the prime space). Opposite the main entrance. In full view of the stairs leading from one main hall to another. Next to the restaurant or, better still, the bar, or adjacent to the toilets. These are normally the best positions.

You have yet another problem. More and more exhibition organizers are insisting that you conform to the standard shell scheme for overall stand design. This tends to produce overall monotony and a very flat top surface view if you pick a high vantage point and assume the role of a prospective customer, looking out over the entire exhibition hall, trying to pick out your stand. A good stand designer can turn this to advantage, giving you a slightly higher 'focal point', even by cheating a little, and 'a focus of interest in a desert of imagination', for your stand design in general.

But don't let the designer get carried away. The object of the exercise is to display and sell your products or services, not his creativity. Make sure the stand itself doesn't look **more** attractive than the products being displayed, otherwise you'll find yourself selling exhibition stands!

Use a professional designer and stand building organizer, because your stand **must** look professional, not as if it's been cobbled together at the last minute by the sales department, who'd forgotten until last week that the exhibition was even taking place. Never, never, never, use existing display units from your front offices or factory. Your stand needs to be an integrated whole, not a series of isolated, disjointed, second-hand bits and pieces. The competition will love it, but your customers and your salesforce will despise it. Better not being there at all.

## The Barriers

The objective of being there is to attract as many people on to your stand as you can during the show (isn't it?). What you do with them once you've got them on to your stand we'll discuss later.

The incredible thing is how many exhibitors seem deliberately to make it as difficult as possible for casual prospects to walk on to their stands. They build barriers around the stand. They restrict the single entrance and exit to thirty-six inches maximum and position a salesman in the centre of the entrance, his feet ten centimetres over the edge, arms folded, 'ready to repel boarders' expression on his gloomy face. (Actually, it's last night's booze-up that's making his head and his feet ache!)

The casual prospect, the majority of people you're trying to catch, won't come near your stand unless he can see clearly as he approaches that he can easily walk on – and easily walk off again without being captured. That's his subconscious talking, and it's a very powerful argument.

So make sure your stand designer bears this firmly in mind.

My prize for barrier building goes to a scaffolding firm at the Materials Handling Exhibition a few years ago. They'd given the job of designing the stand to one of their own draughtsmen with the instructions, 'Build as much of the product into the design as you can.'

The result was a towering mass of scaffolding, within which was the discussion platform and chairs, tables, etc – *five feet off the ground*.

Worse than that. The only access to and from the discussion platform was one set of portable steps, stores variety. The 'gallows steps' deterrent. No casual potential customers will journey up a set of steps, especially to reach a discussion area immediately beneath several tons of scaffolding.

Over five days, I don't think that company logged a single name and address of anyone who wasn't already a customer.

Be open. Be welcoming. Look friendly. No implied threats to life or limb.

## Signs and Colours

Here are a few specifications, because I know from experience they are hard to find elsewhere.

The signs you use on your stand need to be read clearly from a number of different distances, ranging from the other side of the hall – 'Ah! There they are, over there!' – to a couple of feet away – 'That's interesting. I didn't know UWC's widget crusher would do that.'

So the *size* of your lettering needs to be appropriate to the purpose of the sign itself. Here are the minimum sizes and distances for clear reading:

> 20 feet away – lettering 2 inches high (minimum)
> 50 feet away – lettering 3 inches high (minimum)
> 75 feet away – lettering 4 inches high (minimum)
> 100 feet away – lettering 5 inches high (minimum)
> over 100 feet away – lettering 6 inches high (minimum)

If you use polystyrene letters, fire regulations now dictate it must be self-extinguishing grade.

On colour, don't ever get hooked on *just* your house colour. Ten to one you'll ruin your stand if you do. Use colours to accentuate your product displays. Here's another list of colour 'feelings':

Blue is cold
Red is warm
Green is soothing (unless it's acid or 'puke'!)
White is clinical
Yellow is fresh

See the section on Colours in Chapter 8 for more input on this subject.


## Models

I'm not going to talk about the female variety who are rarely properly briefed to do anything useful except look gorgeous and pacify complainers. I want to say a few words about what you can do if you haven't any products to display, because you sell a service.

One such company I can use as an example is Knight Wegenstein Ltd, consultants to the foundry industry. At every

Foundry Exhibition, you'll find KW at the bottom of the steps leading from Hall 5 into Hall 4 at the National Exhibition Centre, a huge yellow KW inverted triangle on the front of their stand, acting as a superb focal point to attract the casual visitor.

On the stand itself is an intricate table top model of an automated foundry, under a sheet of thick perspex. No one can resist a good model. Referring to aspects of the model foundry, KW's stand staff can discuss any aspect of their consultancy services.

I've seen lifting gear specialists with models of building sites full of tower cranes with which the visitors can play games. I've seen testing laboratories with flight simulators and JPS racing cars on their stands as focal points. I've even seen a cleaning services company with a stand comprised of an elaborate model railway.

My favourite services stand didn't use a model, it designed the stand completely as a cafe. Rows of little square tables covered with chintzy table cloths, a tea counter with polished tea urns. Half a dozen waitresses. The stand in question was at the Hanover Fair in 1977. The company actually *cleaned* the Hanover Fair, and about half the factories and offices in West Germany. Every visitor to the cafe was a valid potential customer. Great stuff.


## No Telephones

Why do you want telephones on an exhibition stand? No one from the works should be allowed to contact the stand staff during exhibition opening hours and the stand staff certainly shouldn't want to contact anyone outside whilst they are on duty. When they're off-duty they can find a telephone somewhere else or use the one in your hospitality suite (next subject).

If the telephone is on the specification only because the Chairman likes to use it on the day he visits the stand, take it off the spec. Take his chair and desk away too!

**Hospitality and Hospitality Suites**

During the planning stages you should decide whether to allow boozing on your stand, or to keep it dry and rent a hospitality suite or room, adjacent to the exhibition hall.

That's what we did in 1976 at the Machine Tool Exhibition, long reputed to be 'the wettest show on earth!' No drinks of any kind on the stand, no personal belongings, no off-duty stand staff, no literature, no telephone. Just business.

Any existing customer who walked on to the stand, unless he'd come to see something in particular, was whisked away ASAP to the hospitality suite by his local sales engineer or by one of our hospitality girls (from the Company's sales office, plus two wives of directors). There he could booze in private, out of sight and reach of our competitors at the show. We wooed lots of their customers in that suite and they didn't know a thing about it!

Any existing customer who'd come to the stand to lodge a complaint was in the hospitality suite so fast his feet hardly touched the ground. The last place you need a complaining customer is publicly in the middle of your exhibition stand.

Any potential customer who requested literature was taken to the hospitality suite for a drink, his name and address and requirements written down by the girl on the literature desk in the suite, a large envelope typed on her typewriter in front of his eyes and the literature was in the post that very night, to be on his desk waiting for him when he got back to his office.

'You don't want to carry literature around for the rest of the day, Sir. Let me take your name, address and particulars and we'll get it in the post tonight to your office' (pointing to typewriter).

While I'm on the subject of hospitality, let's consider the kind of hospitality you tend to give your existing customers.

At an exhibition, you have an opportunity to show your gratitude for past business placed, with champagne or something suitable. But you don't necessarily want to go splashing champagne around for the casual punters and the hangers on. Lagers, gin and tonics, teas, coffees, crisps and peanuts will normally do for these people. So how do you separate the two?

You can't totally. But you can go at least half-way – and half-way will show you a big saving in cases of champagne.

Select one day of the show and invite all your existing customers to your stand on that day, and to one of a series of celebrations held that day in your hospitality suite. Not all your customers will be able to attend that day, but a sufficient number will to show you that considerable saving for the rest of the show.

Your top brass always attend on this day, of course. It's the existing customers they need to talk to.

Do this, and you'll find the rest of the days relatively clear of existing customers (whom you can call on any old time – you know who and where they are) so that you can concentrate more fully on capturing the potential customers and your competitors' customers.

Just a note here about private 'At Home' exhibitions, where you invite selected customers and prospective customers to your own show in your own showroom. Take two days for the event and invite your customers on one day and your prospects on the other. Same thing then applies for the booze.


### It Will Start – Whether you Are Ready or Not!

Early on in the planning stages, your exhibition stand team should have sat through the Video Arts Ltd training film or video *It'll be Okay on the Day!* Each member of the team should be in possession of the Video Arts/Andry Montgomery Group booklet – 'What every exhibitor ought to know'.

This booklet is full of check lists for both planning and manning an exhibition stand, and later on in the process you should be showing the stand-manning team the second Video Arts film or video referred to in the booklet – *How Not to Exhibit Yourself!*

One of the check lits in this booklet is for making sure your stand is ready for the opening of the show. The top ten rules of project management:

1 Agree objectives.
2 Establish command.
3 Establish responsibilities.

4  Plan all dates backwards from opening day.
5  Every manager must have his own calendar.
6  Fix key meetings a long way in advance.
7  Circulate information religiously.
8  Chase progress relentlessly.
9  Check budgets regularly.
10  Resist afterthoughts ruthlessly.

(If you're currently contemplating a stand at a major show, nine months ahead, I hate to tell you, but you should have begun the planning three months ago!)

If *you* are the fortunate person to have been designated 'Stand Manager', with the responsibilities of the Captain of a ship, even over the chairman, let us move on to those hectic few days before the opening of the show, when you and your team are working fourteen hours a day in the exhibition hall, frantically trying to get everything ready for D-day.

## What you Can Do and what you Can't Do

If you've been there before, you'll doubtless know the rules – written and unwritten! Don't try to beat the system. If you do, all the exhibition construction labour, the carpenters, the painters, the electricians, the furniture contractors, the carpet layers, the flower people, will down tools in a flash and every other exhibitor at the show will be blaming **you**.

For exhibitions, the Unions rule, okay!

You can 'dress' your own stand, which implies handling anything that is free standing. You can do your own fetching and carrying – they're not proud! But **no tools**. Don't even mend a fuse.

If you use your own workforce to help with the free-standing exhibits, the positioning of the products (but not including the testing and running of anything that's going to actually perform during the show), or the erection of partitions, the workers must belong to the right Unions.

In Britain, most site workers belong to one of three Unions:
UCAT – The Union of Construction and Allied Trades

T & GW – The Transport and General Workers Union (drivers and labourers)

EETPU – The Electrical, Electronic, Telecommunication and Plumbing Union

Most major exhibition halls publish a comprehensive document on what you can do and what you can't. Don't rely on just the information you get from the exhibition organizer – he just hires the hall. If in doubt, go direct to source for the full facts.

A hot tip from me. If you want your stand finished **first**, not last, first thing you do when you get to the exhibition hall is you make contact with the Union organizer or, better still, the Area Convenor, if there's such a body on site.

'My name's John Fenton, UWC, stand number 76 in Hall 4. I'm responsible for the stand. Just thought I'd say hello and find out if there is anything I should know, or can tell you, so that we get the stand finished with plenty of time to spare.

'Who are your people I should talk to for lighting and for final sign touching up?

'Where do I make contact with them?

'Who should I talk to if we encounter any problems?'

He'll get the message. And the tip when the job's completed.

Any bits and pieces you need, extra to the original agreed list with the labour force, you pay 50% of the cash up front, and 50% when the job's done. It's the only way – otherwise you'll stay at the bottom of the list. Don't forget, there are a lot of other stand managers, all trying to be first to finish.

Have at least £200 in cash on you if you're stand manager for a major show in Britain. I don't know what the going rate is for any other country – but I do know there is one.

## Don't Forget the Excitement

One final point before we move on to how to win during the exhibition itself.

Exhibitions should be exciting. Your stand should be exciting. Your stand staff should catch the mood of the show, because it **is** 'Show Business'.

If your stand design is drab, lacking in colour and movement and life, your stand staff will perform likewise.

## Manning the Stand

Manning a stand at a trade exhibition is an incredibly tiring occupation, both physically and mentally. Bear one fact of life very clearly in mind – the guards outside Buckingham Palace are changed every two hours, and they just have to stand there!

Don't expect anyone to be able to put in an eight hour day, for five days, on an exhibition stand **and** be sharp, professional, able to take advantage of every opportunity that presents itself. It can't be done.

You'll need a rota system. Two hours on and two hours off. And by 'off' I mean off and away from the stand, not lounging about taking up very expensive selling space. (The benefits of a hospitality suite again!) You need enough stand staff to make the rota system work, you need a good stand manager who can make the discipline of running a successful stand stick, and you need a good deputy stand manager, just in case of accidents. Then you need the appropriate number of auxiliary stand staff – for reception, clerical duties, technical for demonstrations, specialists and top brass, linguists if it is an International show and you're trying to capture export business.

Don't sort this out *ad hoc*. Plan it well in advance.

If you have any choice in the selection of stand-manning staff, here is a checklist you might find useful. Think about each individual on each of the eight factors, plus sub-factors, before deciding yes or no. If you yourself are on the short list, take it personally and see if you can measure up positively to all eight.

1 Educational background
   general
   technical
   special
   languages
2 Training
   what has been given?
   what is its relevance to the exhibition?
3 Exhibition experience
   types attended
   venues – home/overseas
   duties carried out
4 Contacts
   in location – home/overseas
   customers
   other exhibitors
   exhibition authorities
5 Personality
   behaviour
   appearance
   self-confidence
6 General attitude
   what is it?
7 Attitude to stand duty
8 Attitude to 'exhibitions'

A few comments about this checklist:

On Personality – you need *happy* people; people who look smart, behave professionally, won't frighten the casual visitors.

Try to avoid anyone whose facial characteristics make them look bad-tempered or aggressive or frightening. (I employed a guy once who was so gaunt his face looked like a skeleton with skin in harsh light. I never put him on stand duty.)

On General Attitude – you need the 'Company' person, rather than the loner. The people who have the interests of the business at heart.

On Attitude to Stand Duty – you're looking for the people who see the task of manning an exhibition stand as exciting (for the right reasons) rather than those who consider it a chore.

On Attitude to 'Exhibitions' – you're looking for those 'Company' people who see the exhibition as something that will clearly do the business some good, who understand the things that can be achieved and maybe some of the things that can't!

The rest of this chapter is a true-life story of one business aiming to beat its competitors comprehensively in the exhibition arena. Use this example as a blueprint for your next show.

## D-Day Minus 7

Today, seven days before the exhibition opens, the whole man-ning team attended a **briefing**. It was thorough, thank goodness, lasting all morning. Plenty of time and opportunity for questions.

The main objectives of being at the exhibition were stated, examined, questioned and agreed. Don't often see a unanimous vote in this Company, but we got one here.

Then we went through each of the products we'll be having on the stand, its position, what key benefits we'll need to stress to visitors, the back-up literature for each. The boss had a giant drawing of the stand plan on one wall and a model of the complete stand and exhibits which we could all walk round and view from all approach directions. These helped a lot.

We were made to write down the three main objectives for all the stand-manning staff!

To make direct sales.
To set up appointments for future calls.
To get the names and addresses and interests of every person who sets foot on our stand during the show whom we hitherto didn't know.

Samples of the exhibition enquiry forms we would be using were handed round and a couple of role plays were conducted to test procedure for bugs and gremlins. Another unanimous vote.

The boss appointed the Stand Manager and his deputy and publicly, in front of the whole team, delegated his own authority to the Stand Manager for the duration of the show. I can still hear the boss's words:

'Jim Thomas has the same authority next week as the captain of a ship. His ship will be this exhibition stand. If he needs to throw you over-board, set you adrift on a cutting out or foraging expedition or press gang more hands, that's what he'll do, and he'll speak with my voice. Believe it.

'If I get in the way, he has the authority to throw **me** overboard.

'The discipline on our stand next week is going to help us crucify the competition, steal a lot of their customers, and keep them well away from our customers.

'I look to you all to give Jim 100% support.'

Then we discussed stand security, competitive tactics during the show, procedures for handing in our enquiries twice a day – once at 1 pm and again at close of business – and the diary for special visitors.

Rotas were drawn up and agreed. Hotel reservations were verified. Touch wood, no one looked like going sick or getting married or arrested next week.

The girls who will be handling the hospitality suite and the literature stocks went through their procedures. Another two role plays, one for a drunken complainer. Lots of fun, but everyone got the message.

The boss did his usual thing about getting to bed reasonably early each night. The discussion on how he defined 'reasonably' lasted twenty minutes. When will some of these people grow up?

This time, we didn't get a unanimous vote, but the majority, for no later than midnight, was considerable. And the boss had the Ace anyway – the exhibition party was on the *last* night, with no early to bed stipulation and the opportunity of a lie-in the next morning (clear hotel rooms by 12 noon and pay bill on departure). But if anyone reported unfit for duty at 8.30 any morning during the show, or couldn't pass the walk-the-white-line test, the party was cancelled.

Any other activities, business or pleasure, during the show, were banned for every member of the manning team.

Finally we discussed the competitions we were participating in during the show and the tactics we'd planned for demoralizing our competitors. Exhibitor's badges, tickets and car parking passes were allocated.

This is really going to be a great exhibition. I can feel it already.

## D-Day Minus 1

The one thing about the day before an exhibition opens is that, except for the stand builders' vehicles, you can park easily. So for the familiarization briefing, everyone arrived punctually at the allotted time.

Jim Thomas, as Stand Manager, briefed us all on the stand layout, where the electrical switchboard was sited, where the emergency telephone was locked away (one key only, and Jim's got it), the best route to our hospitality suite so as to avoid our competitors' stands, where we keep our personal belongings, visitors' belongings, the booze and the food in the hospitality suite.

Then we did a conducted tour of the exhibition hall to establish the geography of the place, where the telephones, toilets, bars, restaurants, press office, first aid, lost property and lifts were situated. If we'd had time, I reckon Jim would have organized a 'find-your-way-back-to-base' army style survival test.

Jolly useful couple of hours, though. I'll cut a good half hour off my journey each day as a result. Didn't realize there were so many short cuts and easier ways of getting from A to B and back again.

## D-Day

Well, everything is ready on time. The Royals are opening the exhibition. The visitors are starting to stream in. I feel great. I know what I have to do. I'm armed and ready with survey pad, exhibition enquiry form and a spare in my pocket. Everything's been tested and proved to be working. Now all I've got to do is get the first order of the day and win that bottle of champagne (which I will receive **next** week!)

Seeing that Video Arts film again last night was a good final recap. *How Not to Exhibit Yourself!* Ha. Won't see us making any of those mistakes this time.

Jim even ran a final dress parade before we opened for business this morning. Good job too. Three guys had pens in full view in their breast pockets – sign of a clerk, not a professional Seller! Two chaps and one of the girls were sporting brand new shoes. Bet their feet will be killing them by lunch time.

Fred and Arnold laughed when I told them about my thick wool socks and talcum powder. Let's see who's laughing by mid-week.

First wooden spoon award went to Dave, who at 11.23 precisely sat on one of the visitors' chairs. Harry went into a trance or something at 12.16 and we caught him in a classic prison guard stance, feet ten centimetres over the front edge of the stand, arms folded, 'ready to repel boarders' expression on his face. We pulled his leg unmercifully and he kept saying he didn't know he was doing it. Just shows how easy it is to lose concentration. Those two hour duty rotas are a winner. We must be working at 95% efficiency. But this is only the first morning.

Our lapel badges are winners, too. They each have our name, the Company's name and a question in letters large enough to be seen five or six feet away – 'How can I help you?'

No one believed at the briefing that the question would break the ice with the visitors to our stand the way it is doing. A good 30% are reading the badge, thinking about the question it puts into their minds and start talking to us before we start talking to them. Great! The addition of that first word, 'How' is making us avoid that horribly easy to fall into trap of saying to a visitor, 'Can I help you?' I well remember at our last exhibition how many visitors replied – 'No thanks. Just looking!'

Our exhibition enquiry forms are much better than last time. For the previous exhibition we used a standard form, available from any business stationers. This time, we've designed our own, to make sure we gather precisely the information we need to meet our three main objectives *and* to cut down writing to a minimum.

The discipline/training/security system seems very good, too. A few members of the stand manning team couldn't understand why Jim Thomas is insisting on every single enquiry form filled in with a visitor being given to him personally at 1.00 pm and at close of business each day.

The first lot have just been collected, because few of us thought this system could be made to work. So Jim's just given us a short sharp lecture on the reasons behind the system, and warned us that if anyone doesn't deliver tonight and from then on at the designated times, he/she goes home.

'You don't even hang on to enquiries for your own territories,' Jim said. 'I need to count, analyse and examine every single one. The more people who carry enquiries around, the greater is the

**SALES ENQUIRY**

Seen By ...........................

| | |
|---|---|
| Name of Firm | Date / / |
| Address | |
| Business | ☎ |
| Person(s) | Position |
| Interested in | Department |
| | Quotation/Action Required:- |

Information or Literature Required

Literature Supplied

Mailing List Add:                    Delete:

*Henden Blaise & Co. 21 Shrewsbury Road, Beckenham, Kent.  01-650 1173*
*To Re-Order ask for SALES ENQUIRY PADS*

---

Exhibition _____ Date _____

Seen by _____

Company _____

Address _____

_____

Phone no. _____

Contact 1 _____

Contact 2 _____

Type of industry _____

| ACTION | | |
|---|---|---|
| Standard letter | yes | no |
| Visit A.S.A.P. | yes | no |
| Visit by appointment | yes | no |
| Remarks _____ | | |
| _____ | | |
| _____ | | |
| **Mailing list** | yes | no |

**ENQUIRY GRADE**

---

**SMT-PULLMAX**
**MACH'76 Enquiry**

**Products of interest**

| Notes on specific details | Metal Cutting | Metal Forming |
|---|---|---|
| General Information | ☐ ST 10-220 | ☐ P31-CNC220 |
| Budget Price | ☐ ST 14-220 | ☐ Pullmax Universal |
| Quotation | ☐ ST20-220 | ☐ Pullmax Beveller X91 |
| Time Studies | ☐ VHF/3/3U/3UBS | ☐ Pullmax Ring Roller 731 |
| Demonstration | ☐ Unipré 1000 | ☐ Kumla Rolls PV7H |
| | | ☐ Ursviken Press Brakes |
| | | ☐ Ursviken Guillotine |
| | | ☐ Wikstroms BW300 |
| | | ☐ Wikstroms BW225/4DV |

**Literature taken at MACH'76 stand**
☐ General Catalogue m/c    ☐ General Catalogue m/f

**Reason for Interest**
☐ Expanding production    OTHERS
☐ Replacing existing plant
☐ Seeking to reduce labour force

Name _____ Position _____
Company _____
Address _____
_____
Telephone Number _____ Extension _____
Best Time For Sales Engineer To Call _____

---

danger of losing a few, or having them snatched. Don't underestimate our competitors. The enquiry form that goes missing
might be the one that leads to the biggest order we've ever had.

'I'm not only Stand Manager, I'm also head of security. It's my job to guard these enquiries with my life. They go with me when I leave each night and are locked in the hotel safe. That way, if we get raided at 5.57 pm on the last day (everybody laughed at the thought) we only lose one day's enquiries.

'And there's another reason. I want every one of you to bring in the maximum number of enquiries. So twice each day I'm going to be analysing the forms to see who's performing and who's not. Over the week, I've got eight or nine opportunities to improve anyone's performance – or to replace a real dead-head, if we've got one, with someone who *will* perform. Don't forget the competitions.'

We've accepted the logic and the common sense. But I figure we'll lose Harry by tomorrow night. His mind's obviously on something else – probably that receptionist over on stand 47B.


## D-Day Plus 1

Oops! First blunder. What with the euphoria of the first day, we forgot to tidy up last thing last night and get ready for this morning. Sneaky Jim got here half an hour earlier than anyone else – deliberately, I'm sure – and was doing a prison guard stance imitation at us when we arrived. 'What would have happened if there'd been a rail strike or you'd had a puncture and been late?' he hit us with. 'What would visitors have thought of the mess our stand was in when I got here this morning? We don't take the risk.'

Then he lined us up and checked our trouser creases. Seven pairs of trousers failed the test. But it was all done in the right spirit. Again, we all knew what the rules were for making sure we maximized the return on the exhibition investment.

Today the 'sold' notices are coming out. We decided it was too early on the first day. This is part of our plan to demoralize our competitors. Everyone has been briefed to wax enthusiastic when talking to competitors and other stand staff and to use words like 'Great' and 'Fantastic' and 'Incredible business we're doing' when questioned.

Our 'sold' notices hang on the products on our stand. One of our competitions is to aim to sell every product on the stand every day. More bottles of champagne for the person who sells most each day, *and* for the person who sells the most things across the whole product range, including things not being exhibited.

But the 'sold' notices are not directly connected with the competition. When a product has been sold, okay, a 'sold' notice is hung on it, but the main plan is to show our competitors that we are selling all our products every day (whether or not). They know about our competition; we told them! So every time they look at our stand, they see us doing the great business we're telling them we're doing. And the laughter they hear they take as the laughter of success.

The visitors see and hear our success, too. And everyone likes to back a winner. So we **do** do great business.

Every morning, the 'sold' notices will come off and we'll begin again. By close of business each day, every product on our stand will have a notice hanging on it.

We've other notices, too. Our new products each have a big sign 'new' above them. The word 'new' is the most powerful buying motivator in the English language, and you can tell that it is effective on an exhibition stand by the crowds of visitors who keep flocking around our 'new' products.

## D-Day Plus 2

Today we begin our Competitive Tactics plan. I reckon Industrial Espionage is a more accurate term, but the boss wants to keep things strictly legal.

Volunteers were requested for this activity, because it means working pretty hard during the off-duty two hour periods and doing a quick change act, out of uniform, into civvies and back again.

Everyone volunteered. No one wanted to miss having a crack at our competitors in this way.

We've been given a check list of things to do, things to collect, paperwork to acquire. Nowhere on the check list does it say

anything about making the competitor's enquiry and order forms disappear if we see them lying around, but everyone is clear what to do, nevertheless.

Back on our stand, Jim and his 'security force' are going to make sure that we do it to our competitors but they don't do it to us. A couple of guys I know are planning to try to steal a few things from our own stand just to test our security. You should see their disguises!

**Competitive Tactics Check List**
Make the most of your opportunities.

**Personal Activities**
Interviews
Watch their stand
Attend their lectures
Tell them how well **you** are doing

**Printed Matter**
Collect
sales/technical literature
service literature
performance information
price lists
publicity material/company reports

**Materials**
Obtain
samples
products
components

**Other**
Attend (or take part in)
tests
demonstrations

Tonight, back at the hotel, we're getting together to pool our spy achievements and to plan tactics for tomorrow. Bet no one misses *that* meeting.

## D-Day Plus 3

A guy came on the stand this morning with a camera and flash-gun, looking official. He was just about to take a picture of our latest and greatest new product when Jim pounced on him and asked him for his ID. It turned out he was a publicity assistant from one of our competitors.

Another lecture from Jim. 'Don't take anyone at face value. Ask for verification – a business card will do. If they've gone to the trouble to get bogus business cards printed, you're not likely to stop them anyway. No one's allowed to take photographs other than the official photographer appointed by the Exhibition Organizer. Remember that.'

4.12 pm this afternoon Jim made a lightning swoop! We didn't realize we'd been getting slack. We were all still brim-full of enthusiasm. Best exhibition we've ever had, for business, for not getting bored, for fun. Two days to go and we're already over our main target for orders, appointments and names and addresses logged.

Jim found four full ashtrays, three empty glasses, one item of 'left luggage', one raincoat draped over a visitor's chair, two samples lying on the floor instead of in their show case, three duff spotlight bulbs, one displaced polystyrene letter and a portable radio.

As we were already above targets, Jim let us off. But now we're clearing up ready for next morning three times each day!

Ah well, it's all worth it. Think of all that commission we'll be earning in the months to come – all those enquiries we've got to follow up – and that party on Friday night.

# 13
# How to Win in Retailing

**We want the maximum number of customers beating a path to our door and begging us to sell them more.**

**How? By being nice to our customers, by being happy, by never putting them down or making them feel small – and by using one or two little USPs I'm now going to tell you about.**

The rules for winning in Retailing haven't changed in fifty years.

1 get the maximum number of people to walk into your place of business;
2 sell them the maximum amount of goods while they're with you;
3 give them the kind of attention and service that will make them come back for more on a regular basis.

Rules 1 and 3 apply to winning against your competitors down the road or round the corner. Rule 2 applies to the profit you make from your Retailing. The more profit, the more resources you can allocate to achieving 1 and 3.

In this chapter I'm concentrating on some specific things you can do to increase your USP and gain an edge – to be better and look better in the eyes of your customers. But first, it is important that we establish what your customers are after.

Retailing is essentially a very simple business. The customers buy from you for only six primary reasons:

1 to save money;
2 to maximize usefulness;
3 to enhance personal appearance;
4 to enhance prestige;

5 to enhance comfort;
6 because you are convenient.

Okay, if you are in a specialist business, you may have a different reason; for example, if you are an optician, the primary reason for buying would be to see clearly, but enhancing personal appearance might often be more compelling.

If you sold home gymnasiums, the primary reason for buying might be to keep or to get fit, but secondary reasons might be prestige, comfort and (for the track suit and running shoes) again personal appearance.

I am spelling this out because it is incredible the number of Sellers in retail stores who obviously have never bothered even to think about *why* their customers might want to buy. Nowhere in Selling is product orientation so rampant than in the retail sector – probably because of an abject lack of training.

If you understand the customer's buying motivation, you're sixty per cent of the way towards a successful sale. You'll know which questions to ask; which benefits of your merchandise to stress; which items to demonstrate or to suggest the customer tries on.

You'll also know how best to entice more people into your place of business.

## Price Cutting

We are all very familiar with the multi-coloured fluorescent posters which decorate 80% of the Retailer's window, advertising **'massive reductions'** or **'everything reduced'** or **'50% off'**. Many Retailers set out simply to sell on the basis of lowest price, undercutting their competitors, but also undercutting their own profit margins. A classic case of 'Price Fright' again. No future!

The astute Retailer advertises price cuts only on *selected* lines; goods of universal appeal or need and goods for which the Retailer can negotiate very special terms from the suppliers, either independently or in conjunction with a group of other Retailers in different areas. All other goods sold are at the normal prices. Thus, more people are attracted into the place of business by the advertising; they buy the cut price merchandise and while they are there, they also buy a number of other things. That's the key Convenience reason playing its part.

Strategically placed point of sale displays, adjacent to the cut price items and also the cash till, can add to every customer's order.


## Coffee Service

The higher class tailors and dress shops sometimes provide an all day coffee service and a sitting down area. If this is used in conjunction with the browsing sign, the psychological obligation is quadrupled.

But the coffee *must* be offered as soon as the prospective customer walks into the store. No strings.

'Good morning, Sir, Madam. Terrible day for shopping; will it ever stop raining? We've just put some fresh coffee on, would you and your wife like a cup? How do you like it? Have a look round while I organize things.'

Just like Flo Wright's Saturday car park technique – the coffee is far too hot to drink. So the Retailer has the prospective customers comfortably locked in for at least ten minutes. Worth another 20% on average order value!

Far more Retailers could use this technique to beat their competitors and win more business.


## Invite Browsers

Especially for furniture, carpets, hi-fi, domestic appliances, a professionally painted sign outside the store, on the pavement, works wonders.

The browser browses, but because of the sign inviting him/her into the store just to browse, there is a slight subconscious feeling of obligation which the Retailer can use to break down the normal mental barriers in the prospective customer's mind and to start selling. 'Were you looking for anything in particular?' 'We've another showroom upstairs.'

But don't police the browsers. Don't follow them everywhere. Let them browse properly, once you've told them where you'll be if they want to ask any questions.

## Smiles

Remember the 'Think a Smile' instruction for when you telephone a customer? In Retailing, *smile* is a total concept. You need to be happy every minute of the selling day. And that's hard.

Have a series of prominent posters positioned under every one of your counters and on the back of the staff room door. Have miniatures on every cash till. Run a penalty points competition with a wooden spoon prize for the 'Dismal Jimmy of the Day'. No one will want to win that one!

## Make it EASY to Pay

In 1978, my wife and I were shopping in Beverly Hills, California. She needed some make-up. We found what she needed with no trouble, the sales girl was very helpful and very good.

Then we tried to pay for what we'd bought. It was only a few dollars, so I offered *cash*.

'Oh. Don't you have a charge account with us?' the sales girl asked.

'No, we're visitors from England,' I replied.

'Ah. Do you have a credit card, then?'

'I do, but I'd prefer to pay cash,' I said happily, totally unaware of the financial revolution that had been taking place around me for the past ten years.

The sales girl had been trained not to argue with the customer. She took the offered money, asked us to sit down for a few minutes and disappeared.

*Twenty minutes later*, she re-appeared, very apologetic, very red, with my change and receipt, explaining the reason for the long wait. I won't bore you with the details – suffice it to say that the store had absolutely no system for handling customers who wanted to pay with actual money.

Pardon the old joke, but in Beverly Hills, money is most certainly the poor man's credit card.

The reason I'm telling you this story is to illustrate the Achilles heel of Retailing. It is getting steadily, remorselessly, increasingly more difficult to *pay* for the goods you've decided to buy.

Even Marks & Spencer haven't cracked this problem, although they've cracked just about every other problem in their kind of Retailing. You still have to queue to pay all too often.

When the customer has chosen the goods and is ready to pay for them, *speed* is critically important. Even customers who have taken about an hour to make up their minds expect to be out of the store in a flash once the big decision has been taken. It's a state of mind. If you hold up the paying process, the goods will often go back on the shelves, the customer will stalk out of your place of business in high dudgeon, never, never come back **and** will tell lots of other people about your abject inefficiency. Unjust it might well be. An isolated case it may well be. You've still lost a customer and a few potential customers.

For credit card payments where you've got to telephone for a code number, do the telephoning *in full view of the customer*, not in some back room. If the customer can see what you're doing, patience will be extended.


### The New Recruits

Retailing is full of incompetent sales people, thousands of them. A high proportion are recent school leavers. They are incompetent only because they have received absolutely no training in how to do their new job – the Selling bit especially. A new recruit is dropped in at the deep end and expected to cope with an incredibly difficult and complex series of tasks. Is it any wonder, therefore, that a high proportion of new recruits don't make it, and while they're suffering, kill quite a few good customers into the bargain?

Every customer is an Alsatian at heart. Walk into a retail store and find yourself up against a new, untrained recruit. How do you react to what you see as incompetence? Grr! Every time. Frustration, annoyance, even rudeness. It's instinctive. You walked into that store expecting to be looked after, pampered, wooed into parting with your money. Anything less and your hackles go up.

It's the biggest universal problem. Profit margins in Retailing are so low that more training is next to impossible. New recruits are necessary because of the high turnover of sales staff. The new recruits keep killing the customers. Business keeps going down hill.

I have a simple solution to this universal problem. A lapel badge for the new recruits. It says, '*I'm new but I'm trying*'. It's large enough to be read at ten paces. Any new recruit who refuses to wear it has too big an *ego* for Retailing and is out of a job!

The potential Alsatian customer gets within eye shot of the new recruit's lapel badge, reads it automatically and immediately understands. A beaming smile greets the new recruit, who smiles back. Great business is done. Great confidence is built for that new recruit, who graduates to senior sales assistant and maximum commission well inside three months.

First time customers come back a week later and say to the new recruit. 'How are you doing?'

Everyone wins. The new recruit is a competent, confident Seller, turnover of sales staff falls dramatically, turnover of sales rises dramatically, number of regular customers increases dramatically, competitors wonder what the hell's gone wrong.

And all it took was a lapel badge. At 1984 prices – £65 per 1000!

## Returns Anywhere

A while ago I mentioned Marks & Spencer. Britain's top chain on quality, reliability, value for money, and a few things more. But a lot of years of hard work have been put in to make M & S Number One in its field.

One of M & S's best USPs is that if something doesn't fit, or you change your mind, or the colour doesn't match the coat you had at home, as long as the item is undamaged and unworn, you can take it back to *any* M & S store and exchange it or get your money back. No questions. No delays.

What a lesson this is to many Retailers who don't appear even to have familiarized themselves with the basic statutory rights of the customer under the Sale of Goods Act and a few other recent pieces of Legislation. They fight tooth and nail to avoid accepting anything back and especially giving a refund. And very quickly indeed, the word gets round the area, and within weeks the 'Shop to let' and 'Closing down sale' notices go up.

## You Need Regulars

Every Retailer needs as many *regular* customers as possible. Work hard to add to them.

Regular customers bring in your steady bread and butter

turnover. They recommend your store to other people.

Remember their names. Greet them by name when they call. Offer them monthly account and delivery facilities. When you've learned their interests, write to them from time to time when you have something that you feel is right for them.

The cost of selling to regular customers is less than to passing trade, because it's quicker and their needs are known. Because that all important confidence in you, your name and your merchandise has all gone before.

But don't take your regulars for granted. Losing one is a hundred times as bad for your business as losing a passing trade customer.

### Position, Position, Position

Just as for an exhibition stand, the Hilton Rule applies universally to Retailing. If your store is in the right position, you'll do well. If it is not, you'll spend an arm and a leg on advertising and still maybe not attract as many customers into your place of business as the competitor who has picked the best position.

But what *is* the best position? It depends on the business, of course. I buy my greengrocery from a tiny little lock-up shop in Royal Leamington Spa which is sandwiched between the rear entrance of Woolworth's and Marks & Spencer's stores.

Opposite the tiny lock-up shop is the town's largest furniture store and a car park.

That's position. The tiny lock-up shop is *always* full of customers. It does more turnover than any two other greengrocers in the town. It delivers for its regulars. It takes telephone orders and its sales girls bring the boxes out to your car, which can park for a few minutes to load directly outside the shop. Its pavement displays are mouthwatering.

Its passing trade is tremendous, because greengroceries are mainly impulse buys. So many of the customers of Woolworth's, M & S and the furniture store, and the people who use the car park, buy from that little lock-up shop because it is so **convenient**.

**14**
# How to Stay Ahead and Grow while all around you the Competitors are Falling like Flies

## YES WE CAN!

'When all is said and done, there's more said than done!'

When all is said and done; when you've read this last chapter, if all you do is say to yourself, 'I enjoyed that' and you put this book on your library shelf to gather dust for ever, neither of us will have achieved much, will we?

Everything you need to know about Selling, to be able to make sure you stay ahead and grow, is in this book. Everything you need to know to be able to change your attitude towards the job, work and success, is in this book.

Everything you need to know to be able to change from a Negative to a Positive, from a Sheep to a Wolf, from a Representative to a Professional Sales Executive, from being Poor to being Rich.

And if I may quote Mae West on this last point – and agree wholeheartedly with her – 'I've been rich and I've been poor and believe me baby, rich is best!'

If you're saying to yourself, 'Yes, I see the point, but it looks too much like hard work and I'm busting a gut now, I've no time even to consider changing my way of working like this guy Fenton says I should,' then let me present you with a kind of recap on the whole thing – something that originated from Caterpillar Tractor Corporation as a rather different recruitment advertisement.

## Wanted – a LAZY Seller

So lazy, he takes advantage of every sales aid provided by his Company.

So lazy, he copies the methods of the most successful Sellers.

So lazy, he carefully plans his routes to hold travelling to a minimum.

So lazy, he concentrates his efforts on the customers and potential customers that represent the most business.

So lazy, he frequently makes appointments by phone so he won't be put through the trouble of calling on a customer who's unavailable.

So lazy, he keeps written records on each account so he won't have to strain his memory.

So lazy, he follows up immediately every lead from his Company's sales promotion, figuring that these represent people who are ready to buy.

So lazy, he relies on testimonials, figuring that satisfied customers can say things for him that he can't say himself.

So lazy, he insists on getting a good night's sleep every night, especially exhibition week.

So lazy, he refuses to run errands for his wife during working hours.

If you come across such a person turn him in immediately. **Everybody** seems to be looking for him!

Absolutely right. Everybody IS looking for him. There aren't many positively lazy Sellers about. So if you fear hard work, get your teeth into the techniques described in this book and do it the 'Lazy Seller' way. You'll still be an outstanding competition beater.

## Why are the Competitors Falling like Flies?

I weigh in at 11 stone 5 pounds. That's 159 pounds USA style. I fluctuate between 11st 3lb and 11st 7lb. As I write these last few pages I'm sitting on a hotel patio in Tenerife, and I'm looking down on a pool side filled with grotesquely overweight male and female bodies. I've been here only a week, yet I'm already struggling to keep within my limits. The food is fantastic, and I'm only human.

I used to be 13 stone. The motivation I needed to lose nearly two stone I got by looking ahead three months to the Sales Road Shows I was scheduled to run throughout the autumn of 1982 –

twelve shows across three months. Five hours on stage, just about non-stop. 'What if I keeled over after four hours?' I asked myself.

When you aim to put on a one man show and play to 2,000 people, I tell you, you generate the motivation to make sure it happens. I bought an exercise bike, a rowing machine, installed a 'Spa' hot bath and went on Judy Mazel's pineapple diet. Two miles on the bike every morning, half a pineapple and two cups of black tea (no milk or sugar) – nothing else until lunchtime, and in three months I was thinner and fitter than I'd ever been before, even as a teenager. Stamina energy was what I was building. The ability to keep going for long periods at full stretch. The less weight I carried, the easier it became.

I also already had a major asset in the way I coped with mental pressure. Everyone needs a way of winding down, a way of relieving the frustration of the bad working day, of being able to relax and banish away the problems of the week, so that they can begin again fresh the next morning. For some people it's classical music and a pair of high fidelity headphones. For others it's building model railways. For the more dynamic it's a game of squash in the evenings. I see that as a touch too dangerous at my age. My pastime is a pretty comprehensive set of Ludwig drums and Paiste cymbals, wrapped round with 100 watts per channel of pretty deafening stereo. My only danger is the amount of wax I generate in my ears, but beating hell out of a set of drums to the added therapy of music is right for me.

However you do it, you've got to be mentally and physically **fit** to succeed in this exciting business we call Selling.

You need a hobby, a way of relaxing from the pressure of business. One that fits your metabolism. But it cannot be a very time consuming one. You need all the time you can get for building your career.

## Life is Full of Forks in the Road

And this is one of them!

Take the correct road at this fork and you'll never look back.

Take the wrong road and you'll stay more or less where you are now, until you get to another fork in the road, further ahead.

Then you'll have another chance to choose the right road. And another chance at another fork in the road, even further ahead. That's life.

But all the time you're getting older. If you're also getting wiser, you'll know you should have taken maybe a different road at a fork in the road some way back. What this means is that **now** has to be a better time than the next fork, or next year, or next first of the month, doesn't it?

If you **want** it to happen; if you want to be successful, not average; if you want to be rich, not poor; if you want to beat the **hell** out of your competitors; **you**, no one else, **you** have got to **make** it happen.

It's **your** future!

You've got to overcome every bit of your natural resistance to change. Maybe you should remember that the only thing in life, other than death, that is permanent – is change.

Don't fight it. Practice instead the words of C. F. Kettering 'My interest is in the **future**, because I am going to spend the rest of my life there.'

As you read this page, **today** is the beginning of the rest of your life. Live it successfully. Get great fun out of it. Do great business. Build great businesses. And leave your competitors far, far behind.

**You can do it.**

# Index

John Fenton
**How to Double Your Profits Within the Year** £2.95

John Fenton's unique plan is applicable to all types of business and will help you to *at least* double your profits within twelve months. You will be convinced, in the few hours it takes to read this book, that the title's claim is a modest understatement. The book is an extended memo, written by a managing director to his team of top managers. To give a few examples, it shows you how:

* to choose which customers generate profit
* to recruit the right people
* to improve production efficiency
* to price for maximum profit
* to control your sales force

This fascinating guide is required reading for all managers.

John Fenton
**The A–Z of Sales Management** £2.95

*The* book for the sales manager. If you are responsible for a sales force, John Fenton can help you – no matter how successful or experienced you are – to improve your own and your team's performance. This book covers the full range of activities and requirements, and includes:

* credit control
* decision making
* expense accounts
* planning and control systems

and much more. Whether you are a marketing manager, managing director or manager of a small business, this book will help you. And if you've got ambitions . . .

John Adair
**Effective Decision-Making** £2.95

Few managers devote enough attention to the *thinking* processes
they should apply to their jobs. Yet long, energetic hours at work are
wasted if business decisions are not logical, clear and correct.
*Effective Decision-Making* is the definitive guide to the crucial
managerial skill of creative *thinking*. John Adair draws on examples
and case studies from business, recent history, sport and
entertainment in showing how to sharpen analytical management
skills.

Heinz M. Goldmann
**How to Win Customers** £2.95

*How to Win Customers* is not just a book about selling. It is a
step-by-step training course – definitive, practical and complete – on
the improvement of sales techniques. It should be read by everyone
concerned with sales and it can also be used for personal evaluation
and improvement, discussion groups, and for role-playing exercises
on sales courses. No one who reads it can fail to learn from it.

John Winkler
**Bargaining for Results** £2.50

Skilful bargaining is crucial to business success, especially when
money is tight. John Winkler, one of Britain's leading marketing
experts, presents the key to effective negotiation – the methods to
adopt and when to employ them. The approach is highly practical,
using case histories, illustrations and helpful maxims in a book
specially designed for business managers.

## Pricing for Results £2.95

Bad pricing decisions ruin the sales prospects of any product. The
author's unique appreciation of the price mechanism has served him
to win many commercial battles. Here he passes on his expertise, in
an approach recommended for all finance and sales directors/
managers, key account negotiators, general managers and marketing
students. How to set prices; how to present prices; how to discount
prices; how to negotiate prices. The concluding Free Chapter shows
how to organise for pricing decisions once the Winkler techniques are
mastered.

## Reference, language and information

| | | | |
|---|---|---|---|
| ☐ | **The Story of Language** | C. L. Barber | £2.50p |
| ☐ | **North-South** | Brandt Commission | £2.50p |
| ☐ | **Test Your IQ** | Butler and Pirie | £1.50p |
| ☐ | **Writing English** | D. J. Collinson | £1.50p |
| ☐ | **Illustrating Computers** | Colin Day and Donald Alcock | £1.95p |
| ☐ | **Dictionary of Famous Quotations** | Robin Hyman | £2.95p |
| ☐ | **Militant Islam** | Godfrey Jansen | £1.50p |
| ☐ | **The War Atlas** | Michael Kidron and Dan Smith | £5.95p |
| ☐ | **Practical Statistics** | R. Langley | £1.95p |
| ☐ | **How to Study** | H. Maddox | £1.95p |
| ☐ | **The Limits to Growth** | D. H. Meadows et al. | £2.50p |
| ☐ | **Your Guide to the Law** | ed. Michael Molyneux | £3.95p |
| ☐ | **Ogilvy on Advertising** | David Ogilvy | £6.95p |
| ☐ | **Common Security** | Palme Commission | £1.95p |
| ☐ | **The Modern Crossword Dictionary** | Norman Pulsford | £3.50p |
| ☐ | **A Guide to Saving and Investment** | James Rowlatt | £2.95p |
| ☐ | **Career Choice** | Audrey Segal | £3.95p |
| ☐ | **Logic and its Limits** | Patrick Shaw | £2.95p |
| ☐ | **Names for Boys and Girls** | L. Sleigh and C. Johnson | £1.95p |
| ☐ | **Straight and Crooked Thinking** | R. H. Thouless | £1.95p |
| ☐ | **Money Matters** | Harriet Wilson | £1.75p |
| ☐ | **Dictionary of Earth Sciences** | | £2.95p |
| ☐ | **Dictionary of Physical Sciences** | | £2.95p |

| | | |
|---|---|---|
| ☐ **Pan Dictionary of Synonyms and Antonyms** | | £2.50p |
| ☐ **Travellers' Multilingual Phrasebook** | | £2.50p |
| ☐ **Universal Encyclopaedia of Mathematics** | | £2.95p |

Literature guides

| | | |
|---|---|---|
| ☐ **An Introduction to Shakespeare and his Contemporaries** | Marguerite Alexander | £2.95p |
| ☐ **An Introduction to Fifty Modern British Plays** | Benedict Nightingale | £2.95p |
| ☐ **An Introduction to Fifty Modern European Poets** | John Pilling | £2.95p |
| ☐ **An Introduction to Fifty Modern British Poets** | Michael Schmidt | £1.95p |
| ☐ **An Introduction to Fifty European Novels** | Martin Seymour-Smith | £1.95p |

All these books are available at your local bookshop or newsagent, or can be ordered direct from the publisher. Indicate the number of copies required and fill in the form below

12

.......................................................................................................................

Name_____
(Block letters please)

Address_____

_____

Send to CS Department, Pan Books Ltd, PO Box 40, Basingstoke, Hants
Please enclose remittance to the value of the cover price plus:
35p for the first book plus 15p per copy for each additional book ordered
to a maximum charge of £1.25 to cover postage and packing
Applicable only in the UK

While every effort is made to keep prices low, it is sometimes
necessary to increase prices at short notice. Pan Books reserve
the right to show on covers and charge new retail prices which
may differ from those advertised in the text or elsewhere